Black Theology

SCM CORE TEXT

Black Theology

Anthony G. Reddie

scm press

© Anthony G. Reddie

Published in 2012 by SCM Press
Editorial office
Invieta House
108-114 Golden Lane
London EC1Y 0TG, UK

SCM Press is an imprint of Hymns Ancient & Modern Ltd
(a registered charity)
13A Hellesdon Park Road
Norwich NR6 5DR, UK

www.scm-press.co.uk

British Library Cataloguing in Publication data

A catalogue record for this book is available
from the British Library

978-0-334-04156-6
Kindle 978-0-334-04470-3

Typeset by Manila Typesetting
Printed and bound by
CPI Group (UK) Ltd, Croydon, CR0 4YY

This book is dedicated to
Noah and Sasha
My wonderful nephew and niece
God bless!

Contents

Acknowledgements

This book has been a long time coming, and for that there is no one else to blame but myself. There has been many a false start, followed by furrowed brows and deep sighs, as deadlines have come and gone and still the book remained unfinished. So my first and most heartfelt thanks go to Dr Natalie Watson, the Senior Commissioning Editor at SCM, whose infinite patience with me has been hugely reassuring. I can only hope that the wait has been worth it.

Many thanks are due to my former colleagues at the Queen's Foundation for Ecumenical Theological Education. It would be invidious to single out specific individuals at this juncture, but suffice it to say that there have been many people at Queen's whose encouragement and support has been invaluable.

I am also grateful to my Black Theology colleagues across the world, particularly friends at the AAR, whose brilliance has inspired me and also reminded me of my limitations. Black Theology has been a consuming passion for the last twenty years. But as this book will testify, I am as much an educator as I am a theologian, perhaps more so! My passion has been not solely concerned with how to understand and develop Black Theology but, of even greater import, to try and capture its essence as a movement of liberative praxis – the commitment to embody transformative change.

In this regard my even greater thanks go to the many often faceless, ordinary Black people with whom I have engaged in order to prepare this book. I was once told by a music teacher (whose efforts were sadly wasted on me) that music theory was great in itself but wonderful melodies did not come alive until someone had the courage to pick up an instrument and attempt to bring the musical score to life. I am indebted to the many people whose courageous lives of struggle have given life to Black Theology and have proved it is a movement of liberative praxis. I can only hope that this book has done you justice.

I am grateful to my colleague Carol Troupe for proofreading and suggesting judicious editing of the text. She has also been the best of colleagues and a rock in times of great uncertainty.

Then there is my family. My parents, my siblings, my gorgeous nephew and niece and my many cousins!

Finally there is God, who simply is. . .

Introduction

They say that confession is good for the soul. Well, then, here is my confession. This book has been a long time coming, and I have apologized profusely to the publishers for this fact. The reason for this long gestation has been entirely self-inflicted. I took on the task of writing an introductory textbook to Black Theology a number of years ago – more years than I care to remember. SCM Press has a fine tradition of producing excellent introductory surveys to various (particular) fields of theological endeavour. In surveying these various texts, I realized pretty quickly that I had a problem. The problem lay with me and not with these other texts, I hasten to add.

I realized that the book I was expected to write would cause me some major headaches. It was not that I could not write a conventional textbook. The problem lay in the nature of the task itself. Namely, that Black Theology was not conceived to be *just an academic theological discipline*. I will say a little more about this in the first chapter (that follows this Introduction), but for now it is important that I say a few words about the overall aim of this book.

Black Theology was never intended to be simply an academic discipline and, in many respects, it does not operate as one at the time of writing.[1] Believing this to be true, it occurred to me some time ago that trying to write a conventional textbook as if Black Theology was simply another academic subject seemed odd. The more I tried the less successful I was at writing a conventional textbook in the style of the other texts in the series. At one point I was genuinely on the point of giving up and abandoning the project, such was my despair and unhappiness.

---

1 As I shall demonstrate, Black Theology has developed very much as a subset of other disciplines, be it 'Systematic' or 'Constructive' theology or 'Christian Ethics'. It has never been a stand-alone academic discipline in its own right. It is rare that one will find courses or modules created in the name of 'Black Theology'. There are no scholarly societies so named (there are analogous bodies like 'Society for the Study of Black Religion' or areas focused on 'Black Church Studies', but neither of these can be directly equated with Black Theology, although they share much in common). There is only one scholarly journal that carries the name of Black Theology. (See the following link for more details on *Black Theology: An International Journal* – http://www.equinoxjournals.com/BT/about/submissions.)

In the final analysis, I decided to go back to my own formative introduction to Black Theology in the early 1990s. Why had Black Theology so galvanized my life and completely re-orientated my whole being, so much so that I had abandoned what had formerly been my heart's desire?[2] I believe what had captured me had been the creative intent of Black Theology. Namely, it was not solely an academic discipline, which is not to suggest that brilliant thinkers and exponents of Black Theology are in short supply. On the contrary, in such figures as James H. Cone, J. Deotis Roberts, Dwight Hopkins and Anthony Pinn, Black Theology has among its ranks some of the most incisive and brilliant minds of the twentieth and twenty-first centuries.

What made Black Theology compelling news for me was not simply that it had brilliant exponents who could explain this radical departure from the normative, White Euro-American model of faith and religion I had imbibed thus far; it was the fact that it spoke to the realities of my life. As a Black person born into and socialized within the White-majority country of England, my life had been dominated by the twin challenges of the internal acceptance of oneself, coupled with the external struggle of challenging White supremacy and racism. The latter made the former anything but self-evident and normative. I had grown up witnessing the ways in which many ordinary Black people were often forced to make sense of their lives against a backdrop of racism and anti-Black sentiments.

Black Theology gave me a reason to want to remain a part of the Christian faith. It provided me and a whole generation of academically inclined Black people in Britain with the belief that the genesis of our contextual struggles had nothing to do with God, meaning they were neither ordained by nor were they sanctioned by God. That God was not synonymous with White power and Black suffering. On the contrary, Black Theology taught me that it was through Black self-determination and Black power that God's truest presence and activity was to be felt.

Yes, I did end up becoming an academic because of Black Theology, but, more importantly, I also became an activist as a result of my exposure to it. Black Theology provided an underlying methodological framework for directing the ethics and analysis of many ordinary Black people as they have engaged in faithful forms of active resistance to racism and White supremacy in Britain. I know that it has done the same for activists in Southern Africa (particularly South Africa), the Caribbean and in the United States of America.

One of the architects of Black Theology is the African American historian Gayraud Wilmore. In one of his later books, Wilmore outlines dual perspectives for understanding Black Theology. He argues that Black Theology

---

2 Elements of this narrative can be found in two of my previous books. See Anthony G. Reddie, *Black Theology in Transatlantic Dialogue*, New York: Palgrave Macmillan, 2006, pp. 1–13, and *Dramatizing Theologies: A Participative Approach to Black God Talk*, Oakwood and London: Equinox, 2006, pp. 33–7.

can be understood as a scholarly discipline, seeking to provide a rational account for interpreting the meaning of God, in the light of Black suffering and oppression. But, secondly, it is also a mode of liberative praxis.[3]

In using this latter term, I am talking about the need to link faith-based forms of theological reflection with committed attempts to bring about liberative change, via one's accompanying action and activism. The combination of the two elements is more than the sum of its parts.[4] Praxis – the nexus of theological reflection and action, for the purposes of bringing about liberative change, hence the term 'liberative praxis' – should be central to the very identity and intent of Black Theology. Theory alone will not do, and neither will action by itself.

This book is written, therefore, with two aims in mind. In the first instance, like all introductory texts to any particular subject, it seeks to describe and explain the basic rationale of the discipline. Namely, when it began, how it works, what are the key ideas and who are the major players in the scholarly development of Black Theology. If this was the sole aim of the book then writing it should not have caused the amount of trouble it subsequently did. The second aim has proved far more difficult. Namely, to demonstrate by means of Transformative, Popular Education, how Black Theology can remain rooted in the lived experiences of and be committed to the daily struggles in which ordinary Black people are engaged. In effect, how can Black Theology remain true to the very basis of its existence as outlined by Gayraud Wilmore?

The genesis of this work

At the outset of this book I feel it is incumbent on me to say something about me. For, as a contextual liberation theologian and educator, I am of the convinced opinion that all theology should be and indeed is embodied, that the person doing theology has an intense relationship with the shape and form of their attempts to talk about God and the truth of God's revelation and activity with human beings. This compulsion to say something about me is also informed by my ongoing interest in and commitment to Womanist approaches to theological method. Womanist theology is an approach to and a form of contextual, liberation theology that arises from the experiences

---

3 Gayraud S. Wilmore, *Pragmatic Spirituality: The Christian Faith through an Afri-centric Lens*, New York and London: New York University Press, 2004, pp. 155–66.

4 One of the architects of Black Theology in Britain is Emmanuel Lartey who is a practical theologian by training. Lartey offers a brilliant and concise exposition of the praxis mode of theological reflection that underpins all forms of 'liberative praxis'. See Emmanuel Y. Lartey, 'Practical Theology as a Theological Form', in James Woodward and Stephen Pattison (eds), *The Blackwell Reader in Pastoral and Practical Theology*, Oxford: Blackwell, 2000, pp. 128–34.

of Black women. Its main exponents come from the United States of America, although there are important Black scholars in this country who might be described as Womanists.

Womanist theology[5] has challenged all people who might dare to use the descriptor of 'theologian' in their title to consider how personal experience and narrative – one's own position as an individual agent in history – shape one's outlook on and experience of the world. What are the ways in which gender, sexuality, class, nationality, religion and so on influence the process of doing theology?

As a Black male subject, born of Caribbean parents, in the West Yorkshire city of Bradford, in what ways have my own formative experiences helped to shape my identity, which as a corollary has exerted, if only subconsciously, my attempt to undertake constructive talk about God and faith?

How this book works!

Black Theology has been a consuming passion for approaching 20 years. I would credit it with enabling me to stay within the orbit of organized religion and the Church. At the time of my politicization and burgeoning interest in Black history and the mis-education of Black people[6] at the hands of White western power structures, in the early 1990s, Black Theology enabled me to remain within the Church with some integrity, given the churches' own ambivalent role in such oppressive moments from history. This text is an attempt to explain the basic workings of Black Theology and to demonstrate its continued importance in the twenty-first century.

In writing this text, my emphasis has been not simply on outlining the basic tenets of this discipline, it is also to argue for its very reason for its

---

5 Womanist theology is the theological articulation of God as understood through the lens of the experiences of Black (predominantly African American) women. It seeks to address the tripartite jeopardy of being Black, female and poor in the wealthiest nation in the world. Significant Womanist theological texts include: Jacquelyn Grant, *White Women's Christ and Black Women's Jesus*, Atlanta, GA: Scholar's Press, 1989; Delores Williams, *Sisters in the Wilderness: The Challenge of Womanist God-Talk*, Maryknoll, NY: Orbis, 1993; Kelly Brown Douglas, *The Black Christ*, Maryknoll, NY: Orbis, 1994; Emile Townes, *Womanist Justice, Womanist Hope*, Atlanta, GA: Scholars Press, 1993; Renita J. Weems, *Just a Sister away: A Womanist Vision of Women's Relationships in the Bible*, Philadelphia: Innisfree Press, 1988; Katie G. Cannon, *Black Womanist Ethics*, Atlanta, GA: Scholars Press, 1988; Stacey Floyd-Thomas (ed.), *Deeper Shade of Purple: Womanism in Religion and Society*, New York and London: New York University Press, 2006; and Monica A. Coleman, *Making a Way Out of No Way: A Womanist Theology*, Minneapolis: Fortress Press, 2008.

6 See the seminal work of Carter G. Woodson for his ground-breaking work, *The Mis-Education of the Negro*, Trenton, NJ: Africa World Press, 1990 [1933].

being and to demonstrate how it can and has engaged with the lived experiences of ordinary Black people.

My reasons for taking this approach are several. In the first instance there is a major challenge presented to Black Theology by Alistair Kee and his pronouncement that Black Theology has died or is dying.[7] While I reject outright Kee's tendentious polemic, his acerbic attack on the discipline and the movement calls for a renewed attempt to restate the central convictions and perspectives that are outlined by Black Theology. Second, I think the approach I have taken, in terms of seeking to engage with ordinary Black people, for the purposes of raising their critical consciousness, as possible agents for change, is one that has been prompted by the essential crisis that lies at the heart of this movement in the three principal centres in which it has been developed. I will outline these three challenges shortly. But, first, I should state that this approach is also my idiosyncratic means of making sense of an entity that has enlivened my own life and religious faith for many years.

Combining Black Theology with Transformative Popular Education

Transformative Popular Education in the context of this work alludes to a critical process of reflection and action on how oppressive theories and forms of knowledge are constructed and enacted. It is an invitation to ordinary learners (of all ethnicities) to critically assess the veracity of particular truth claims and the processes that produce seemingly all-powerful, interlocking systems and structures that constrict and inhibit the God-given selfhood of ordinary Black people.

Using Black Theology as a model for illustrating the illusory dimensions of the White, Euro-American western world order, this work seeks to enable ordinary Black people to pose critical questions and to gain important insights on truth and knowledge. It does so in the hope that what accrues from this educative process is a form of learning that is transformative. As bell hooks has observed, transformative knowledge can give rise to new, distinctive forms of thinking, which, as a corollary, can assist in reshaping one's perception of reality that is not conditioned or silenced by the hegemonic, patriarchal constructs of imperialism and male-centred control.[8]

So this book is not like the other textbooks in this series. The difference in its approach is not purely a result of my own idiosyncratic journey as an academic – although I am sure this has played a part in some respect. In more substantive terms, this book is an attempt not only to describe and explain

---

7 See Alistair Kee, *The Rise and Demise of Black Theology*, London: SCM, 2008.

8 bell hooks, *Teaching to Transgress: Education as the Practice of Freedom*, New York: Routledge, 1994, pp. 93–128.

Black Theology but also seeks to demonstrate how it can engage with the experiences of ordinary Black people. In terms of the latter, Black Theology becomes a transformative methodology for raising the critical awareness of those at the grass roots. As I will demonstrate in the first chapter, the book draws on the use of experience-based forms of learning, in which the learner is an active participant, and from which new insights and knowledge emerge. These insights are then linked to the theoretical ideas and themes that have been central to Black Theology from its inception. The aim, then, has been to create a book that is not only descriptive of the main ideas and themes of Black Theology but also propositional, meaning it seeks to *propose* an agenda for the discipline.

The seven chapters in the book do not offer a straightforward narrative for Black Theology. Rather, each chapter seeks to raise a central issue or concern in the subject, highlighting not only the key ideas but also, of equal importance, how it can and has engaged with the lived experiences and realities of Black people at the grass roots.

Chapter 1 explains the basic identity and workings of Black Theology, as a constituent member of the wider family of 'theologies of liberation'. Of particular importance is the identification of the underlying ideological frameworks employed by Black Theology in critiquing the normative approaches to Christian theology as they have arisen from the western tradition of Christianity. It is important that the reader understand that as a theology of liberation, Black Theology is not simply any theology undertaken by a Black person. Rather, it is a liberation theology that seeks to critique existing and seemingly normative, oppressive forms of Christian theology and practice, including those developed and expressed by Black people themselves!

Chapter 2 describes the nature and purpose of Black Theology. This chapter uses the first of a number of experiential exercises that provide an activity-based metaphor for explaining both the workings of and the basic intent of Black Theology in light of this particular theme. This chapter demonstrates how Black Theology, as an academic discipline and as a form of liberative praxis, has attempted to 'tell a new story' about Black experience and existence, in the light of the Bible and the Christian theological tradition.

Chapter 3, through the use of another participative exercise, will offer two differing approaches to how Black Theology has been undertaken. These two approaches are not offered as definitive or representative models. Rather, they provide a kind of case-study for how Black Theology has sought, in its different guises, to engage with the experiences of Black people. This chapter makes a special case for looking critically at how Black Theology engages with the material cultures produced by Black people as an expression of their lived experiences and humanity.

Chapter 4 looks at the central importance of Jesus in Black Theology. This chapter does not provide a comprehensive evaluation of differing models of Black Christologies in Black Theology. Instead, it articulates why Jesus Christ remains pivotal to Black Theology, because of the pragmatic and experiential basis on which this discipline and liberative praxis movement is based. Once again, the chapter is built around a participative exercise.

Chapter 5 takes an alternative perspective to that identified in the previous chapter. If Black Theology has offered a surfeit of ideas on Jesus, it has perhaps under-performed when it has come to the Holy Spirit/the Spirit of Liberation. In fact, the very dual nomenclature I have just provided, in many respects, outlines the very nature of the problem with which Black Theology has grappled. If the very embodied nature of Jesus has been central to Black Theology, which is essentially a practical theology for liberative change, then the uses and abuses of the Spirit as a reason for pious inaction has been problematic. And yet, as this chapter demonstrates, Black people have utilized the Spirit as an immediate and dynamic force in fuelling their activism for social change.

Chapter 6 demonstrates how Black Theology has always engaged in critical and sceptical readings of society. It has sought to debunk and challenge the supposedly common-sense and accepted reasons for societal ills in general and Black peoples' problems in particular. It is, perhaps, in this area that Black Theology has sought to challenge conventional and accepted wisdom that has often been provided by mainstream White Euro-American Christianity. Essentially, Black Theology has always asked 'the Why Question'[9] when it comes to particular social arrangements and the workings of power in many of the societies in which Black people live in the West.

In Chapter 7, all of the aforementioned is brought together by means of an analysis of a specific social issue. This chapter outlines how Black Theology can be used to enable ordinary Black people to critique so-called 'common-sense wisdom' in order to give life and practical expression to some of the central concerns of Black Theology. The chapter focuses on the role of the Bible in asserting what are the contemporary social ethics for ordinary Black people, and demonstrates how Black Theology, using all the tools at its disposal, can chart a new, more liberative approach to life that is inspired by religious faith.

---

9 See Anthony G. Reddie, 'Editorial', *Black Theology: An International Journal* 45:2 (2006), pp. 134–5.

1

Black Theology and God as Subversive Ideology

In this chapter, I shall be looking at how Black Theology can be understood in terms of its subversive approach to understanding God. Black Theology is a heterogeneous movement, in which different perspectives and notions of how one undertakes the theological task exist.

There are other ways of conceiving Black Theology in methodological terms. For example, the philosophical or human sciences schools of Black Theology would not identify 'liberation' as a main theme for conceiving Black Theology. Neither would they be overly reliant on Christian-inspired themes and their constant recourse to the Bible and the norms of liberation as understood from within the Judaeo-Christian framework. I will look in more detail at the differing ways in which Black Theology is undertaken, looking in particular at what some scholars have called the 'hermeneutical school'.[1] I will explain this term shortly. My work very much rests within this more dominant, Christian theological approach to undertaking Black Theology.

In aligning myself with the most dominant of the three approaches outlined by Ware, namely, the 'hermeneutical school', I want to assert that this model is most representative of the bulk of scholars who would identify themselves with the cause of Black Theology. In making this claim, I in no way wish to diminish the importance and value of other approaches to or perspectives on Black Theology. Even if one does not anchor one's methodological approach with an ongoing dialogue with the Christian tradition or use liberation as the dominant generative theme, I am still convinced that the broader notions of emancipation and full life remain the overarching goal for all forms of *genuine* Black Theology, as conceived within the tripartite typologies outlined by Ware. It is also worth noting the comparative schemas developed by many Caribbean theologians such as Kortright Davis, Noel L. Erskine and Lewin Williams.[2] South

---

1 See Frederick L. Ware, *Methodologies of Black Theology*, Cleveland, OH: The Pilgrim Press, 2002, pp. 28–65.

2 See Kortright Davis, *Emancipation Still Comin'* Maryknoll, NY: Orbis, 1990; Noel L. Erskine, *Decolonizing Theology: A Caribbean Perspective*, Maryknoll, NY: Orbis, 1981; Lewin Williams, *Caribbean Theology*, Frankfurt: Peter Lang, 1994.

African Perspectives include Allan Boesak, Itumeleng J. Mosala and Buti Tlhagale.[3]

This chapter is an attempt to outline the broad parameters of the meaning, methodological perspectives and major themes of Black Theology. While it offers a broad, inclusive and representative understanding of Black Theology, it is influenced also by the perspectives, biases and subjective views of the author, who is an educationalist and a leading Black theologian in Britain. It seeks to outline the way in which the person of God has been conceived, in largely ideological terms (that is, for socio-political purposes and outcomes), by Black Theology. Black Theology by its very nature argues for the God of equity and justice, not equality and fairness. This is an ideological point of departure or starting point.

This chapter illustrates how Black Theology emerges from the faithful, critical reflections of Black people as they seek to make sense of their existential or lived realities in the world, and as such it is essentially an experiential theology. With this thought in mind, then, I will show how the incorporation of particular models of experiential, transformative pedagogy have assisted Black people to understand more clearly the emotive force and polemical, ideological thrust of Black Theology.

What is Black Theology?

Black Theology can be broadly understood as the self-conscious attempt to undertake rational and disciplined conversation about God and God's relationship to Black people in the world, looking at the past and the present, and imagining the future.[4]

The God that is at the centre of Black Theology is one who is largely, although not exclusively, understood in terms of God's revelation in 'Jesus Christ' in the light of the historical and contemporary reality of being 'Black'. The understanding of Blackness, or indeed of being Black, is one that is often seen in terms of suffering, struggle, marginalization and the oppression of Black people.

---

3 See Allan Boesaka A., *Farewell to Innocence: A Socio-Ethical Study on Black Theology and Black Power*, Maryknoll, NY: Orbis, 1997; Itumeleng J. Mosala, *Biblical Hermeneutics and Black Theology in South Africa*, Grand Rapids, MI: Eerdmans, 1989; Itumeleng J. Mosala and Buti Tlhagale (eds), *The Unquestionable Right to Be Free: Black Theology from South Africa*, Maryknoll, NY: Orbis, 1986.

4 An important aspect of Black Theology is the extent to which it attends to existential realities of lived experience of Black people within history, both in the past and present epochs. This emphasis upon the lived realities of Black people is one that seeks to displace notions of theology being 'distant' and unresponsive to the needs of ordinary people in this world, and is less concerned with metaphysical speculations about salvation in the next. For a helpful discussion on this issue, see Dwight N. Hopkins, *Introducing Black Theology of Liberation*, Maryknoll, NY: Orbis, 1999, pp. 1–14.

Black Theology is understood as a branch of the wider family of 'theologies of liberation'. This title refers to a group of socio-political theologies that seek to reinterpret the central meaning of the God event within history, particularly, in terms of the life, death and resurrection of Jesus the Christ. They provide a politicized, radical and socially transformative understanding of the Christian faith in the light of the lived realities and experiences of the poor, the marginalized and the oppressed.[5]

This enterprise named 'Black Theology' has branches across the world. The most obvious and perhaps significant examples can be found in such diverse places as North America,[6] the Caribbean,[7] South America (particularly, Brazil),[8] Southern Africa,[9] in mainland Europe, particularly in the Netherlands,[10] and of course in Britain, especially through the prism of the Black Theology journals.[11] In these differing contexts, the point of departure

---

5 For an important recent text that delineates the comparative developments in 'theologies of liberation', see Marcella Althaus-Reid, Ivan Patrella and Luis Carlos Susin (eds), *Another Possible World*, London: SCM, 2007.

6 For the best overview on the historical development of Black Theology in North America, see James H. Cone and Gayraud S. Wilmore (eds), *Black Theology: A Documentary History, 1966–1979*, Maryknoll, NY: Orbis, 1979, and James H. Cone and Gayraud S. Wilmore (eds), *Black Theology: A Documentary History, Vol. 2, 1980–1992*, Maryknoll, NY: Orbis, 1993.

7 One could argue that there is a semantic problem with naming the theory and practice of contextualized, liberative praxis-based approaches to theology that emerge from within the Caribbean context as 'Black Theology' as the term 'Black' was eschewed in favour of the alternative naming strategy of 'Caribbean theology'. Given the plural realities of the Caribbean, where the term 'Black' might be understood to pertain to only one section (albeit the numerical majority) of the population, has meant that its usage has proved problematic in this context. Nonetheless, one can point to a number of texts that include work that clearly engages with the overarching, substantive and thematic ideas that are replete within Black Theology. See Noel L. Erskine, *Decolonizing Theology: A Caribbean Perspective*, Maryknoll, NY: Orbis, 1983, and Lewin Williams, *Caribbean Theology*, New York: Peter Lang, 1994.

8 See Antonio Sant'Ana (National Ecumenical Commission to Combat Racism, Brazil), 'Black Spirituality: The Anchor of Black Lives', and Diana Fernandes dos Santos (Youth of the Methodist Church, Brazil), 'Black Heritage in Brazil', in Dwight N. Hopkins and Marjorie Lewis (eds), *Another World Is Possible: Spiritualities and Religions of Global Darker Peoples*, London: Equinox, 2009, pp. 293–9 and 300–4, respectively.

9 Mosala, *Biblical Hermeneutics and Black Theology*; Mosala and Tlhagale (eds), *The Unquestionable Right to be Free*.

10 See Theo Witvliet, *A Place in the Sun: An Introduction to Liberation Theology in the Third World*, London: SCM, 1985; The Womanist Theology Group, 'A Womanist Bibliodrama', in Paul Grant and Raj Patel (eds), *A Time to Act: Kairos 1992*, Birmingham: A Joint Publication of Racial Justice and the Black and Third World Theological Working Group, 1992, pp. 25–32.

11 *Black Theology in Britain: A Journal of Contextual Praxis* began in October 1998 and ran for seven issues, ending in 2001. The journal was relaunched in 2002 as *Black Theology: An International Journal*. Both journals were founded by the overarching

for Black Theology is the reality of being 'Black' in the world and the experience that grows out of this lived actuality of how the world treats you as a person of darker skin. This reality is then explored in dialogue within the overall framework of the Christian faith. This relationship between Black experience and Christianity continues, for the most part, to be the effective conduit that constitutes the ongoing development of Black Theology across the world.

Black Theology has grown out of the ongoing struggles of Black peoples to affirm their identity and very humanity in the face of seemingly insuperable odds.[12] African American scholars, such as Asante, estimate that upwards of 50 million African people were transported between Africa and the Americas over a 400-year period.[13] Inherent within that Black transatlantic movement of forced migration and labour was a form of biased, racialized teaching that asserted the inferiority and subhuman nature of the Black self.[14] The continued struggles of Black people that arise from the era of slavery can be seen in the overarching material poverty and marginalization of Black people across the world.[15]

In addition to the structural and disproportionate material poverty of Black people is the more psychological phenomenon that is the continuing tendency of Black people to internalize the damaging effects of such racialized demonization within the confines of the fragile human psyche.[16] The internalization of this demonized instruction has led to Black people

movement that is 'Black Theology in Britain' and have remained important conduits for the dissemination of Black Theology in Britain (and across the world). Among the Black scholars based in Britain who have written for the journal are Valentina Alexander, Joe Aldred, Mukti Barton, Robert Beckford, Kate Coleman, Lorraine Dixon, Ron Nathan, Michael Jagessar, Emmanuel Lartey and Anthony Reddie.

12 See Dwight N. Hopkins, *Down, Up and Over: Slave Religion and Black Theology*, Minneapolis: Fortress, 2000, pp. 11–36.

13 See Molefi Kete Asante, 'Afrocentricity and Culture', in Molefi Kete Asante and Kariamu Welsh Asante (eds), *African Culture: The Rhythms of Unity*, Trenton, NJ: First Africa World Press, 1990, pp. 3–12.

14 See Eric Williams, *Capitalism and Slavery*, London: André Deutsch, 1983.

15 See Dwight N. Hopkins, *Heart and Head: Black Theology, Past, Present and Future*, New York: Palgrave Macmillan, 2002, pp. 127–54.

16 The issues of Black self-negation have been explored by a number of Black pastoral and practical theologians. See James H. Harris, *Pastoral Theology: A Black Church Perspective*, Minneapolis: Fortress, 1991; Carroll A. Watkins Ali, *Survival and Liberation: Pastoral Theology in African American Context*, St Louis: Chalice Press, 1999; Homer U. Ashby Jr, *Our Home Is over Jordan: A Black Pastoral Theology*, St Louis: Chalice Press, 2003; Archie Smith Jr, *Navigating the Deep River: Spirituality in African American Families*, Cleveland, OH: United Church Press, 1997. In the British context, see Emmanuel Y. Lartey, *In Living Colour: Intercultural Approaches to Pastoral Care and Counselling*, London and Philadelphia: Jessica Kingsley, 2003; Anthony G. Reddie, *Nobodies to Somebodies: A Practical Theology for Education and Liberation*, Peterborough: Epworth, 2003.

directing the fire of their repressed and disparaged selves onto their own psyche and that of their peers with whom they share a common ancestry and ethnic identity.[17]

Black Theology as an academic discipline and, as a form of concrete faith-based practice, takes as its point of departure the reality of Black suffering in history. For many Black theologians, the brutal realities of the transatlantic slave trade provide the essential backdrop against which the ongoing drama of Black suffering in history is played out.[18]

Black Theology is, then, the deliberate attempt to connect the reality and substance of being Black and the development of ideas surrounding Blackness with one's sacred talk of God and God's relationship with the mass suffering of humanity who might be described as being Black people. It is important to note that the 'invention' of Blackness, as opposed to being 'African', is part of the ongoing development of human reconstruction that is a post-Enlightenment-modernist conceit.[19] Namely, that via the new forms of knowledge and understanding of truth that emerged from the Enlightenment, Euro-American thinkers constructed a notion of African people as 'less than' and 'different from' the thinking and interpretation of what it meant to be 'White'.[20]

Black Theology, then, is an action-based form of conversation about God that seeks to respond to the deep-seated racialized depictions of people of darker skin within the cultural imagination of Euro-Americans.[21] One may argue as to the appropriateness of using the term 'Black' as opposed to 'African' and, therefore, pose the concomitant question as to why slavery and suffering should feature so starkly within the framework of Black Theology. What about the African presence that existed long before the horrors of the transatlantic slave trade?[22] These questions, of course, are very valid ones and aspects of this intricate debate and conversation have been explored by thinkers within the Black Theology in Britain movement.[23]

---

17 Cornel West, *Race Matters*, Boston: Beacon, 1993, pp. 11–15.

18 See Hopkins, *Down, Up and Over.*

19 See Emmanuel C. Eze (ed.), *Race and the Enlightenment: A Reader*, New Malden, MA, and Oxford: Blackwell, 1997.

20 The latest work in this area at the time of writing is J. Kameron Carter, *Race: A Theological Account*, New York and London: Oxford University Press, 2008; Willie James Jennings, *The Christian Imagination: Theology and the Origins of Race*, New Haven and London: Yale University Press, 2010. See also Stephen G. Ray Jr, 'Contending for the Cross: Black Theology and the Ghosts of Modernity', *Black Theology* 8:1 (2010), pp. 53–68.

21 For an excellent treatment of the phenomenological features of 'race' and the attempts of Black Theology to respond to it, see Dwight N. Hopkins, *Being Human: Race, Culture and Religion*, Minneapolis: Fortress, 2005.

22 See Robin Walker, *When We Ruled*, London: Every Generation Media, 2006.

23 See Berrisford Lewis, 'Forging an Understanding of Black Humanity through Relationship: An Ubuntu Perspective', *Black Theology* 8:1 (2010), pp. 69–85; William Ackah, 'Back to Black or Diversity in the Diaspora: Re-Imagining Pan-African Christian Identity in the Twenty-First Century', *Black Theology* 8:3 (2010), pp. 341–56.

While the terms 'Black' and 'African' have much in common and often work as synonyms, there are nonetheless some significant differences between the two.[24] While 'African' may automatically translate into 'Black', not everything that is 'Black' necessarily translates into African.

While this work seeks to provide a comprehensive and representative overview of Black Theology, it is influenced also by the very distinctive context of the UK, where I live and work. The term 'Black' can be used in two specific ways within the British context, for example. For many people who use the term 'African' with which to name themselves and would indeed describe themselves as being 'African' or being of 'African descent', these descriptors could also echo to the term 'Black'. In effect, one could easily (if one so chose) substitute the term 'Black' for 'African' without any substantive loss of meaning to the person or persons being described. To articulate a position that uses the term 'African' is to connect oneself to a geographical area, a political and philosophical idea (as in the case of Afrocentricity)[25] or the historical phenomenon of a land mass and the peoples associated with it.

But to use the term 'Black' in a theological sense is to argue for a specific and intentional commitment to the cause of human liberation and societal transformation from *all elements that might be considered oppressive irrespective of the source from which that oppression has emerged.* I have put part of the last sentence in italics for this is of crucial import in understanding the central force of Black Theology. Black Theology is the attempt to reflect upon the presence and agency or activity of God in connection with the suffering and oppression of people of largely African descent. The latter believe and understand that their faith in a liberative God forms the basis for their fight against all the structured and systemic elements that oppress them and cause them to suffer.

The cause of Black suffering might well be elements or activities that have their basis in African cultures, such as female genital mutilation, for example. The 'Black' in Black Theology is committed to challenging all forms of oppression, even that which may have an African cultural basis to it. Black Theology is more than simply African cultural retention, or the reification of African cultural tropes, nor is it reducible to notions of African inculturation.[26] This is to say that Black Theology is not simply concerned with the

---

24 See 'The Prologue', in Anthony G. Reddie, *Working against the Grain: Re-Imaging Black in the 21st Century*, London: Equinox, 2008, pp. 1–8.

25 Afrocentricity is an overarching religio-philosophical framework adopted primarily by Diasporan Africans to construct an approach to Black existence that is informed by a corporate, collective and consistent unitary set of ideas and cultural norms that define what it means to be a Black African human being. For further details, see Molefi Kete Asante, *Afrocentricity*, Trenton, NJ: Africa World Press, 1980.

26 In order to see the difference between Black Theology and African inculturated theologies, see Emmanuel Y. Lartey, 'Theology and Liberation: The African Agenda', and Dwight N. Hopkins, 'Theologies in the USA', in Althaus-Reid, Petrella and Susin (eds), *Another Possible World*, pp. 80–93 and 94–101 respectively.

identification of Black cultures as specific and tangible elements in Black life and the need to infuse religious ideas in terms of such cultural practices. That is not to say that none of the aforementioned can be understood as Black Theology or that they do not contribute to the development of Black Theology, but they are not necessarily understood as Black Theology either. This is the case, particularly, if such cultural factors are the cause of patriarchy, sexism, hetero-normativity and essentialized discourses that eschew the reality of Black cultural diversity and heterogeneity or difference.

Using the term 'Black' as opposed to 'African' is also to take seriously the Diasporan routes or migratory journeys (most accurately to be seen as physical and economic forced migration) of people of African descent. The term 'Black' was (and remains) a deliberate and intentional naming strategy for people primarily of African descent living away from the continent of Africa, who were struggling under the yoke of racism and other forms of structural injustice at the hands of White people with power in the West.

The Black Power Movements[27] in the USA, the Caribbean and Britain,[28] for example, sought to draw on the African roots of Black life, while seeking to respond to the reality of being Black in an era when slavery and colonialism had drastically changed the very nature of what it meant to be a Black person in the world. Black Power drew on the nature of African cultures as part of its rationale, but did not limit itself solely to the provision of describing oneself as African in any strict historical sense.

Black Power as a concept predates the formal development of the Black Power Movement in the 1960s. The development of Black Theology as an

---

27 The 'Black Power Movement' came into full fruition in the 1960s, across the world, particularly in the USA and the Caribbean. The central ideas of the Black Power Movement included the attempt of Black peoples of African descent to develop a framework and a form of practice in which there was a marked sense of 'African pride', a commitment to 'self-determination' and a desire to challenge the racism, paternalism and arrogance of White authority and control that had exploited and oppressed Black peoples for centuries. Important antecedents of the Black Power Movement can be found in the life and work of figures such as Marcus Garvey and Franz Fannon. For further information on these figures, see Amy Jacques Garvey (ed.) *The Philosophy and Opinions of Marcus Garvey*, vol. 3, More Philosophy and Opinions of Marcus Garvey, selected and edited from previously unpublished material by E. U. Essien-Udom and Amy Jacques Garvey, London: Cassell, 1977. See also Tony Martin (ed.), *Message to the People: The Course of African Philosophy*, Dover, MA: Majority Press, 1986; Theodore G. Vincent, *Black Power and the Garvey Movement*, San Francisco: Rampart Press, 1972; Wilson Jeremiah Moses (ed.), *Classical Black Nationalism: From the American Revolution to Marcus Garvey*, New York and London: New York University Press, 1996. See also Frantz Fanon, *Black Skin, White Masks*, New York: Grove, 1967: London: MacGibbon & Kee, 1968. See also Steve Bikos, *I Write What I Like: A Selection of His Writings*, ed. Aelved Stubbs, London: Heinemann Educational, 1979.

28 For an excellent overview of the movement of Black Power and anti-colonial struggle, see Hakim Adi and Marika Sherwood (eds), *Pan-African History: Political Figures from Africa and Diaspora since 1787*, London: Routledge, 2003.

academic discipline emerges largely from the work of James H. Cone who sought to combine the Christian-inspired activism of Martin Luther King Jr with the militant Black nationalism of Malcolm X in order to create a Black Theology of liberation.[29] The term 'Black' as opposed to the terms 'Afro' or 'African' is used in order to denote the explicit ideological and liberationist perspective of this theological formulation.

In the UK, the term 'Black' is used in a dual sense. The more obvious use of the term refers to Black people of African descent who have experienced oppression, suffering and poverty in a world run by and organized for the benefit of White people with power. The other, alternative understanding of the term 'Black' that sits alongside the first is one that draws upon the sense of a shared experience of marginalization, oppression and hardship, in which other peoples, who might also be described as being marginalized, share a common experience of struggle. The term 'Black' within this book does not refer simply to one's epidermis, but is also a political statement relating to the sense of a lived experience within the world that often overlooks the needs and concerns of darker-skinned peoples. In this second understanding, 'Black' has come to represent the common struggle of all persons from minority ethnic groupings seeking to reflect on and challenge White hegemony.[30]

Michael Jagessar and I describe 'Black' in the context of 'postcolonial Britain' as being a socially constructed, marginalized 'other' in the body politic of this nation.[31] That, in effect, in a nation whose indices for belonging and acceptance are still predicated on assumptions around normative 'Whiteness', to be 'Black' and/or to organize oneself around the conceptual realities of 'Blackness' is to adopt the position of the 'other' or, to quote the former British Prime minister Margaret Thatcher, to be 'the enemy within'.

So the 'Black' in Black Theology in Britain, for example, becomes a symbolic totem that unifies all minority ethnic peoples who have been oppressed and marginalized in economic, political, cultural and gendered ways and who desire, in and through their belief in God, to change and transform the world.

This transformation that Black people seek is one that better represents and reflects the 'Kingdom of God' or 'God's rule' or 'Reign' or the 'Economy of God' – different terms for a specific time within history and beyond it, when justice, freedom and liberation will be available for all people and not just some. The motif of the coming Kingdom or 'Reign of God', and the

---

29 See James H. Cone, *Black Theology and Black Power*, New York: Harper San Francisco, 1989 [1969], and *A Black Theology of Liberation*, Maryknoll, NY: Orbis, 1990 [1970].

30 See A. Sivanandan, *Communities of Resistance: Writings on Black Struggles for Socialism*, London: Verso, 1990, on the rise of coalition politics in post-war Britain.

31 See Michael N. Jagessar and Anthony G. Reddie (eds), *Postcolonial Black British Theology: New Textures and Themes*, Peterborough: Epworth, 2007, pp. xiii–xv.

need for oppressed Black peoples to work in solidarity with God in anticipation of this moment in history, is one that resonates throughout the entire literature of Black Theology.

In a very real sense one can say that the underlying rationale for Black Theology as an academic discipline in addition to its attempt to convert its ideas into concrete practice rests and falls on the belief in the possibilities of transformation – in the possibilities of individual and collective change for justice and equity for all poor people across the world. If God is not one of justice then Black Theology ceases to have any intellectual meaning or any practical application to the lives of Black peoples across the globe.[32]

Black Theology and the Christian faith

Black Theology is a broad movement that encompasses a variety of perspectives and methods. For example, not all scholars who seek to work within the framework of Black Theology would necessarily describe themselves as people of Christian faith.

Indeed, Black theologians have attempted to write within a variety of religious frameworks and none. In seeking to outline the definitional dimensions of Black Theology, we need to acknowledge that there is a growing wealth of literature that has explored Black Theology from within other religious paradigms, including Rastafari,[33] Hinduism[34] and traditional African religions.[35] In the USA, Anthony Pinn has sought to use humanism as a vehicle for exploring notions of Black Theology, which reject the traditional theism of Christian-inspired theology.[36]

While noting these significant alternative versions of Black Theology, it is equally important to realize that most writing and reflection in the area of Black Theology in Britain, however, has been dominated by a Christian purview. At the heart of Black Theology within the Christian framework

---

32 This central theological question pertaining to whether God can be best (if ever) understood as one of liberation whose predisposition is to be in actual solidarity with poor, marginalized and oppressed Black peoples has been challenged most vociferously by William R. Jones, *Is God a White Racist? A Preamble to Black Theology*, Boston, MA: Beacon, 1998, and Anthony B. Pinn, *Why Lord? Suffering and Evil in Black Theology*, New York: Continuum, 1995.

33 See William David Spencer, *Dread Jesus*, London: SPCK, 1999.

34 Michael N. Jagessar, 'Liberating Cricket: Through the Optic of Ashutosh Gowariker's Lagaan', *Black Theology* 2:2 (2004), pp. 239–49.

35 See Marcus Louis Harvey, 'Engaging the Orisa: An Exploration of the Yoruba Concepts of *Ibeji* and *Olokun* as Theoretical Principles in Black Theology', *Black Theology* 6:1 (2008), pp. 61–82.

36 See Anthony B. Pinn, *Why Lord?* and *African American Humanist Principles: Living and Thinking like the Children of Nimrod*, New York: Palgrave Macmillan, 2004.

is the concept of 'liberation'. In using this term, I mean to suggest that the word 'Black' comes to represent God's symbolic and actual solidarity with oppressed people, the majority of whom have been consigned to the marginal spaces of the world solely on the grounds of their very Blackness.[37]

Black Theology is committed to challenging the systemic frameworks that assert particular practices and ideas as being as they should be (that is, normative – usually governed by the powerful), while ignoring the claims of those who are marginalized and are powerless, often demonizing the perspectives of the latter as being aberrant or even heretical.[38] This process of seeking to change the actual workings of the world and to assist the oppressed and the marginalized to be free 'in this world' and in the world to come is one that is understood as 'liberation'.

The methodological point of departure in my understanding of Black Theology aligns itself with the most well-known and representative of the different traditions of Black Theology, namely the 'hermeneutical school'.[39] The term 'hermeneutics' comes from the world of biblical studies and can be understood as the art or science of interpretation, particularly interpreting what one might term 'sacred texts'. This school of thought is one that seeks to locate Black Theology within the Christian tradition. Scholars in the 'hermeneutical school' seek to rethink and reinterpret the meaning of Christian faith and the work of the Church in the light of the liberating ministry of Jesus the Christ, which in turn is correlated with the very real existential struggles of Black people. This model of Black Theology seeks to utilize the tools within Christian tradition in order to create a liberative framework for articulating the quest for Black freedom. However, this branch of Black Theology is the most representative of the bulk of scholars who would identify themselves with the cause of Black Theology.

Central to the Christian perspective on Black Theology is the position and role of Jesus. Black Theology has always been an essentially Christocentric movement. What I mean by this term is that Black Theology has taken as its definitive central point the person and work of Jesus and his relationship with the suffering and struggles of the grass-roots proletariat in the first-century epoch of Judaea.[40] The relationship of the 'Jesus of history' in his context is then juxtaposed with the 'Christ of faith's' continued involvement in the lives of the economically marginalized and the socio-political and cultural oppression of Black people in the contrasting eras of modernity and postmodernity.

---

37 Cone, *Black Theology of Liberation.*

38 See Kwok Pui-Lan, *Postcolonial Imagination and Feminist Theology*, Louisville, KY: Westminster John Knox, 2005.

39 See Ware, *Methodologies of Black Theology*, pp. 28–65.

40 See William R. Hertzog II, *Parables as Subversive Speech: Jesus as Pedagogue of the Oppressed*, Louisville, KY: Westminster John Knox, 1994.

The concentration on Christology in Black Theology is not to suggest that Black Theology does not believe in the doctrine of God as Supreme Creator or in the Holy Spirit as Sustainer; but there is a definite sense that Jesus is the focus of theological reflection within Black Theology across the world. For many, the most important person in the Christocentric development of Black Theology has been the African American Black theologian, James H. Cone. Cone's landmark trilogy of books in the late 1960s and early 70s, *Black Theology and Black Power*, *A Black Theology of Liberation* and *God of the Oppressed*,[41] remain the dominant texts in outlining the importance of conceiving Christology from the perspective of disenfranchised and oppressed Black peoples across the world.

Despite the central importance of James Cone to the development of Black Theology, Black Theology did not begin with his writings in the late 1960s and 70s. Instead, we have to look to the era of slavery and the mass incarceration of enslaved Africans for the birth of Black Theology. When enslaved Africans began to reimagine their existence and their destiny and sought to fight for their freedom, using the frameworks of a reinterpreted Christian faith as they did so, these people were engaging in the very first documented examples of Black Theology.

A nascent model of Black Theology can be found in the actions of Sam Sharpe. Sharpe was a Baptist deacon who initiated one of the largest rebellions against slavery in the Caribbean, when he and other enslaved Africans fought for their freedom in the Christmas period of 1831. This early model of Black Theology can be seen in Sharpe's declaration that Jesus was a liberator, and that human beings were created by God for freedom.[42] Biblical texts like Luke 4.16–19 or Matthew 25.31–46 became 'proof texts' that God, as reflected in the life and teachings of Jesus, was on the side of the oppressed and their suffering, and against the perpetrators of the slave trade. So, long before the great Latin American liberation theologian Jon Sobrino wrote his landmark text *Jesus the Liberator*,[43] enslaved Africans were already working with an acute, practical, experiential theological framework attuned to their existential realities – albeit not written down in the form of a systematic theology! This Black radical tradition in Christianity – Black Theology – continues in the present day. Black people have continued to reinterpret the meaning of the Christian faith in order to challenge illegitimate White power (and Black power, also, when it should be called to account) and to proclaim freedom for all people.

---

41 See James H. Cone, *God of the Oppressed*, New York: Seabury, 1975.

42 See Anthony G. Reddie, *Black Theology in Transatlantic Dialogue*, New York: Palgrave Macmillan, 2006.

43 See Jon Sobrino, *Jesus the Liberator: A Historical-Theological View*, Maryknoll, NY: Orbis, 1993.

Helping people to understand Black Theology

As I have illustrated, Black Theology did not begin with the intellectual musings of a people who had the luxury of being able to reflect benignly on their comfortable existence, imagining what God might be like. Conversely, Black Theology emerged from the fiery furnace of oppression and hardship. In the midst of the tumultuous struggles, pains and sufferings, Black people began to imagine and then struggle for a better world, a new existence in which there would be justice, dignity and freedom for all people, including themselves.

To understand Black Theology one needs to understand the reality of what it means to be exploited, oppressed, overlooked, ignored and consigned to death, mainly on the grounds of the colour of one's skin, which in turn is informed by the prejudices and discriminatory practices of others! What does it mean to be considered a 'nobody' in the world?

In order to understand Black Theology we have to engage with our emotions. It is essential to engage with our affective domain, in other words, we have to find ways in which to engage with the emotional and feeling centres of the self, as opposed to relying purely on our intellectual and thinking processes – that is, cognition.

Much of my own work over the last several years has been concerned with helping predominantly Black and White students to understand the central ideas of Black Theology. In this work, I have often relied on a participative approach to doing Black Theology, which has been drawn from the arena of Christian education, as a branch of practical theology.[44]

This approach to undertaking Black Theology has been used in order to help others to 'get it', that is, to see and to feel the necessity for Black Theology. This work has largely been done in theological education, where my pedagogical and polemical charge for Black Theology has been an inductive rationale that seeks to change hearts and minds, rather than the mere deductive *raison d'être* of simply seeking to provide more and better information. My approach to undertaking Black Theology is one that seeks to use models of transformative learning and participative group reflection (what I call a 'participative process' or method) as a way of explaining and developing new ways of understanding Black Theology and the concomitant practice of engaging in radical and liberative God-talk in the light of Black suffering, struggle, marginalization and oppression. In effect, my approach to teaching Black Theology rests upon the struggling for truth through activity-based learning as a means of creating new knowledge and ways of perceiving the truth.

---

44 For development of this approach to doing Black Theology, see Anthony G. Reddie, *Dramatizing Theologies: A Participative Approach to Black God-Talk*, London: Equinox, 2006.

One of my favourite exercises for enabling adult learners to understand something of the central force of and the necessity for Black Theology is entitled 'What Do You See?'[45] The aim of the exercise is to assist adult learners in seeing how one's position and reality in the world leads inevitably to particular ways of imagining the divine, and the resultant relationship of the divine to the situation and the context in which the individual or any group of peoples live.[46]

As a way of assisting the learner to come to terms with the most foundational of ideas and concerns that are central to Black Theology I am going to introduce this exercise, and describe how it has been used as a means of teaching Black Theology – that is, enabling others to 'get it'.

Exercise: 'What Do You See?'

For the exercise you will need a central object around which the various participants will sit. You will also need a number of pieces of paper; most usually A4 sheets have been used in the past. These pieces of paper will be affixed to the central object at regular intervals across its body, so that, when people are sitting in a circle around it, no one person or group of people can see all the pieces of paper and what is written on them. I will talk a little more about the slogans on the pieces of paper in a short while. For the exercise to work, I have sometimes used a large circular item like a laundry basket or, more recently, a more portable item like a series of A2 boards that can be pinned together to make a three-sided freestanding object that stands on top of a coffee table. On the board or on the laundry basket (or something similar) you should place a series of A4-sized pieces of paper that are comprised of different colours. Most times, there are five pieces of paper. Each piece of paper has a letter written on the top of it. Usually, the letters simply read 'A', 'B', 'C', 'D', 'E' and are written across the top of each sheet. Depending upon the size of the object, I then place the sheets on which the letters are placed at regular intervals around the central/circular object.

On each piece of paper, underneath the letter, I usually write a short pithy statement. Examples of statements I have used include: (1) 'A woman needs a man like a fish needs a bicycle'; (2) 'God has no hands except our hands'; (3) 'If wishes were horses, then beggars would ride';

---

45 This exercise was first developed and published in my first book. See Anthony G. Reddie, *Growing into Hope Vol. 1, Believing and Expecting*, Peterborough: Methodist Publishing House, 1998, pp. 5–6.

46 A major thematic thrust of this work is the Irish-American practical liberation theologian and religious educator, Thomas H. Groome. See *Christian Religious Education: Sharing Our Story and Vision*, San Francisco: Jossey-Bass, 1999 [1980], and *Sharing Faith: A Comprehensive Approach to Religious Education and Pastoral Ministry*, San Francisco: HarperSanFrancisco, 1991.

(4) 'To educate a man is to educate an individual. To educate a woman is to educate and liberate a nation'; (5) 'To overcome is to undertake'.

- As the facilitator of the group, I will stand next to the central object on which the letters are situated. I then ask all the other participants to form a circle around the central object.
- When all the individuals are seated in a circle around the central object, I uncover the central object and then ask the various participants seated in their various places around the circle, 'What do you see?' Each person, depending upon their particular vantage point, position or perspective, will see something slightly different than the person sitting next to them or close by. None of us see things the same way. This central fact is a result of how the various participants are seated, namely, in a circle around an object that has different pieces of paper placed at different points on the object itself. The exercise in figurative terms looks something like the diagram below.
- The exercise continues with me asking selected individuals how many A4 sheets of paper exist on the central object? In most cases, I have placed five such pieces of paper (but it could be more or less depending on the size of the group). Depending upon where individuals are sitting, they may be able to see one, two, three or in some exceptional cases even four of the A4 pieces of paper. One of the most basic points of learning that emerges in the early proceedings of the exercise is

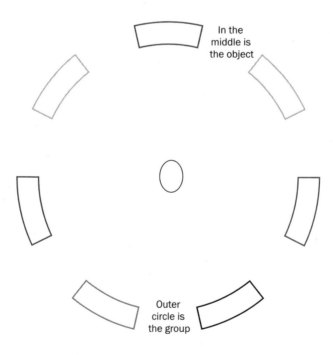

In the middle is the object

Outer circle is the group

that no one person or group of people can see everything that exists on the central object. Some individuals can see letters A, B C, others can see only the E, others C and D, or whatever combination, depending upon their particular vantage point in the circle. While most people can only see particular letters, if they are even remotely observant, they will be aware that there are more letters/pieces of paper in existence than what they can necessarily see for themselves. Why is that the case? Well, simply put, if each person listens to what the others on the opposite side of the circle, for example, are saying, then they will be aware that others can testify to the existence of other letters/pieces of A4 sheets that they themselves cannot see.[47]

Thus, many if not most of the group participants will know that more letters/pieces of paper exist than what they can see, simply because they will learn from other people. The first obvious point of learning from the exercise is that no one position has the monopoly on knowledge. The sum of what the group 'knows' derives from the sharing or pooling of knowledge between the different participants. This simple 'fact' may seem a benign or even an axiomatic truth, but when one considers the various ideologies or religious traditions that assert that their one perspective or position has the monopoly on truth,[48] often asserted through the prism of 'revelation' and notions of election, it does not take much imagination to see the radicality of this seemingly innocent assertion.[49]

---

47 This initial learning point in the exercise demonstrates the limitations of empiricist forms of epistemology. Namely, that rational, materialist, objective knowledge construction, often the favoured method since the Enlightenment, is of great import but has its limitations when one seeks to make sense of so-called truths such as beauty, love and the aesthetic appreciation of the other. This is of particular import when one considers the role and importance of revelation to our ways of knowing and the construction of religious and theologically derived knowledge and truth. This issue is addressed very well in David Willows, *Divine Knowledge: A Kierkegaardian Perspective on Christian Education*, Aldershot: Ashgate, 2001.

48 Kelly Brown Douglas, an African American Womanist theologian, argues that embedded within Evangelical Christianity is the concept of a 'Closed Monotheism', in which the rubric of salvation is reserved for those who claim allegiance to the saving work of Jesus Christ. The truth claims of other religious traditions are rejected as being of a lesser substance or altogether false, depending upon the branch of this tradition to which one adheres. See Kelly Brown Douglas, *What's Faith Got to Do with It? Black Bodies/Christian Souls*, Maryknoll, NY: Orbis, 2005, pp. 42–9.

49 One of the crucial elements of learning that emerges from this, the first part of the exercise, is the sense that there is an inherent form of ethnocentrism to many forms of religious faith in that the construction of knowledge within the prism of revealed truth leads almost inexorably to notions of preference for some and exclusion for others. Religious scholars such as John Hull have argued that only a form of critical openness to the 'other', formed from within the orbit of an inclusive liberal theological ethic, can safeguard against the worst excesses of religiously derived models of superiority, which

The exercise now becomes a more ideological one when the facilitator, me, then arbitrarily decides that only one letter is of any importance from this point onwards in the game. From this point forward, I usually decide that those who can see the letter 'E' (I have tended to choose the letter 'E' in order that it can stand for Europe or 'E' for Enlightenment) are charged with the task of describing the letter on the piece of paper facing them, and to interpret it for those who cannot see it. This is 'their burden', to evangelize and civilize those who are less enlightened, having not received the revelation of being able to witness to the 'E' for themselves. The slogan that accompanies the 'E' usually states, 'If wishes were horses, then beggars would ride'.

As the exercise now develops, I charge those who cannot see the 'E' to remember that the only letter that matters is the one they cannot see. They are told repeatedly that the letters they *can see* are worthless and without any merit, and they are forbidden to speak about or mention them again for the remainder of the exercise.

As the exercise develops, it soon becomes obvious that particular members of the group that cannot see the 'E' will not acquiesce and accept the superiority of a letter which they cannot grasp the truth of in any empirical sense. What I mean by this statement is that those who cannot see the 'E' can only take the accounts of those who can see it on trust. Those who cannot see the 'E' (which is the majority of the people in the exercise) are forced to accept the superiority of something of which they cannot be a part, while being instructed or even forced to deny that which is a direct part of their own immediate experience – that is, the letters that are immediately before them.[50]

When I have used the exercise with a variety of people in many workshops, across the length and breadth of the UK and in other countries also, it soon becomes patently obvious that there is an inherent unfairness and irrationality in the set-up of the game itself. Those participants who cannot see the 'E' begin to question the inherent unfairness and illogical premise of the exercise. Why should only one letter and those who can see it be deemed superior to all the others? Why is there this kind of arbitrary

---

as a corollary leads to the negation of the other. See John M. Hull, 'Critical Openness in Christian Nurture', in Jeff Astley and Leslie J. Francis (eds), *Critical Perspectives on Christian Education*, Leominster: Gracewing, 1994, pp. 251–75.

50 This exercise has been used as a means of highlighting the ethnocentric compliance of Christianity in its decision within the formative years of this religious tradition to work primarily within the framework of Greek Hellenistic thought, at the expense of other religio-cultural frameworks. See Robert E. Hood, *Must God Remain Greek? Afro-Cultures and God-Talk*, Minneapolis: Fortress, 1990. In the exercise many of the participants who cannot see the 'E' have remarked on the naturally polarizing tendencies of existing within a religious/ideological set-up where one group is deemed to be the sole possessor of truth. It is this form of missionary-based evangelical theology that Black Theology seeks to displace.

division between 'some' who are given great privileges in the game, simply because of an accident of where they are seated, versus those who are not so blessed? Hopefully, many of you can see the direct parallel between the set-up in the game and White, ethnocentric, evangelical mission theology?

Often, when I have enacted this exercise, I have 'upped the anti' in colloquial terms, by asserting that not only are the non-E symbols of no value but also those who follow them are savage and demonic.[51] I have then given permission to those who can see the 'E' to resort to punitive measures in order to convince those that cannot see it to acquiesce to the power of the former. Those that can see the 'E' often invoke a variety of coercive measures in order to 'persuade' their fellow participants in the exercise to 'see' the superiority of that letter.

On occasions, some have resorted to powerful forms of evangelical preaching, seeking to exhort their fellow game-players to resist the claims of the untruths that confront them, namely, the other non-E letters in the exercise, in order to convert these 'heathens' to the one true 'enlightenment'[52] – namely, that of the 'E'. Yet on other occasions, those trying to exhort their fellow participants to change their minds have simply used the threat of violence, plus various forms of intellectual coercion, such as the questionable theories of election, with which to 'win over their converts' to their way of thinking.

Hopefully, as I have described the workings of the exercise, you will begin to see the metaphorical basis of this participative activity. As the exercise develops, many of the participants begin to experience and feel some of the dynamics of oppressive structures and frameworks and how these elements impact upon those caught up within them.

For those who can see the 'E', their actions often vary from easy compliance[53] to subtle forms of resistance, to the notion that they are superior to

---

51 Robert Warrior, a Native American scholar, has argued that it was precisely this form of closed monotheistic notion of 'Manifest Destiny' and election that enabled White Euro-American Protestants to commandeer the land from native peoples on the basis that the gods/God followed by the latter were aberrant and therefore, as a corollary, the people who followed such deities were themselves dangerous and not deserving of liberty or respect. See Robert Allen Warrior, 'A Native American Perspective: Canaanites, Cowboys, and Indians', in R. S. Sugirtharajah (ed.), *Voices from the Margin: Interpreting the Bible in the Third World*, London and Maryknoll, NY: SPCK/Orbis, 1995, pp. 277–85.

52 It has been interesting to witness the different forms of interpretation those who can 'see' the 'E' invoke when trying to convince their fellow participants who cannot see that letter. Some will state that 'E' stands for 'Enlightenment' or 'Europe' or 'Education'. Of course it needs to be said that the favoured letter does not have to be an 'E' but for the sake of argument and tradition I have usually resorted to the 'E' when playing this particular game/exercise.

53 I once used this exercise in a theological college setting with a former police officer who was training for ordained ministry. This individual could see the 'E' and most expertly showed great skill and subtlety in coercing, cajoling and using terrorizing tactics to get others to accept his will regarding the superiority of the 'E'. In the debrief following

others. What has always fascinated me when using this exercise is the extent to which it has proved all too easy for those given power in the exercise arising from an arbitrary accident of seating to begin to believe the myths of their superiority! Most of the participants who can see the 'E' soon learn not to question their alleged and spurious superiority.[54] Others, in the context of the game, grow to enjoy and even love their status as the superior beings. Of course, one should add that there are many who can see 'E' but resist the temptation to exploit their supposedly exalted position.[55]

In terms of the majority of participants who cannot see the 'E', their actions are also quite varied. Most, if not all of them, will try to resist the imposition of those who can see the 'E'. Some resist by means of simply asserting their right to self-determination and the fact that they can see other letters aside from the 'E' that is being imposed upon them. Scholars such as Valentina Alexander[56] and Robert Beckford have termed this form of resistance 'passive radicalism'. This mode of anti-oppressive struggle is one that is based on a form of a pneumatologically inspired connection with the Divine, whom the oppressed come to believe has created them to be free, through the power of the Spirit and Spirit-filled forms of religio-cultural practices. This form of assertion is an expression of an innate belief that it is a fundamental right on behalf of those who are being oppressed to seek to claim their freedom with God in and through the power of their religious association with the Supreme Being.

The freedom they claim is one that asserts their innate connection with a deity whose love and concern for them might not give rise to any concrete or material change in their existential realities, but nonetheless it bolsters their thinking and imagination to resist the imposition of others. In effect, this is an internalized form of resistance, where the ontological basis of Black humanity is preserved from the contaminating stain of the oppressor.

---

the exercise he was of the view that his former career as a police officer had fitted him well for the supposed 'game-playing' in this exercise.

54 James H. Cone argues that the greatest sin in Christian theology has been the silence of most White people to the vicious lie and unpalatable untruths of White supremacy. See James H. Cone, 'Theology's Great Sin: Silence in the Face of White Supremacy', *Black Theology* 2:2 (2004), pp. 139–52.

55 It can be argued that, in the context of the game, the minority who can see the 'E' and yet refuse to collude with the oppressive and exploitative structure of the game and the spurious superiority of their position are the ones who can be seen as exemplifying the radical change agents advocated by James Perkinson, who challenges White people to exercise a form of group traitor-like existence in the desire to stand against White supremacy and in solidarity with oppressed Black peoples. See James W. Perkinson, *White Theology: Outing Supremacy in Modernity*, New York: Palgrave Macmillan, 2004.

56 See Valentina Alexander, 'Passive and Active Radicalism in Black Led Churches', in Michael N. Jagessar and Anthony G. Reddie (eds), *Black Theology in Britain: A Reader*, London: Equinox, 2007, pp. 52–69; Robert Beckford, *Dread and Pentecostal: A Political Theology for the Black Church in Britain*, London: SPCK, 2000, pp. 46–8.

Passive radicalism has tended to be most visible and operative within the Black Pentecostal movement within Britain, although evidence of it can be found in other Black peoples, particular older individuals.

Conversely, 'active radicalism', where those who are marginalized and oppressed seek to confront the oppressive and dehumanizing structures in a more deliberate and explicit manner, can also be witnessed in the exercise. This occurs when those who cannot see the 'E' seek to adopt more confrontational measures for seeking to challenge the unfair and biased system of the game. Active radicalism is the form of resistance fiercely advocated by James Cone, in the very first self-articulated book on Black Theology. Cone seeks to provide a theological rationale for the militant activism of the Black Power Movement that was a powerful resource for Black self-determination and Black pride in the second half of the 1960s in North America.[57] One can witness aspects of active radicalism in Walter Rodney's ground-breaking 'Rasta inspired text' *The Groundings with My Brothers*,[58] also published in 1969.

In using this exercise, I am not suggesting that the participants who engage with it are suddenly and miraculously enabled to 'get' Black Theology in all its terms. Clearly, that would be a nonsensical and risible contention. I am also at pains to stress that the exercise is essentially 'only a game' and can, at best, only seek to reflect in an approximate manner the broader realities of White hegemony and Black suffering. It cannot mirror the true complexities, horrors and sheer absurdity of racism, racialized oppression, sexism, patriarchy and heterosexism. What it can and has done is to begin to sensitize and make participants politically aware of the ways in which mainstream, White Euro-American theology has been used to restrict and oppress Black people and other peoples from the global South.

Second, the exercise seeks to work as an active form of metaphor, in that it invites participants to make connections between the game, their experiences and emotions that have arisen from taking part in this activity and the theological reflections that follow. It is in this nexus of reflections on the exercise, and the further thoughts around the development of Black Theology, that the central truths of this theological movement begin to emerge for the learner.

Black Theology reflections from the exercise

The importance of this exercise is that it assists in making us aware of the many differing perspectives on knowledge and truths that exist in our world.

---

57 Cone, *Black Theology and Black Power*, pp. 5–61.

58 See Walter Rodney, *The Groundings with My Brothers*, London: Bogle-L'Ouverture Publications, 1990 [1969].

The exercise – 'What Do You See?' – challenges participants to see how particular standpoints and perspectives govern how we understand and accept
what is truth! Essentially, what one learns from the exercise, which is itself
a central tenet of Black Theology, is that all philosophical claims for truth
(epistemology) are invariably linked to the realities of power. That is, truth
is not only some kind of objective and tangible reality, but it is also subjective and intangible! What you believe and claim to be true is very much
dependent on how much power and influence one has to insist that one's
truth claims are legitimized.[59] The exercise enables those who experience
marginalization and any resultant oppression to ask whether truth resides
solely with those with power who can see the 'E'. The understanding of
Black Theology that arises from this exercise is one that reminds us all of the
continued erroneous belief at the heart of the globalized world order, that
only one set of people essentially matter in the world.[60]

This exercise has been used as a means of showing the relationship between theology and ideology. I have often linked this exercise to a later experiential, participative form of embodied theological game-playing entitled
'Re-defining the Norm'. In the latter exercise participants are challenged to
reconstruct a narrative using partial pieces of the story that are available to
them, while another group has all the pieces of the story at their disposal.
The exercise demonstrates how knowledge and truth claims are often po-
liced and controlled by those with power.

Very often as Black people in marginalized contexts we have had to continue
to press for the veracity of our experience in all forms and manner of discourse –
whether in writing, speech or in militant forms of protest – in order to challenge the systemic workings of the world, simply in order to be heard.[61] This
struggle is often a debilitating one. It requires Black people to challenge the
systemic workings of White hegemony in order that our marginalized presence
is realized. It is the pernicious pressure of this ongoing struggle that has led to
various forms of pathological behaviour being ascribed to Black people.[62]

---

59 See Reddie, *Nobodies to Somebodies*, pp. 132–40.

60 The Sri Lankan theologian Tissa Balasuriya has commented on the economic capi-
talistic Euro-American world (although, since he wrote his article, China and India have
become members of this elite world financial undertaking) and claims that it is constructed in order to benefit a few at the expense of the many across the globe. See Tissa
Balasuriya, 'Liberation of the Affluent', *Black Theology* 1:1 (2002), pp. 83–113.

61 See Paul Grant and Raj Patel (eds), *A Time to Speak: Perspectives of Black Christians in Britain*, Birmingham: A joint publication of Racial Justice and the Black Theology
Working Group, 1990. See also Grant and Patel (eds), *A Time to Act*.

62 A number of Black pastoral theologians have sought to develop theoretical and practical resources that seek to help and assist in the holistic development and growth of the
Black psyche. See Homer U. Ashby Jr, *Our Home Is over Jordan*; Smith Jr, *Navigating
the Deep River*; Watkins Ali, *Survival and Liberation*; Edward P. Wimberly, *Moving from
Shame to Self-Worth: Preaching and Pastoral Care*, Nashville, TN: Abingdon, 1999.

Black people seeking faithful change have had to learn the hard lessons of keeping faith and maintaining dignity, integrity and self-worth against all the odds. This can be a hugely difficult and thankless task, and probably explains why some Black people decide to opt out of White, western-inspired epistemologies, as they will claim that the knowledge base inherent in these systems is one that is arbitrary and outside their own experiences.[63] This can be seen in various forms of religious Black nationalism. At the opposite end of the religious continuum, one can see the attraction of pietistic modes of spiritual resistance to White hegemony and globalized and indeed localized oppressions.[64] This becomes all the more operative when one witnesses the entrenched nature of the interlocking power systems that incarcerate the Black self and make any semblance or even notion of change appear to be a seemingly impossible one.[65]

These existing reflections have since been supplemented by an extensive knowledge base accrued from the countless 'performances' of this exercise. The exercise has been used to raise questions of epistemology. How do we know what is true when widely divergent truth claims exist? This exercise also demonstrates the ideological nature of knowledge and truth.[66] As many Black people have always stated, 'It's not what you know, it's who you know and who knows you that counts.'[67] The exercise has been used to

---

63 This can be witnessed in varying forms of Black religious nationalism that will eschew any contact or accommodation with White Euro-American thought forms. For an excellent scholarly work that outlines these various developments, see Algernon Austin, *Achieving Blackness: Race, Black Nationalism and Afrocentrism in the Twentieth Century*, New York and London: New York University Press, 2006. See also Nathaniel Samuel Murrell, William David Spencer and Adrian Anthony McFarlane (eds), *Chanting Down Babylon: The Rastafari Reader*, Philadelphia: Temple University Press, 1998.

64 Robert Beckford addresses some of these concerns in one of his earlier books. See Beckford, *Dread and Pentecostal*, pp. 178–82.

65 The notable African American Womanist ethicist Emilie Townes provides a penetrating analysis of the interlocking, systemic and embedded nature of evil within the workings of the globalized White Euro-American world order, where what passes for truth and justice is constantly being disguised and distorted, for the benefits of White hegemony. See Emilie M. Townes, *Womanist Ethics and the Cultural Production of Evil*, New York: Palgrave Macmillan, 2006.

66 Harry Singleton constructs a comparative analysis of the differing and yet complementary theological methods of Juan Luis Segundo and James H. Cone, in order to demonstrate how their respective work constructs robust theological models that expose the death-dealing religio-political ideologies of the rich and powerful. See Harry H. Singleton III, *Black Theology and Ideology: Deideological Dimensions in the Theology of James H. Cone*, Collegeville, MN: The Liturgical Press, 2002.

67 I first encountered this salient truth when I was undertaking earlier research looking at the means by which Black Theology when used within a Christian education framework (to create a Black Christian education of liberation) could become a vehicle for conscientization and empowerment of Black youth in Britain. This can be seen in the development of an experiential learning exercise entitled 'Re-defining the Norm', which

demonstrate how arbitrary claims for the superiority of one position over and against others inevitably leads to tyranny and oppression. This exercise enables participants to experience the 'abject nothingness' of non-being, which arrived through the pernicious epoch of the transatlantic slave trade.

In the context of the exercise, those who have been disenfranchised through their position of not being able to see the 'E' have naturally rebelled at the sheer absurdity of the premise at the heart of the game. How can it be that some people should be deemed superior to others on the basis of the accident of an arbitrary position? From experience, the more powerful, erudite or socially advantaged the participant in 'real life', the more they have reacted with anger and frustration at their position of marginalization and exclusion in the game. I have witnessed very well-connected and educated White people react in a kind of repressed pent-up fury at the privations heaped upon them as they have been deprived of autonomy, respect or perceived intelligence, within what is a simple exercise or game lasting no more than an hour! When one cannot see the 'E', nothing in your reality, including the letters you *can see* is afforded any value or merit whatsoever. Suddenly, one is reduced to being an object.[68]

The sharp sense of learning for many White participants in this exercise has arisen from the realization that this seemingly 'innocent game' suddenly maps onto a larger set of realities and experiences for Black and Asian people in Britain and across the world, which are anything but a game. The brutal realities of slavery, colonialism, racism, neo-colonialism, globalization, patriarchy, sexism and homophobia that have affected millions of Black people the world over are not trivial incidences that can be overcome by stating, 'I don't like this game, I'm not playing any more!'

On only one occasion when using this exercise have I encountered this phrase. On that occasion, a very conservative and repressed White woman training for the Anglican ministry got up and proceeded to walk out of the room. In response to her retort that 'she wasn't playing any more', I said 'And your actions show the necessary empathetic skills for ministry how again?'

Conversely, when Black and Asian people have taken part in the game and found themselves on the side of the oppressed unable to see the 'E', they have often revelled in the exercise. For many of them, this exercise is simply a faint echo of the continued reality of oppression and hardship many of

---

became the central enacted metaphor for framing the essential truth in the contention that it is 'who you know and who knows you' that helps to shape what we come to understand as truth. See Reddie, *Nobodies to Somebodies*, pp. 134–40.

68 See Anthony B. Pinn, *Terror and Triumph: The Nature of Black Religion*, Minneapolis: Fortress, 2003, for an excellent treatment on the absurdities of racialized forms of oppression in which the Black self is reduced to 'absurd nothingness' and the Black body becomes a mere object on which notions of inferiority and primitivism are projected.

them face on a daily basis. When responding to the debriefing[69] that follows the 'action' part of the exercise, one Black participant said:

> Sitting on the other side of the circle and finding that what I can see and know to be true is completely disbelieved and ridiculed; this simply reminds me of the many times I've been stopped by the police whilst driving my BMW. It doesn't matter how much I try to explain what I know to be true about me and this car, the policeman still looks at me like I am an idiot who is incapable of telling the truth.[70]

The inescapable connection between a seemingly simple and innocent game and the larger experiential truths of Black life is one that lies at the heart of this exercise and my use of it as a way of enabling ordinary Black people to understand Black Theology.

Black Theology seeks to respond to the question of how and in what ways God cares about and is in solidarity with peoples who are oppressed and marginalized on the basis of their God-given, God-created Blackness. How can faith in God and the attempt to live in harmony and relationship with that God become the basis for oppressed peoples to imagine, to hope and indeed to live with the new consciousness or awareness of their place in history in the light of this new reality, as the basis for life?[71]

This experiential, practical, activity-based approach to Black Theology is one that attempts to engage learners in an embodied, emotional and literal fashion, in the central dynamics of issues concerning power, 'race' and knowledge claims for truth. This is especially the case if one asserts that its truths emanate from some process of revelation from a divine being. In the words of the great African American religious historian Robert Hood, 'Must God remain Greek?' Why is it that the bulk of revelation in Christianity has

---

69 It is essential that participants are enabled to debrief and come out of role when the active part of the exercise is completed. I have always sought to give participants opportunities to explore their feelings and reflect on their thoughts as they attempt to make sense of the exercise in which they have been immersed. This and the many other exercises and dramas I have written attempt to connect the resultant emotions and thoughts that have emerged in the game-playing with a larger set of realities and experiences that have impacted upon Black people in the world, in both contemporary and historical periods in history. This method for undertaking Black Theology lies at the heart of my participative approach to this subject. Reference is made to debriefing or 'coming out of role' in the introduction to Anthony G. Reddie, *Acting in Solidarity: Reflections in Critical Christianity*, London: Darton, Longman and Todd, 2005, pp. xvii–xxii.

70 This statement was made during a performance of this exercise in a community church setting in North London in 2000.

71 My earlier attempts at creating an accessible and participatory-based approach to assisting people to understand the importance and relevance for Black Theology can be found in Reddie, *Growing into Hope,* vols 1 and 2.

been safely ensconced within Hellenistic or Greek-derived thought forms, often at the expense of African-derived forms of knowledge and truth?

The questions posed by Black Theology on these important issues are vital because this model of Christian-inspired theological reflection represents the sacred faith-inspired thinking and action on the life of Black people, detailing their hopes, aspirations and beliefs for another world, within and beyond the present reality, in which their existence is one largely of struggle, oppression and sheer hardship.[72]

One should approach Black Theology as a very different entity from the mainstream of White Euro-American God-talk. When James H. Cone or Womanists like Jacquelyn Grant helped to give voice to a radical Black Jesus, focused on rethinking the basic tenets of Christianity, they did so in order to provide resources for the mass of suffering and oppressed Black humanity. Their scholarship and the activism of those that followed them was a plea to create a model of Christian-inspired thinking and action that would give voice to the cries of pain, frustration, hardship, sorrow, joys and the sheer unquenchable life force of Black people to survive and thrive in a world in which they are often treated as mere objects and not subjects.[73] Black Theology represents a committed and rational response to the challenges of being a Black human being in a world run by White people with power for the benefit of others like themselves.[74]

The experiential dimension of Black Theology is summarized in one of my favourite sayings, first expressed to me by my mother – namely, 'Who feels it, knows it'.[75] Black Theology seeks to pose the critical question regarding Black existence – 'What have we felt?' This question is followed by the corollary, namely, 'what have we known to be true?' The second question naturally grows out of the implications of the first. In the light of what we have felt, in what way does that basic foundational question give rise to the challenge to seek meaning and truth from one's continued existence of struggle in the world? And let us not be persuaded by neo-conservative apologists who will point to the disproportionately small number of Black successes as the basis for arguing that the unremitting reality of marginalization, economic poverty, societal indifference, disproportionate levels of ill health, poor provisions for education and psycho-psychotic nihilism are not the lot of the bulk of Black peoples the world over. The election of a Black president in the USA was indeed a cause for much celebration, but

---

72 This notion of 'another world' being possible is addressed with great eloquence by a number of Black (in the wider political sense) scholars from across the world. See Hopkins and Lewis (eds), *Another World Is Possible*.

73 I am indebted to Inderjit Bhogal for his insights on the developmental process of oppressed and marginalized people moving from a reactive mode of survival to a more proactive sense of seeking to thrive and indeed thriving within the present world order.

74 See Hopkins, *Heart and Head*, pp. 127–54.

75 See Reddie, *Dramatizing Theologies*, pp. 22–4.

let us not forget that he largely had to disavow his very Blackness in order to do so.[76]

Black Theology has not died, as some recent doomsayers have predicted,[77] but it is definitely in need of re-energizing.[78] Black Theology must reaffirm its commitment to the massed ranks of ordinary Black people consigned to the margins of the so-called New World Order.[79] The vision for the ongoing protesting and iconoclastic presence of Black Theology in the world remains undimmed. The systemic and systematic workings of the present globalized world order that leaves the few who are able to see the 'E' in a position to control the world's resources while the many who cannot see the 'E' are consigned to lesser status has not abated. Black Theology, to my mind, remains the most potent of faithful frameworks for reimagining a world that has peace, justice and equity at the centre of its daily operations for all people, regardless of the colour of one's skin. Long may that struggle continue! Long live Black Theology!

Questions

1. What are the strengths and weaknesses of this approach to theology?
2. Some people will argue that by placing greater emphasis upon action and transformation rather than doctrine Black Theology seems to downplay Christian tradition in favour of contemporary relevance. Is this a problem? If yes, then why? And if not, then why not?

---

76 It is worth noting that Barack Obama in his Democratic nomination acceptance speech, of 28 August 2008, did not once make reference to or mention that he was 'Black' or 'African American'. In his reference to Martin Luther King Jnr's famous 'I Have a Dream' speech, no reference was made to the fact that King's speech was in the context of the fight for civil rights and anti-racist struggle, or that speaker of those eloquent words was also a Black man or 'African American' like the person invoking the speech in the first place. See http://uk.youtube.com/watch?v=dtL-1V3OZ0c.

77 See Alistair Kee, *The Rise and Demise of Black Theology*, London: SCM, 2008.

78 This form of re-energizing and challenge can be seen in a number of comparatively recent texts, such as Linda E. Thomas (ed.), *Living Stones in the Household of God: The Legacy and Future of Black Theology*, Minneapolis: Fortress, 2004; Iva E. Carruthers, Frederick D. Haynes III and Jeremiah A. Wright Jr (eds), *Blow the Trumpet in Zion: Global Vision and Action for the 21st Century Black Church*, Minneapolis: Fortress, 2005.

79 Although the term has a long derivation going back to the end of the First World War and the foundation of the League of Nations, I am using this term in the light of the more recent usage by George Bush Sr as reported in the *Time Magazine* cover story of the 11 December 1989. The notion of the new world order of western globalized power has been addressed from within the context of religion and theology by Dwight Hopkins *et al*. See Dwight N. Hopkins, Lois Ann Lorentzen, Eduardo Mendieta and David Batstone (eds), *Religions/Globalizations: Theories and Cases*, Durham, NC, and London: Duke University Press, 2001.

3. Black Theology takes a very critical and sceptical view of existing knowledge claims of truth that emanate from the status quo. Is this scepticism justified? What do you say to those who argue that it undermines 'traditional' faith and trust in religious authority?
4. Taking the metaphor of the game as 'real life', is there anything helpful we can say to those who cannot see the 'E'?

2

The Nature and Purpose of Black Theology: Telling a New Story

In this chapter, I want to look at one of the central concerns of Black Theology, namely, the attempt to rethink the very meaning of the Christian faith in order that it become consistent with, and relevant to, the realities of Black life as it is lived within history. Essentially, Black Theology is concerned not with protecting assumed truths or with providing a spiritualized understanding of history and human experience. Rather, its central concern is the need to provide the necessary resources for fruitful and flourishing living for all people, but particularly for Black people of African descent. Central to the very nature of Black Theology is the relationship it creates between the Black experience of suffering and hardship and the belief that the God revealed in Jesus Christ is in solidarity with those who experience oppression and marginalization. James Cone puts it like this:

> For if the essence of the gospel *is* the liberation of the oppressed, from socio-political humiliation for a new freedom in Christ Jesus (and I do not see how anyone can read the Scriptures and conclude otherwise), and if Christian theology *is* an explication of the meaning of that gospel for our time, must not theology itself have liberation as its starting point or run the risk of being at best idle talk and at worst blasphemy?[1]

In this chapter, I want to show how Black Theology seeks to reinterpret the very meaning of the Christian faith for the sole and explicit purposes of fighting for Black liberation in this world.

As we have seen from the outset of this book, Black Theology proceeds from the experience and reality of Black suffering in the world. In the light of the historical reality of Black suffering, Black Theology has sought to reinterpret the meaning of God that is revealed in the person of Jesus, in order to create a radical religious movement that is committed to the liberation of Black people. The basic *raison d'être* of Black Theology has been

---

1 James H. Cone, *God of the Oppressed*, New York: Seabury, 1975, pp. 51–2.

to challenge racism[2] and to confront the biased self-serving interpretation of the Christian faith that has given voice to and enabled the flourishing of White supremacy. Black Theology has challenged the alleged neutrality of Christianity, recognizing the ways in which White Euro-American churches used the Christian faith to assert the inferiority and lesser status of enslaved Africans.[3]

One of the central practices in Black theologians' armoury has been the use of suspicion in their interrogation of the accepted orthodoxies of Christian doctrine and church teaching. This 'hermeneutic of suspicion' is one that seeks to critically evaluate and critique normative assumptions around what is purported to be truth. Black theologians have critiqued the normativity of accepted beliefs, often seeing the assertion of such truth as owing more to the controlling dictates of church authority and power than any corroboration in and through the Holy Spirit. They have offered radical alternatives to understanding many of the central tenets of Christian theology, rethinking seemingly inviolate concepts and truths, for the sake of improved Christian praxis and liberation for the poor and the marginalized.

Like other 'theologies of liberation', Black Theology is governed by the necessity for orthopraxis (right action) as opposed to orthodoxy (right belief). Black theologians such as Cone, Hopkins and others have argued that priority is placed on God's spirit of liberation in the bodies and the consciousness of oppressed Black peoples rather than in fossilized doctrines often created by the powerful.[4]

This radical rereading of the essential meaning of the Christian faith operates for two primary reasons. First, in order to confer meaning on the often miserable existence and struggle of so many ordinary Black people in the world, in which 'hopelessness' and 'suffering' seem to go hand in hand with what it means to be Black in the world. And second, to challenge the biased distortions of the Christian faith itself, which lent itself to and became complicit in the marginalization and oppression of Black people the world over. Black Theology offers a no-holds-barred explication for a new understanding of God, in effect telling a new story of how this God in Christ has recognized and continues to be in solidarity with poor Black people across the world.

Similar to the use of an experiential exercise in the previous chapter, on which I subsequently reflected, I would now like to offer another exercise

---

2 See James H. Cone, 'Theology's Great Sin: Silence in the Face of White Supremacy', *Black Theology* 2:2 (2004), pp. 139–52.

3 See Anthony B. Pinn, *Terror and Triumph: The Nature of Black Religion*, Minneapolis: Fortress, 2003, pp. 1–80.

4 See Cone, *God of the Oppressed*, and Dwight N. Hopkins, *Heart and Head: Black Theology–Past, Present and Future*, New York and Basingstroke: Palgrave, 2002.

for use in a similar manner. This exercise has been used as a way of seeking to explain the lived experience of struggle and suffering that has led to Black people rethinking the very meaning of God and God's relationship to Black humanity. This reinterpretation operates from a critical perspective on how so-called truth and knowledge are constructed by those with power, which in turn is then used to validate particular forms of religiously inspired action. There is no stronger motivation and justification for any action than the powerful words of 'God told me to do it'. Black Theology has sought to tell another story, one that arises from the reality of their experiences of suffering and struggle, which are qualitatively different from the accounts that have arisen from the dictates of those with power. Elsewhere, I have spoken of the knowledge validation of Black Theology that emerges from the notion of 'Who feels it, knows it'.[5]

The following exercise has been used as a means of enabling participants in the workshops I have led in predominantly poor communities, often with Black people, to understand the hermeneutical (interpretative) enterprise of reassessing the meaning of God and faith, in the light of Black suffering and struggle.

Exercise: 'Paying the price'

For this exercise you will need the following resources:

a cup or mug
a small milk pan
an empty biscuit tin
a waste-paper basket
a washing-up bowl
a small ball (such as a table tennis ball)
chalk or tape to mark starting line.

Mark the 'starting line' and place the washing-up bowl a short distance from it. Place the waste-paper basket at a greater distance from the line. Continue like this, with the containers decreasing in size being further away from the starting line. Establish who in the group is right- or left-handed (this will be important during the activity). The object of the game is to gain the most points by throwing the ball into any of the containers. Contestants have to try and get to 100 points. Each person gets five throws. Throwing with your weaker hand doubles your points. The further away the object, the more points you score. Points are as follows: washing-up bowl = 1; waste-paper basket = 2; biscuit tin = 5; milk pan = 10; and cup = 20. Will people go for the easy options or risk going for the higher points?

---

5 Anthony G. Reddie, *Dramatizing Theologies: A Participative Approach to Black God-Talk*, London: Equinox, 2006, p. 22.

When the activity is over, bring the group back together. Discuss the choices people made. Who went for the easier targets? Who took up the challenge of the harder targets or threw with their weaker hand? Who won?

The activity brings up issues about taking the easy option or taking on a challenge or risk. Were you more likely to win aiming at the bowl or the cup? Does either choice provide guaranteed success? Do you think you were right to take the risk even if you didn't win?[6]

Post-exercise reflections

In this exercise, I wanted to find a playful and participative means of enabling those with whom I was engaging to understand the overarching learning outcome of the game. Namely, that the challenge to achieve the hoped-for end result in the game can be likened to the realities of Black struggle for so many people across the world. But of equal importance is the belief that this struggle is also replicated in the life and death of Jesus himself.

The exercise invites the participants to make an immediate assessment of how they are going to operate within the activity. Are they going to play it safe and aim for the smaller objects, in the realization that in doing so they are condemning themselves to likely dissatisfaction and frustration? When I have used this exercise with ordinary Black people, particularly young people under the age of 20, many have immediately grasped the nature of the exercise itself. They have seen the need to embrace the challenge that is posed in the game.

I remember one of the first occasions I used this exercise. I was leading a workshop for a number of Black, African Caribbean young people in Birmingham. We were meeting in the youth centre of a large Black majority church. Assisting me in leading the session was a much older Caribbean woman in her in early sixties. She had come to the UK from the Caribbean in the early 1960s as part of the '*Windrush* generation'.

As the young people began to engage with the exercise in an enthusiastic and vibrant manner, one began to witness the clear generational tensions between them and this older Black woman youth leader. As the young people all began to hurl the small ball at the container that was furthest away,

---

6 This exercise was first published in Anthony G. Reddie, *Growing into Hope, Vol. 2; Liberation and Change*, Peterborough: Methodist Publishing House, 1998, p. 58. It was subsequently adapted by Carol Troupe for use in non-confessional religious education lessons in state schools. The version I am using here is Carol Troupe's adapted version. It is used with her kind permission. This exercise is taken from Carol Troupe's website, *Living Out Faith*. This site contains teaching and learning materials that explore how Black Christian faith (informed by the central tenets of Black Theology) can be expressed and lived out by ordinary Black people. For further details, see http://www.livingoutfaith. org.uk/index.php.

namely, the cup (often using their weaker hand as they did so), so this older woman became increasingly exasperated. She felt the young people were being 'unrealistic' and 'over-ambitious' in attempting to get the small ball into the furthest container. She wanted them to play it safe.

And yet when I asked her if she had played it safe in her youth, she replied with an emphatic 'No'. She had left the small Caribbean island of Nevis in order to attain better prospects in the so-called 'Mother Country' of the Empire, namely, the United Kingdom. She had left her small village on the coast with only a few pounds in her purse, one suitcase and an address in Birmingham, where she hoped to arrive, in order to meet her parents she had not seen for nearly ten years.

As she was enabled to reflect on her own experiences of some 50 years past, it was clear that the exercise mirrored the continued commitment of Black people to engage in the struggle to change their existential realities, realizing that accepting the status quo was not an option. The restless energy of Black people to undertake the necessary struggle for change is what lies at the heart of Black Theology. The praxis (faithful action) of Black Theology rests upon this dynamic interplay between Black agency (self-determined activity born of one's own free will and choice to act) and the spirit of liberation that is God, revealed in Jesus Christ.

The exercise seeks to represent, in metaphorical terms, the challenges presented to Black people by a world governed by White exploitative power and the resultant outcome, which is racism. In order to achieve the hoped-for sense of liberation and social transformation, Black people, empowered by their belief in a God of liberation, have accepted the challenge of trying to 'win through' in order to realize their goals. Trying to accept the status quo and not accept the challenge of trying to 'win through' is not an option. African American Black theologian Dwight Hopkins puts it like this:

> Black theological spiritual practice fundamentally means social transformation of wicked structures and destructive systems that hold a boot to the necks of poor Black people in the United States. Any talk about the spirit in the black church that leaves unjust social relations in place serves a devilish way of life that breeds monopoly capitalism, the second-class status of women, the harmful military presence of the United States abroad, and, of course, racial supremacy over African Americans and other people of color.[7]

The exercise offers an accessible means of enabling ordinary Black people to reflect critically on the nature of Black agency in the world. In what ways have Black people sought to engage in faithful struggles in order to bring

---

7 See Hopkins, *Heart and Head*, p. 78.

about systemic change? CaribAmerican Black theologian Delroy Reid-Salmon argues that the Jamaican national hero Sam Sharpe represents an emblematic figure in the Diasporan African struggle for justice and equity.[8] Reid-Salmon cites Sharpe as being willing to 'pay the price' of liberation as the natural consequences of seeking to stand up against injustice.[9]

Alongside the iconic figure of Sam Sharpe in Jamaica, one can also point to the equally heroic figure of Nat Turner. The latter led a rebellion against slavery, in Virginia in 1831. Like Sharpe, he also paid with his life when attempting to fight for the freedom of Black people.

In the exercise, it has been interesting to note the means by which the majority of the participants opt for the most striking forms of engagement, namely, seeking to undertake the most difficult aspect of the game. While some others do attempt to make progress by means of throwing the ball at the nearer objects,[10] most opt for the more daring approaches.

Most of the participants recognized that in order to score the most points it was essential that they attempted the hardest option available to them. Most failed in their quest to get the ball into the cup from such a distance. Others, having failed with their initial throws, adopted a more pragmatic approach on later throws and attempted to secure some points by attempting the easier options. But even in the case of the latter, these pragmatic throws were only temporary tactics, occupying no more than two of the five throws available to them. Most participants usually settled for one or two safe throws and then concentrated their efforts on securing the higher, maximum points by aiming for the smaller receptacles the furthest distance away.

One of the most important insights that has arisen from the exercise is the reflection on the part of many of the participants that, on hindsight, they would not change their actions irrespective of whether they were successful or not. Namely, that even inevitable failure (in all the years I have been using the exercise to conscientize and empower ordinary Black people, no one has ever reached the magical 100 points) is not the worst element in the activity. For many, the worst outcome is simply not to attempt the struggle at all.

The set-up of the exercise invites the participants to take risks. The attraction of gaining the 100 points and so attaining the prize (I have always offered a real set of inducements for those participating) is tantalizing. The

---

8 See Delroy A. Reid-Salmon, 'Faith and the Gallows: The Cost of Liberation', in Anthony G. Reddie (ed.), *Black Theology, Slavery and Contemporary Christianity*, Aldershot: Ashgate, 2010, pp. 151–64.

9 Reid-Salmon, 'Faith and the Gallows'.

10 Which was affirmed in the first instance by the youth leader in the exercise – like notions of passive and active resistance as detailed in the previous chapter, all forms of struggle are legitimate.

THE NATURE AND PURPOSE OF BLACK THEOLOGY

desire to win through is real. The Black participants taking part in the game cannot help but engage with the challenge that is set before them. The intensity of the actions of the participants is increased the younger they are; teenagers are the most vociferous players in the game!

Black Theology reflections

The exercise seeks to provide an experiential means of enabling participant-learners to get a sense of how the lived experience of struggle and suffering has informed Black Theology. In the first instance, it is noteworthy to realize the ways in which enslaved Black peoples were able to relate their existential experience of suffering with biblical texts.

For many Black and other marginalized and oppressed people, Isaiah 53 has been a pivotal text as it taps into their experiences of struggle and oppression.[11] This passage in Isaiah has generated a great deal of debate for many years. Some have said that the person mentioned in the passage is Jesus. The passage foretells the sacrifice and suffering he would undergo in order that humankind might be reconciled to God. In contrast, others have argued that we should not bring our knowledge of later events as described in the New Testament (particularly the life, death and resurrection shown in the four Gospels), and use them to understand what an earlier passage might have meant. Could previous authors writing long before Jesus' birth really be thinking about him when they wrote this passage?

Within Black Theology a number of writers have located within the suffering of Jesus a sense of divine solidarity with their own historical and contemporary experiences of unjustified and unmerited suffering. Scholars such as Douglas, Cone and Terrell[12] have all explored the theological significance for Black people of Jesus' suffering on the cross as foretold in Isaiah 53.

Writing with reference to this theme, Terrell states:

Yet the tendency among Black people has been to identify wholly with the suffering of Jesus because the story made available to them – Jesus' story – tells of his profound affinity with their plight. Like the martyrs, they are committed to him because his story is their story. Jesus' death by crucifixion is a prototype of African Americans' death by *circumscription*.[13]

---

11 See James H. Cone, *A Black Theology of Liberation*, Maryknoll, NY: Orbis, [1970] 1990, pp. 110–28. See also Jacquelyn Grant, *White Women's Christ and Black Women's Jesus: Feminist Christology and Womanist Response*, Atlanta, GA: Scholar's Press, 1989, pp. 205–22.

12 See Kelly Brown Douglas, *The Black Christ*, Maryknoll, NY: Orbis, 1994; Cone, *God of the Oppressed*, pp. 108–95; JoAnne Marie Terrell, *Power in the Blood? The Cross in the African American Experience*, Marykmoll, NY: Orbis, 1998.

13 Terrell, *Power in the Blood?*, p. 34.

This radical identification with the undeserved suffering of an innocent individual has exerted a powerful hold on the imagination of many Black people and other marginalized and oppressed groups in the world.[14]

A number of biblical texts, particularly those in Mark's Gospel, provide textual evidence for the nature of Jesus' struggle. Some of the most salient texts include Mark 10.32–45 or Mark 8.27–33 and Mark 9.30–32. In these texts, we see Jesus contemplating the challenge and struggle that awaits him. Black Theology seeks to recast this struggle of the impending crucifixion not as death to achieve spiritual salvation for sinful humanity, as is often depicted in many traditional notions of the cross. Rather, the nature of Jesus' struggle in confronting the cross is beautifully summarized by David Isiorho as 'Jesus died because of our sins and not for them'.[15] He argues that Jesus died in solidarity with all those oppressed peoples for whom the struggle for liberation necessitated them facing their own contemporary crosses.[16]

The way of the cross for Jesus was not in order to fulfil the desires of 'God the Father' to wash away the sins of fallen humanity. Rather, Jesus dies the death of a subversive agitator whose courageous opposition to the imperial greed and colonial corruption of the Roman government and Jewish religious complicity gives rise to the symbolic power of sacrificial death for the sake of others. This death echoes that of so many Black people in history, whose struggle to overcome injustice is reflective of, and indeed is often inspired by, Jesus' own sacrifice. Womanist theologian Jacquelyn Grant argues that Jesus is a co-sufferer with ordinary poor Black people as they seek to confront unjust systems and powers in their efforts to fight for their freedom.[17]

Black theologians and their Womanist counterparts have sought to rethink the traditional categories of Christian theology in order to seek to make sense of their continued realities of poverty, marginalization and oppression over the past four hundred years. James Cone's most recent book seeks to link the sheer murderous absurdity of lynchings in the life experiences of African Americans in the United States with the cross of Jesus. Cone seeks to tell 'another story' of God's interaction with humankind by means of a re-appropriation of the cross in the light of Black suffering via the brutal realities of lynching. Cone states:

---

14 See Robert Beckford, *Jesus Is Dread*, London: Darton, Longman and Todd, 1998, and Riggins R. Earl Jr, *Dark Salutations: Ritual, God, and Greetings in the African American Community*, Harrisburg, PA: Trinity Press International, 2001, pp. 1–16.

15 Verbatim comment made by David Isiorho at the national Black Theology in Britain conference at the Queen's Foundation for Ecumenical Theological Education, July 2008. This comment was made in response to the paper he had presented, critiquing many of the traditional notions of Christ's sacrifice, particularly those that adhere to notions of 'penal substitution'. This paper was subsequently published in *Black Theology*. See David Isiorho, 'Black Identities and Faith Adherence: Social Policy and Penal Substitution in the Epoch of the SS *Empire Windrush*', *Black Theology* 7:3 (2009), pp. 282–99.

16 Isiorho, 'Black Identities and Faith Adherence', pp. 284–92.

17 See Grant, *White Women's Christ and Black Women's Jesus*, pp. 212–18.

The cross has been transformed into a harmless, non-offensive ornament that Christians wear around their necks. Rather than reminding us of the 'cost of discipleship', it has become a form of 'cheap grace', an easy way to salvation that doesn't force us to confront the power of Christ's message and mission. Until we can see the cross and the lynching tree together, until we can identify Christ with a 'recrucified' black body hanging from a lynching tree, there can be no genuine understanding of Christian identity in America, and no deliverance from the brutal legacy of slavery and white supremacy.[18]

This central intent of Black Theology in rethinking the normative understanding of the meaning of God as revealed in Jesus Christ has not simply been an esoteric, academic undertaking. This attempt to tell a new story has not been done simply to provide more erudite and articulate thoughts in order to demonstrate that Black people can think.[19] Rather, the deconstructive work of Black Theology has been undertaken in order to provide impetus for the necessity and inevitability of struggle. To quote James Cone once more:

> We conclude, then, that survival is a way of life for the black community. Black theology is a theology of survival because it seeks to interpret the theological significance of the being of a community whose existence is threatened by the power of nonbeing.[20]

Black Theology responds to concrete realities of Black struggle and suffering in the world and seeks to tell a new story regarding God's relationship with these marginalized and dispossessed peoples in order to reinterpret and offer meaning to these depressing realities of Black life.

One of the critical starting points of Black Theology has been the reality of Black peoples' struggle to understand themselves in the light of the ongoing nature of Black suffering, pain, marginalization and oppression. In the exercise, a number of the participants noted that how the activity had been constructed made it inevitable that they would act in a certain manner. Namely, that the desire to struggle to win through in the exercise became almost self-evident from the moment it was explained to them.

---

18 James H. Cone, *The Cross and the Lynching Tree*, Maryknoll, NY: Orbis, 2011, pp. xiv–xv.

19 It is important to note that this fact in itself is an important subtext for all forms of Black intellectual inquiry, as it was once thought that Black people lacked the capacity for critical, scholarly discourse. See Emmanuel C. Eze (ed.), *Race and the Enlightenment: A Reader*, New Malden, MA, Oxford: Blackwell, 1997.

20 Cone, *Black Theology of Liberation*, p. 16.

As a transformative, popular educator, of course, this form of construction in the exercise was quite deliberate. It was my intention to almost force the participants to engage with the exercise in an assertive manner. I developed the exercise in this way in order to try (as best one can, using any type of learning activity) to replicate the nature of the dialectical struggle (the challenge of reconciling opposing and often conflicting entities in order to achieve a semblance of resolution) that has faced Black people since the era of slavery. This critical challenge that has confronted Black people has often been termed 'double consciousness'.

W. E. B. Du Bois and double consciousness

The notion of competing realities is not a new phenomenon for Black people. One of the first people to wrestle with this phenomenon was W. E. B. Du Bois in his now classic text *The Souls of Black Folk*, first published in 1903. Du Bois detailed a phenomenon he termed 'double consciousness'. In using this term, Du Bois was speaking of the struggle that confronted Black people. It was a struggle within the Diasporan African tradition to reconcile two opposing realities at war within the Black mind.[21] This struggle for truth was one between two competing forces. Namely, whether one is determined by self-affirming – an internalized form of subjectivity that Pinn calls the quest for 'complex subjectivity'[22] – or by an all-embracing externalized form of rejection and objectification. Du Bois's most memorable comment in this book, which has to a great extent helped to define Black religious Diasporan theories on Black people over the course of the last century, was that 'the problem of the twentieth century is the problem of the colour line'.[23]

In the first instance there is the internalized vision held by Black people themselves, in which they see themselves in largely positive terms, as they attempt to construct an image for their self-determination in the world. This internalized vision is placed alongside the external world of White power and influence in which Black people have to deal with issues of degradation, demonization and dispossession. These two 'unreconciled strivings'[24] have continued to fight their tumultuous struggle within the battlefield of the Black mind.

In seeking to tell a new story, Black Theology has used the work of scholars such as Du Bois as a means of examining and addressing deep-seated issues that have long affected Black people. These include substantive issues relating to notions of identity that affect children of the African Diaspora.

---

21 W. E. B. Du Bois, *The Souls of Black Folk*, New York: Bantam Books, 1989, p. 3.
22 Pinn, *Terror and Triumph*, pp. 82–107.
23 Du Bois, *Souls of Black Folk*, p. xxxi.
24 Du Bois, *Souls of Black Folk*, p. 3.

For example, there are questions related to the sense of dislocation felt by many Black children in Britain and in other parts of the African Diaspora, as to whether they belong within White-majority western societies.[25]

This sense of dislocation is manifested in both psychological and physical terms. The forebears of these children were plucked from the ancestral cradle of Africa and transplanted to the Caribbean and the Americas. In the light of the rupture and breach in African Diasporan history, the past five centuries have been a perpetual and substantive struggle for self-definition – a search for a sense of identity that has not been dictated and imposed by White power.[26]

Du Bois understood the complexity of this dangerous duality within Black people. The struggle to accommodate internalized subjectivity and external objectification carried within it the calamitous seeds for ongoing mental ill health and widespread pathology. Du Bois understood the potency of biased racialized doctrines that asserted the subhuman character of the 'negro'. The struggle to resist the pernicious nature of this assault upon Black personhood became the dominant motif in Black religio-cultural discourse since the epoch of slavery. Du Bois wrote in 1946:

> The experience through which our ancestors have gone for four hundred years is part of our bone and sinew whether we know it or not. The methods which we evolved for opposing slavery and fighting prejudice are not to be forgotten, but learned for our own and others' instruction . . . The problem of our children is distinctive: when shall a colored child learn the color line? At home, at school or suddenly in the street? What shall we do in art and literature? Shall we seek to ignore our background and graft on a culture which does not wholly admit us, or build anew on that marvellous African . . . heritage?[27]

---

25 There has long been a 'back to Africa' motif to Black life in the West, as many Black activists have argued for a return to Africa, the ancestral home of all people of African descent. Arguably, the biggest ever movement that sought to encapsulate such hopes and dreams as a socio-political reality was that formed by Marcus Mosiah Garvey in the early part of the twentieth century. For more details on the Garvey movement, see Colin Grant, *Negro with a Hat: The Rise and Fall of Marcus Garvey*, New York and London: Oxford University Press, 2008. For an assessment of Garvey's movement, in terms of Black Theology, see Charles Lattimore Howard, 'Black Stars and Black Poverty: Critical Reflections upon Black Theology from a Garveyite Perspective', *Black Theology* 9:3 (2011), pp. 312–33.

26 See the work of the great African American historian Carter G. Woodson for work that reflects on the notion of the identity struggle of Black people that often arises from various forms of mis-education organized and perpetrated by White power. See Carter G. Woodson, *The Mis-Education of the Negro*, Trenton, NJ: Africa World Press, 1990 [1933].

27 W. E. B. Du Bois, *The Education of Black People: Ten Critiques, 1906–1960*, New York: The Monthly Review Press, 1973, p. 44.

Du Bois was chiefly a social scientist, and his early scholarly pursuits following his doctoral studies at Harvard University in 1895 were mainly concerned with using the insights of academics such as Max Weber to rebut the post-Enlightenment social scientific basis of racial theory. Du Bois soon realized that empirical social science could not bear the burden for responding to the ongoing negation and oppression of Black people.

Black religionists who pre-dated Black Theology's attempt to tell a new story

Pre-dating Du Bois's attempts to respond to the plight of Black people, religious activists such as Richard Allen and Edward Blyden[28] had used Christian teachings and a nascent Black Theology as their means of responding to the struggle for Black subjectivity. Richard Allen, a former slave, became the founder of the African American Episcopal Church (AME), which seceded from the American Episcopal Church because of the endemic racism of the latter ecclesial body.[29] Henry McNeal Turner, a descendant of Allen in the AME Church, began to construct an explicit African-centred conception of the Christian faith, arguing that an alignment with Africa should become a primary goal for Black Americans. This focus upon African ancestry would enable subjugated objects of Euro-American racism to find a suitable terrain for the subversive activism that would ultimately lead to liberation – the seeds of the academic model of Black Theology.

Pinn acknowledges the link between the African-centred teachings of the AME Church and the later Black nationalism of Marcus Garvey and the *Black Star Line* 'Back-to-Africa' movement of the early twentieth century.[30] The importance of this reinterpretation of the Christian faith is that it provides an alternative perspective on the relationship between religious faith and human suffering. In effect, these independent Black church leaders were using Black Christian faith as a means of developing an alternative narrative that would seek to make sense of Black struggle and suffering.

A central motif in the development of Black Theology has been its insistence on reinterpreting the basic meaning and intent of God. This has largely taken on a christological or Jesus-focused approach given the centrality of Jesus to the Christian faith as a whole.

---

28 See Edward Blyden, 'Africa's Service to the World: Discourse Delivered before the American Colonization Society, May 1880. The Scope and Meaning of "Ethiopia"', in Cain Hope Felder (ed.), *The Original African Heritage Study Bible*, Nashville, TN: James C. Winston Publishing Company, 1993, pp. 109–21.

29 Anne H. Pinn and Anthony B. Pinn, *Fortress Introduction to Black Church History*, Minneapolis: Fortress, 2002, pp. 32–43.

30 Pinn, *Terror and Triumph*, pp. 90–3.

This hermeneutical approach to Black Theology owes much to the pioneering work of James Cone. Reflecting on Cone's use of the Bible as a source and norm for undertaking Black Theology, Michael Joseph Brown writes:

> Although Cone, as a follower of Karl Barth, believed in the biblical grounding for his theological perspective, confirmation was not to be found in the writings of mainstream biblical scholarship. In response, Cone wrote his own biblical interpretation of Black theology.[31]

Like Cone and the majority of those Black theologians who are within the 'hermeneutical school', the Bible remains an essential source and norm for undertaking Black Theology.[32] The early Black church leaders cited by the Pinns in their introduction to Black church history were concerned with attempting to ally the biblical witness of a liberative God as depicted in the Bible with the troubled and contested nature of Black existence and experience. This work was undertaken in order to fashion an alternative meaning and intent for the Christian faith.

Rereading the Bible as central to 'telling a new story'

Although Black Theology is often undertaken by scholars who have been trained as systematic theologians or ethicists, a good deal of Black Theology work has sought to engage with the Bible as one of the key sources for seeking to develop a liberative model of the Christian faith that arises from the realities of Black suffering. One of the key reasons for using the Bible as an important source for doing Black Theology[33] lies in the relationship between the realities of Black suffering in history and the analogous examples of such experiences from within the biblical text.

Black theologians have sought to read the Bible in the light of the realities of Black suffering as a means of exemplifying the radical liberative qualities of God that would seem to demonstrate God's relationship with human suffering. The liberative dimension of the God of the Bible is one that seems to echo to the

---

31 Michael Joseph Brown, *The Blackening of the Bible: The Aims of African American Biblical Scholarship*, Harrisburg, PA: Trinity Press International, 2004, p. 18.

32 Frederick L. Ware, *Methodologies of Black Theology*, Cleveland, OH: Pilgrim Press, 2002, pp. 28–56.

33 This is in addition to the pragmatic perspective, which asserts that the Bible remains an important element in Black Christian practice, from within the Black church. See my previous reference to Gayraud Wilmore's notion of 'pragmatic spirituality', where essentially he is arguing that Black Theology is a 'practical' or pragmatic discipline, whose sole *raison d'être* is to proclaim the liberative qualities of God for the *sole* purposes of Black liberation.

metaphorical struggles of 'paying the price' for liberation that are replete within the experiential exercise I described at the beginning of this chapter. I have often encouraged participants to reflect on what biblical texts and stories would appear to resonate with and speak to the realities of suffering and struggle that have been the experiences of most Black people for the past 400 years.

As we have seen from the exercise at the beginning of this chapter, the struggle for Black liberation is not a timid or a passive affair. It requires the necessity of faith – in oneself and in God – to undertake the critical challenge of seeking to overturn the oppressive realities of the status quo that impinge on the individual or community.

Participants in the exercises, in addition to many of their forebears, will testify to the synergy that exists between Diasporan African suffering during the epoch of slavery and the experiences of the Israelites in the Hebrew Bible, more commonly known as the Old Testament. The Exodus narrative – God's decisive entering into history in order to liberate God's people from the shackles of bondage and slavery in Egypt – has been a key theme in Diasporan Black thought and Christian reflection. Randall Bailey, a renowned African American Hebrew Bible scholar, explores the relationship of African American spirituals and 'Old Testament' texts in his exploration of how enslaved Africans established a relationship between the immediacy of their suffering and such realities within the Bible.[34] Citing Bailey's reflections on 'Go Down Moses',[35] as an example of a well-known spiritual that evokes the narrative of the Exodus, I would argue that this text remains one of the most powerful examples of Black theological synergy between the historicity of Black suffering and the Bible.[36] James W. Peebles writes:

> This practice of singing and dancing among the Africans was allowed as they endured the four hundred years in American captivity. The African/Edenic captives began to sing about the 'Deliverer' whom they once knew in their native folktales, like Moses, the deliverer who had once brought them from the land of captivity in Egypt. 'Go Down Moses' became a popular slave song even among the white slaveholders. The slave songs of the African/Edenic captives were drawn from the rich memory brought with them from the land across the waters.[37]

---

34 See Randall C. Bailey, 'But It's in the Text! Slavery, the Bible and African Diaspora', in Anthony G. Reddie (ed.), *Black Theology, Slavery and Contemporary Christianity*, Farnham: Ashgate, 2010, pp. 31–46.

35 A version of 'Go Down, Moses', complete with 25 verses, can be found in *Original African Heritage Study Bible*, Felder (ed.), pp. 1845–6.

36 Bailey, 'But It's in the Text!', pp. 34–6.

37 James W. Peebles, 'The Africology of Church Music', in Felder (ed.), *Original African Heritage Study Bible*, pp. 1841–66 (1842)

The importance of the Exodus as a narrative of liberation can be seen in the ways in which it has permeated into the popular culture of Diasporan African peoples. For example, in African Caribbean cultures, one can witness the use of the Exodus narrative in Bob Marley's iconic 1977 album of the same name.[38] In both African American and African Caribbean history, we have Black people of African descent who have experienced the degradation of capture, in the form slavery and forced removal from their homeland to a place of exile. The ongoing memory of Caribbean and American slavery is one that continues to have a deep resonance within the life experiences of people in these contexts.

In attempting to reread the Bible, Black Theology has been greatly indebted to Black biblical scholars. The work of Black biblical scholars has been utilized as a means of seeking to develop an alternative hermeneutical framework (the basis on which people interpret sacred texts for meaning and truth) that will assist Black people in understanding the place of God in the midst of the struggles for justice and liberation.

Contextual challenges in rereading the Bible

In the next section of this chapter I will look at some of the critical issues that are significant in how ordinary Black people seek to reread the Bible. This is important as it is essential that ordinary Black people are enabled to re-engage with and reinterpret biblical texts as a means of creating an alternative narrative for the purposes of Black liberation. The first part is a more general reflection on the role of the Bible in Black life and how Black Theology (informed by specialist biblical studies) can speak to these ongoing realities. The final part of the chapter is a more concrete example of how Black Theology has been used to enable ordinary Black people to learn to tell another story, via their engagement with the Bible.

What has been important in this consideration is how the ideas and concerns of Black Theology can assist ordinary Black people to continue the faithful challenge of seeking to bring their lived experiences into critical conversation with sacred narratives. In a previous publication regarding Black existential experience and our ongoing relationship as people of African descent with the Bible, I wrote:

My belief in the sacredness of the Black self is such that the existential realities of Black experience sit in dialogue alongside the Biblical text

---

38 Bob Marley and The Wailers, *Exodus*, London: Island Records, 1977. For more details on this iconic album, see http://en.wikipedia.org/wiki/Exodus_(Bob_Marley_%26_The_Wailers_album).

and are not subservient to it. As I have often said to Black participants in the workshops and classes I teach, when having to defend my theological method; 'Black experience has an integrity of its own, which is not subservient to the Biblical text. I have no evidence to believe that when the author of any biblical text was writing, they had my reality as a Black person in mind as they were doing so.[39]

The latter statement has been made in the light many years of struggle and painful reflection for myself and for countless numbers of Black people throughout the world. Like many Diasporan Africans, I was brought up in a God-fearing, church-attending Christian household. My mother, a working-class Jamaican woman from the rural areas of the western parish of Portland, insisted that all her children attend church on a Sunday – there was no negotiation in the Reddie household regarding this. The world in which I was nurtured and socialized was one that echoed to the religio-cultural frameworks provided by the Bible. My mother and other older matriarchs would quote from it habitually – Psalm 23 was and remains a favourite with my mother and many of my aunts.

Yet the unswerving fidelity to the Bible of my youth has been replaced with a more critical striving, restlessness of spirit and intellectual struggle in more recent times. This restlessness of spirit has arisen as a result of on-going, nagging questions regarding the relationship of the Bible to my life and that of other Black people and has refused to dissipate. In the present era, the desire to 'tell another story' via the Bible has thrown up a number of sharp challenges regarding the continued relevance of this sacred text to Black life. The question remains, namely, what has the Bible got to do with Black bodies? And why are we so sure that these ancient texts written in far-off epochs, in contexts barely recognizable to ourselves, should have the final word on contemporary ethics and Black socio-political praxis in the twenty-first century, or indeed any century?

Yet, many ordinary Black people remain, much like myself, stubborn creatures of habit. I have grown to become much more critically sceptical of the claims made for the Bible or the normative posture it has occupied in Diasporan African life and the certitude we often hold towards it as being the 'Good Book'. And yet, when we think in terms of 'telling a new story', the critical question of 'whose story' gets told cannot be ignored. So, I now wonder how helpful is the 'Good Book' if you are a marginalized and ob-jectified lesbian, gay, bisexual and transgendered (LGBT) other? I wonder how 'good' this book is if you are an indigenous person of the land who has suffered from invasion and forced removal from the soil of one's ances-tors at the behest of the 'Good Book' that sees your spirituality and innate

---

39 Anthony G. Reddie, *Working against the Grain: Re-Imaging Black Theology in the 21st Century*, London: Equinox, 2008, p. 109.

subjectivity as aberrant or transgressive? And yet, despite all these hugely important caveats, I have to tell you that as I write this piece from my desk at work, I have a copy of an NRSV Bible laid open at the Psalms on my bed in my flat, in order to ward off unclean spirits while I am absent from my home. Do not ask me to deconstruct this for you.

Do not ask me to consider the extent to which this is simply a form of learnt behaviour or an example of the debilitating false consciousness many of our Marxist friends have warned us about, or even a culturally retentive example of the superstition that permeates the Black self in exile in Babylon. For whatever reason, I continue to undertake this practice, learnt from my mother and grandmother; I have retained it in my life – namely, that one places an open Bible at the Psalms on one's bed when absent from the room. The reasons for doing so lie in the belief that there is a sacred form of power that resides within the 'Good Book' to fight powers and principalities and elements unseen and yet deeply real within our lived experience of the world.

One of the important aspects of this task is the need to instil an appreciation of what is still more commonly known as the 'Old Testament'. The Old Testament has always exerted a powerful hold on the imagination of Black people. To quote my old class leader from the church in which I first received my call to preach, 'Anthony, Jesus may have saved our souls, but it is Moses and Old Testament prophets who taught us how to fight our oppressors.' It is significant, therefore, that this text majors on Israel's Scriptures.

It is imperative that Black people are encouraged to engage with the sheer messiness and interdisciplinary playfulness with which they have learnt, via their lived experiences, to engage with the Bible. I am sure I am not the only person whose position towards the 'Good Book' displays creative and complex levels of idiosyncrasy, paradox, contradiction. In the light of our suffering and struggles – our attempts to 'pay the price' for Black liberation – Black people have demonstrated their ability to hold in tension seemingly disparate sources of truth, that is, the tension between holy texts and messy contexts. I am referring here to the ongoing interaction between Black contexts and myriad experiential settings that arise from such religio-cultural environments and the supposed, alleged fixity of Holy Scripture.

When looking at the ways in which ordinary Black people have engaged with the Bible in the past (and in our present time), we can deduce that there are myriad ways in which they have engaged with the Bible. The incorporation of alternative ways of perceiving truth has long been a part of the theological and interpretive repertoire of Black people as they have engaged with what many take to believe as sacred text. Sadly, it is through the dictates of largely although not exclusively evangelical neo-Pentecostalism that many Black people have been encouraged, even forced in some cases, to relinquish this commendable flexibility in how they read the Bible and do theology. It is important to keep on reminding ordinary Black people that fundamentalism is a relatively modern invention over the greater span of history in which people have been interpreting biblical texts. It is important to hold in mind the fluidity and the imaginative panache with which Black peoples have been enabled to engage with biblical texts, seeking to locate our reading strategies within the real, complex world in which we live.

For me, one of the key telling concerns is the need to engage in an honest fashion with the ongoing challenges of relating to the Bible as Scripture. Such has been the complex interaction between what happens within the pages of Scripture and the cultural apparel and socio-religious performance of Black people that is brought into a critical relationship with the text; one might be tempted to see this ongoing nexus as one that responds to riffs of the jazz musician.

In many respects, one could argue that the challenge of engaging with the Bible in the light of human experience represents a delicate balancing act between competing notions of truth: the truth that emanates from lived experience and that which comes from a sacred text. At best, these two elements work in harmony, but we should not disguise the dissonance and discord that can exist when these perspectives are brought into conversation. Black people's engagement with the Bible represents enduring struggle between seemingly binary opposites. The challenge in linking the messy, changing nature of human experience with the allegedly 'pure' and 'eternal Word of God' can be likened to the nexus between time and eternity, between immanence and transcendence, text and context, continuity and change, centre and margins, rule-bound conventions and the modern tendency towards free-form self-expression. These tensions are not new, of course. I am sure that enslaved Africans being worked to death on the plantations in the Americas and the Caribbean wrestled with such conundrums. Who was this God that was revealed in the pages of the Bible for them? What on earth did this God of and in the Bible have to say to the painful realities of their lives? How did they hold in tension such disparate elements as the holy and the ordinary, matter and spirit? These questions represent the most fundamental of all existential concerns.[40]

As we will see in the final chapter, when we look at a particular contemporary issue in the light of Black Theology, the Bible remains a highly contested issue in the ongoing 'culture wars' in many western societies. Central to these arguments seemingly parochial questions represent a significant challenge to all religious and non-religious communities alike in their engagement with sacred text. Namely, what are the limits between normative readings and heterogeneous, culturally inspired forms of interpretation?

In short, how elastic are biblical texts and does it matter if we even break them altogether? The challenges that face many ordinary Black people in

---

40 See Dwight N. Hopkins, *Being Human: Race, Culture, and Religion*, Minneapolis: Fortress, 2005, pp. 81–117.

their engagement is one that can be assisted by means of making recourse to such resources as *The Africana Bible*.[41] *The Africana Bible* represents the collective talents of some of the most outstanding Black biblical scholars in the world, who engage with 'Israel's Scriptures' (what one might term, loosely, the 'Old Testament' in more common parlance), bringing these texts into conversation with Black cultures from across the world.

In their engagement with ancient material, the editors have rightly rejected any sense of the conventions and restrictions of the so-called 'orthodox canon'. They have encouraged various contributors to mine the wider corpus of Israel's Scriptures, seeking to highlight and illuminate the alternate narratives and theologies that have often been considered to be beyond the limits of acceptability. Perhaps one might even argue that the editors and contributors to this text in engaging with non-canonical material offer us alternative and expansionist notions of God and God's activity in the world.

As the Caribbean biblical scholar Oral Thomas has argued, it is preferable that we see biblical texts as contested earth-bound constructions of how people have attempted to talk about God, than as uncontested pearls of inspired wisdom spoken by God that have fallen from the sky.[42] In effect, for a Black liberationist ethic to flourish, we need to move beyond the strictures that the Bible is the 'Word *of* God' to one that argues for it being the faithful 'Word *about* God'.

The Africana Bible has, to my mind, become one of the first biblically related texts produced within the academy that has managed to capture something of the elusive and seemingly contradictory manner in which Africana culture has conjured and manoeuvred with both the form and content of the Scripture in order to produce an interactive text that almost does the impossible – capture lightening in a jar – that is, bottles and traps for one moment the extravagant flexibility that Black people and their concomitant cultures at their best have brought to the alleged fixity of the Bible.

One can see elements of this complexity in the ways in which many Caribbean people, for example, have wrestled with the biblical text within the patterns of the contextual, lived colonial and postcolonial settings in which they have resided. Michael N. Jagessar has remarked that one has to make an important distinction, for example, between 'biblical literalism' and 'biblical realism' as differing interpretative frameworks by which Caribbean people engage with biblical texts. Jagessar cites the latter as being part of the complex repertoire of Caribbean people in their ability to read biblical texts in a seemingly literal fashion. The outworkings of such reading strategies, however, express themselves in liberationist, hope-filled declarations

---

41 See Hugh R. Page Jr (Gen. Ed.), *The Africana Bible: Reading Israel's Scriptures from Africa and the African Diaspora*, Minneapolis: Fortress, 2010.

42 See Oral A. W. Thomas, *Biblical Resistance Hermeneutics within a Caribbean Context*, London: Equinox, 2010.

of life that are, nevertheless, linked squarely to the contextual realities of their lives. That is, biblical realism is not a retreat from reality by immersing oneself in a literal reading of the biblical text. Rather, it is a reading of the text in a way that reinforces the contextual struggles of life and questions the presuppositions one often holds about God that are often not attested to by experience or conviction. Jagessar states:

> The example I often use is the way the Haitian Creole Bible translates the verse 'With God all things are possible' (Matt. 19.26 and Mark 10.27). The translators use a French Creole word *Dejage* which puts a different spin on the text to read 'With God we can make do'. For Haitians and their history it would seem a lie to say with God all things are possible. Their reality has told them a different story.[43]

The added strength of *The Africana Bible* is its emphasis upon the creative and expressive skills of African Diasporan perspectives, in all their glorious multiplicity. With its focus on Diaspora, *The Africana Bible* provides an important resource for exploring different locations of power within the sacred text. This form of contested struggle for truth within the text is also reflected in the relationship of often powerless readers to the officially sanctioned power of the Bible itself. Namely, there remains a critical exchange between the Bible, which is imbued with the weight of authority and power across the ages, and the often powerless lives of ordinary Black people who continue to read it, often with a fanatical sense of devotion.

I have cited *The Africana Bible* for special attention in this section of the work because I felt it offers important resources that speak to the ongoing challenges for how we enable ordinary Black people to handle the Bible. I know that, in the strict demarcation of academic disciplines within the academy, there are many Black theologians who will find my engagement with the Bible, as a non-biblical specialist, a little troubling. In response to such challenges I need to remind us, once again, of the central point of this text. Namely, to hold in tension twin identities of Black Theology, as an academic discipline and a religious and social movement, committed to Black liberation. In terms of the latter, there is the necessity to recognize that, for many ordinary Black Christian people, the Bible represents the foundational element in their theology. To attempt to undertake any critical form of Black Theology without engaging with the Bible is to run the risk of having one's activities dismissed as 'intellectual nonsense'.

While I am not in agreement with Garth Baker-Fletcher and his seemingly conservative position regarding the Bible, in terms of its place in Black Theology, I do nonetheless applaud his desire to wrestle with it, in terms of making

---

43 Taken from a personal correspondence with the author.

this discipline relevant to ordinary Black people.[44] The challenge in this section of the chapter, indeed in the whole book, is trying to hold in tension the need to engage with ordinary Black people while acknowledging the limitations and constrictions of the lived Black experience that sometimes leads to inbuilt forms of conservatism and internalized oppression.[45] In terms of the latter, I am speaking of the ways in which ordinary Black people internalize the destructive elements of self-denial and hate that have been levelled at them and then project such elements onto others, often peoples with whom they share a familial or communitarian-based relationship.[46] The helpful limitations of Baker-Fletcher's approach to integrating the Bible within the Black Church and the work of Black Theology can be placed in dialogue with that of *The Africana Bible*. In terms of the latter, it is important to realize that part of the internalized oppressive factors that impact upon ordinary Black people is the difficulty many find in being enabled to challenge the Bible and realize that within its texts there are contested notions of truths and differing perspectives of God.

Within the Bible, we witness an ongoing struggle for truth between notions of insider versus outsider, centre versus the margins, pure versus miscegenation (mixed) and perhaps, most crucially of all, the struggle for the meaning of so-called authentic language about God.[47] These themes are addressed to great effect in many of the essays to be found in *The Africana Bible*, particularly, in the essays written by Bailey, Kirk-Duggan, Masenya and Sadler and Wil Gafney.[48] This work is an invitation to explore what it means to be an African within the context of Diaspora and how one makes sense of the often contested meanings and nuances of what such terms mean when juxtaposed with the Bible.

---

44 See Garth Kasimu Baker-Fletcher, *Bible Witness in Black Churches*, New York: Palgrave Macmillan, 2009, pp. 105–24.

45 See Anthony G. Reddie, *Acting in Solidarity: Reflections in Critical Christianity*, London: Darton, Longman and Todd, 2005, pp. 45–53.

46 Arguably one of the greatest texts to address this issue is Franz Fanon, *Black Skin, White Masks*, New York: Grove, 1967; London: MacGibbon & Kee, 1968.

47 On postcolonial theory, see for example R. S. Sugirtharajah, *Postcolonial Reconfigurations: An Alternative Way of Reading the Bible and Doing Theology*, London: SCM, 2003; R. S. Sugirtharajah, *The Bible and Empire: Postcolonial Consideration*, Cambridge, London and New York: Cambridge University Press, 2005; David C. I. Joy, *Mark and Its Subalterns: A Hermeneutical Paradigm for a Postcolonial Context*, London: Equinox, 2008; Musa W. Dube, *Postcolonial Feminist Interpretation of the Bible*, St Louis: Chalice Press, 2000; Fernando S. Segovia and R. S. Sugirtharajah (eds), *A Postcolonial Commentary on the New Testament Writings*, London: T & T Clark, 2007; and Catherine Keller, Michael Nausner and Mayra Rivera (eds), *Postcolonial Theologies: Divinity and Empire*, St Louis: Chalice Press, 2004.

48 Randall C. Bailey, Cheryl Kirk-Duggan, Madipoane Masenya (ngwan'a Mphahlele) and Rodney S. Sadler Jr, 'African and African Diasporan Hermeneutics', in Page Jr (Gen. Ed.), *Africana Bible*, pp. 19–24; Wil Gafney, 'Reading the Hebrew Bible Responsibly', in Page Jr (Gen. Ed.), *Africana Bible*, pp. 45–53.

These reflections have wrestled with the practical challenges of wrestling with the Bible in order that it become a more radical resource for the ongoing liberative praxis of ordinary Black people. The Bible remains an important source for talking about liberation within Black Theology, and hopefully, as my assessment of *The Africana Bible* has shown, there are creative scholarly resources that have been produced that are enabling the necessary critical rereading for the purposes of telling a new story. The process of telling a new story takes place in dialogue with the Bible not because of any fundamentalist belief that God cannot be found beyond the pages of its sacred texts. On the contrary, as we will see in some of the later chapters, Black Theology's belief in the primary of the Black experience of suffering is such that the seemingly fundamentalist notions that equate the Bible directly with God's own self are summarily rejected. As the 'philosophical school' of Black Theology has demonstrated, one can argue for the self-determination of Black people and their rights to freedom on grounds that do not require the Bible or any biblical mandate for human liberation. But the Bible remains significant because, on pragmatic grounds at least, it is hard to conceive of a mass movement necessary for any effective Black liberative praxis that does not bring on board the Church and ordinary Black people. And the latter are very much orientated around the Bible and its sacred story of God's interaction with humankind. This is salient truth for many ordinary Black people of faith, and, whatever the criticisms one might legitimately make of the Bible, nevertheless it remains foundational to any praxis-based approach to Black Theology that has been conceived thus far.

A dramatic approach to engaging with biblical texts

This second approach is drawn from my own work. In my activist-led scholarly work as a popular educator and a participative Black theologian, I have often resorted to dramatic exercises, not unlike the ones used in this book. I have done this because of the way in which it enables ordinary people to become active participants in the creation of new forms of knowledge. On occasions when the issue at hand is somewhat emotionally fraught and is mired in controversy, making use of a dramatic exercise has proven useful in enabling ordinary people to step into role or character and pretend that they are just 'playing a game'.

Dramatic exercises, of the kind used in this book, can be creative ways of enabling people to interact with one another and with the subject/topic of concern that is at the heart of the dramatic exercise. Educators have long asserted that drama and dramatic exercises provide a creative means of developing interaction and involvement, which leads to greater engagement for the learner. I have been concerned to find a means by which ordinary Black people can be enabled to enter into a process of teaching and learning in which their presence and interaction is central to the overall educational enterprise.

Drama and dramatic exercises require that people are actively engaged in a process of discovery. In addition to the aforementioned, in using this approach I am able to explore a range of ideas and concerns in a way that would be very difficult in conventional prose. Drama usually comes alive by means of conflict and intellectual and emotional struggle. In playing the game the various participants are forced to go beyond the limitations of their initial thoughts in order to engage with the emotions that are newly emerging through the process of the exercise and the resultant drama.

The Bible offers numerous challenges and opportunities, many of which get lost, because of the way in which we often approach this book. Part of the challenge of seeking to tell a new story via the Bible lies in the way in which it has been domesticated, made safe, in order not to trouble our material interests and current bias. Part of the reason why the Bible is often domesticated also arises because we are so far removed from the ancient periods in which the various texts were first constructed. The Bible has become the book of the Church, and we are overly familiar with it. These collections of writings, written over a long period of history, are not recently constructed texts as we sometimes believe them to be.

What often confronts us, therefore, is a huge contradiction. On the one hand, many Christian believers, often nurtured within the life of the Church, feel that they know what the Bible is about. They read and feel that they know God. This familiarity often leads the Church to 'domesticate' the Bible – that is, to make it safe, palatable and comfortable for our times. God becomes 'one of us' who can be used to justify our prejudices, boundaries and views of the world.[49] Yet, on the other hand, our distance from the times in which the Bible was written often leads people (at best) to misunderstand what the Bible says or (at worst) to distort and misrepresent God as understood in the pages of Scripture. One of the ways in which biblical scholars, theologians and Christian educators have attempted to respond to these issues has been by 're-contextualizing' the Bible. By this, I mean trying to retell the various stories of the Bible in another setting or situation from the one in which they were first written. This new setting can unsettle us – it can put us off our guard and disturb our complacency. Suddenly, what we thought we knew is pushed aside in the face of a new perspective with which we are unfamiliar. This forces us into new ways of thinking and so leads to new learning. Writers such as McCrary[50] have attempted to put Bible passages into completely new settings and forms from the ones in which they were first set, in order that they should speak to us in different ways for our present situation.

---

49 See Anthony G. Reddie, *Nobodies to Somebodies: Practical Theology for Education and Liberation*, Peterborough: Epworth, 2003, pp. 132–40.

50 P. K. McCrary, *The Black Bible Chronicles: From Genesis to the Promise Land*, New York: African American Family Press, 1993, and *The Black Bible Chronicles: Rappin' with Jesus*, New York: African American Family Press, 1994.

This example of ordinary Black people's engagement with the Bible arises from a piece of group work that was undertaken subsequent to the exercise that was used at the beginning of this chapter. This particular dramatic exercise asked individuals to reflect on their engagement in the opening activity – the struggle to try and throw the ball into one of the containers. The exercise is not important in itself. It serves primarily as a metaphor for the kinds of lived experiences of struggle that are commonplace for many Black people. Reflecting on the symbolism of the exercise, these Black participants were invited to consider who the biblical people are that might have inspired them in their everyday, lived experiences as Black subjects living in the White-dominated country of Britain.

The previous reflections on drama and exercises have been offered as a means of placing the following reflections in context. Having worked with a number of ordinary Black people on the opening exercise, I want to show how using drama and improvisation can be used to enable them to reflect more critically on their lived experience. Namely, that using Black Theology as a theological framework for enabling them to reread the Bible, ordinary Black people can create alternative interpretations of lives, moving them from debilitating levels of passivity to greater forms of liberative praxis.

Central to this worked example is the exercise of getting ordinary Black people to link their lived experiences of struggle with that of a 'heroic' biblical character. From this exercise emerged improvised pieces of drama as ordinary Black people imagined themselves as biblical characters, but then reread these characters back into their present-day experiences. In effect, the people were challenged to reread the Bible in the light of their lived experiences and then expose their lives to scrutiny from the glare of the Bible itself, in terms of the character they had been playing in the improvised exercise.

This type of improvised dramatic approach to theological reflection draws upon a long tradition of Black religious educators using the Bible as a means of addressing social and cultural issues within Black communities.[51] In developing this approach I was very much influenced by the work of African American Womanist religious educator Lynne Westfield, who has developed interactive and participative ways of enabling ordinary Black people of faith to engage with biblical texts for liberative purposes. Westfield seeks to enable Black people to create a critical coming together of their corporate and communal narratives of the faith community alongside the sacred texts that orientate the peoples' identities as a worshipping and believing entity. This nexus then creates the faith-based dynamism that

---

51 As far back as the late 1960s, Black religious educators were linking Black Biblical Studies with a nascent Black Theology in order to create educational programmes that sought to reinterpret the Bible for the purposes of Black self-determination and liberation. See Jeffrey N. Stinehelfer, 'Dig This: The Revealing of Jesus Christ', *Religious Education* 64:6 (1969), pp. 467–70.

motivates a people who are seeking theological and religious frameworks for their liberation.[52]

The participative approach that is integral to this biblical-inspired model of Black Theology-based reflections is one that seeks to conscientize Black people. It speaks to the challenges laid out in the previous chapter of this book, namely, why is Black Theology worth pursuing? Why does it continue to have relevance for, and can it speak to, the continued marginalization and exploitation of Black people?

Black Theology reflections

Having reflected on the importance of drama as a means of engaging with Black people, I would now like to share some reflections on how this method has been used in the context of helping participants to 'tell a new story' using the Bible. Unlike some of my previous work where I have scripted short plays for use with Black people, on this occasion I asked the individuals to reflect on the historic spiritual 'Go Down Moses' in order to create their own improvised form of drama.

Using Randall Bailey's reflections on how enslaved Africans 'read against the text' as a means of establishing a basis for fighting for their liberation, a group of ordinary Black people were encouraged to imagine themselves as part of a biblical text.[53] Given that Black Theology emphasizes the importance of personal experience, participants were asked to reflect on how they imagined themselves as a Moses in the many contemporary contexts in which they live. What did it feel like to have to stand up against a Pharaoh? Individuals were asked to write down a number of different scenarios in which they had been challenged to 'speak truth to power' and to push themselves forward to 'pay the price' for the struggle for liberation and change.

A number of individuals spoke of the occasions when they had spoken up against racism in either the workplace or in the Church. Listening to the different accounts, it was fascinating to see the ways in which the biblical text of Moses' encounter with Pharaoh (Exod. 7.16) had inspired them to believe that the cost of mounting such a challenge against 'White power' was the price to be paid for standing up for justice.[54]

---

52 See N. Lynne Westfield, *Dear Sisters: A Womanist Practice of Hospitality*, Cleveland, OH: Pilgrim Press, 2001. See also N. Lynne Westfield, 'Life-Giving Stories: The Bible in a Congregation', in Vincent L. Wimbush (ed.), *African Americans and the Bible: Sacred Texts and Social Textures*, New York and London: Continuum, 2000, pp. 577–87.

53 See Bailey, 'But It's in the Text . . .'.

54 Lerleen Willis offers an interesting account of how many Black people see their Christian faith as an integral part of their psychological armoury in dealing with racism in their places of work. See Lerleen Willis, 'The Pilgrim's Process: Coping with Racism through Faith', *Black Theology* 4:2 (2006), pp. 210–32.

The challenge for the participants was to identify what had enabled Moses to stand before Pharaoh and to utter his prophetic challenge.

One of the central issues that emerged from this exercise was that, for the majority of participants, the God of liberation spoke strongly in their minds, more so than fear of the consequences for not speaking up. A number of individuals spoke of the ways in which they were intimidated by the people in power who sought to challenge their perspective on the truth. It was often put to them that they were making a 'big mistake' in challenging authority and that the price to be paid for such disobedience would be severe. And yet, despite such challenges, many spoke of how being challenged to read the Bible in an overtly political manner, linking it to very real socio-political realities, enabled them to find the courage to challenge injustice.

In being challenged to identify the biblical text with their socio-political contexts, many Black people were enabled to tell a new story. This new narrative was one that moved beyond the overly apolitical spiritualized interpretations of Black life that are sometimes put forward as the essential subtext of Black lived experience. It is not uncommon in the accounts put forward by some Black commentators to hear that there is 'the hand of God' or a belief in 'divine providence' for interpreting Black struggle in society. For some Black people, when asked to account for the struggles they had endured living in British society, their response was one of 'God has put me in the fire so that he can refine my faith'. In effect, their understanding of struggle and suffering was one of seeing all such events as within the orbit of God's sovereignty.

While not doubting the spiritual and psychological gains that can be accrued from such forms of interpretations, for the Black participants who took part in this improvised drama it was recognized that such an approach could lead to passivity. That in seeing God as the author of one's social condition, individuals and communities could be led to believe that 'it was God's will' for them to suffer and that such suffering was commensurate with God's intention for Black people. As we will see in more detail when looking at how Black Theology has sought to make sense of Jesus' suffering on the cross, there has been a marked theological challenge in not seeking to spiritualize or valourize suffering as being of God.

An alternative perspective was understood by the participants in this exercise when compared to the dangers of passivity that were mentioned a few moments ago. Through being challenged to link a specific biblical narrative with contemporary experience, many Black people came to realize the importance of reading the text in the light of their own lived experience. Moses' encounters with Pharaoh entailed a clear disparity in power between the two protagonists. Moses' account of what he believed to be true is clearly disputed by Pharaoh. Many Black people have spoken movingly of the occasions when they have had their accounts of the truth ridiculed by those with power.

One of the facets that emerged from the text, when ordinary Black people were encouraged to narrate their experiences of standing up against racism in the light of Moses' encounter with Pharaoh, was the necessity of trusting in their inner voice. In the improvised dramas created by the participants, there were numerous occasions when some of the protagonists found themselves being challenged on their version of the truth. 'Were they sure they had heard what they had claimed?' 'How could they prove it?' 'Did they really want to go through with an official complaint, given that things could get nasty?'

The last question reminds us of the account that was shared at the outset of the chapter when the older Black woman challenged the young Black people on why they were insistent on taking the harder options as opposed to settling for the easier ones much closer to hand. What emerged from the improvisations was the reality that confronting the challenge of racism, speaking truth to the conservative pharaohs of this world, was one that required persistence and perseverance.

The group were encouraged to reflect on their own contextual struggles in the light of the story of Moses. It struck me that Moses was an important figure to use in this exercise because he has always exerted an impression on the popular consciousness of Black people. One of the reasons I think Black people have identified with Moses is due, to some extent, to his status as 'unpromising material'. On the face of it, Moses' formative years do not seem to fit him for the iconic role he would undertake at a later point in his life. As a result of his heroic actions as the leader of a liberation movement, many Black and marginalized peoples have identified with Moses.

Some Black theologians have even identified Moses as being a Black person of African ancestry.[55] The renowned African American singer Isaac Hayes, one of the most popular singers of the late 1960s and early '70s, even dubbed himself a latter-day 'Black Moses' because of his prophetic-like utterances on record. Long before Hayes, women of immense substance such as Nanny of the Maroons (eighteenth-century Jamaican national heroine) and Harriet Tubman (nineteenth-century African American hero) were both seen as Moses-like figures as a result of their leadership qualities.

The challenge presented to those participants who took part in the exercise was to identify who are the Moses-like figures in our present age who have 'paid the price' in seeking to fight for the liberation of their people?[56] Where are we looking to find these people? What are we looking for? Would the people with whom they come into contact on a daily basis be described as 'Moses-like figures' in the present age?

---

55 See Cain Hope Felder, 'Exodus', in Felder (ed.), *Original African Heritage Study Bible*, pp. 85–94, for a Black social and theological reading of Moses as a Black Afro-Asiatic male.

56 See Anthony G. Reddie, 'Pentecost – Dreams and Visions (A Black Theological Reading of Pentecost)', in Maureen Edwards (ed.), *Discovering Christ: Ascension and Pentecost*, Birmingham: IRBA, 2001, pp. 27–42. In this essay I acknowledge Doreen and Neville Lawrence as prophets and leaders of our age.

One of the most intriguing aspects of the reflections from the individuals as they sought to think about Moses' encounter with Pharaoh was the question of 'personal experience'. Normative, classical Christianity claims that an individual can gain a personal experience of God in Christ by means of the Holy Spirit. On the face of it, this claim must seem fantastical to some, yet to others it is an uncontested and irrefutable reality of life.

I have argued that many older Black people living in the UK have a very personalized and literal appropriation of Jesus in their lives.[57] God in general and Jesus in particular are not simply rationalized concepts but are experiential truths. Jesus becomes the best friend, the fellow struggler in solidarity in the midst of myriad trials and tribulations.[58] For many ordinary Black people in the exercise, as they reflected on Moses' task of speaking 'truth to power' and narrating such events in terms of their own lives, the challenge was to account for their own personal experience. What did it mean to believe that one is called to pay the price when the task that lay ahead seemed so impossible? At what point does one begin to question reality when asked to perform or undertake some seemingly impossible task?

The question of personal experience of God and the convictions that arise from it is a particular facet of Christianity that is both one of its enduring strengths as well as being a major weakness. In terms of the former, countless men and women have been inspired by the realness and nearness of God in order to create change in their individual lives and in the lives of others.[59] Yet, as James Cone, the 'founding father' of Black liberation theology, once remarked in an address given at the Queen's Foundation in Birmingham in 1997, the most dangerous people in the world are those who claim to have an untrammelled line of communication to God and know exactly what God wants and what can be construed as God's will. In effect, these are the scary people who later claim, 'God told me to do it', when they are arrested for some extreme atrocity.

So what are we to make of this elusive thing called religious experience? Whose experience counts? Who can be trusted to speak for or about God? Surely not all forms of committed faith-based actions can be deemed to be rational let alone permissible? And what if the challenge to pay the price as outlined in this chapter is one that calls for a committed challenge to the very hierarchy of the Church itself? Some Black people have spoken of

---

57 See Anthony G. Reddie, *Faith, Stories and the Experience of Black Elders: Singing the Lord's Song in a Strange Land*, London: Jessica Kingsley, 2001, pp. 65–72.

58 See Earl Jr, *Dark Salutations*.

59 See Reddie, *Growing into Hope*, vol. 1, pp. 59–78. See also Anne S. Wimberly, *Soul Stories: African American Christian Education*, Nashville, TN: Abingdon, 1996. Wimberly's concept of 'story linking' involves (African American) learners combining their personal narratives with heroic people of faith. The latter are historic and contemporary people who have been inspired by God to achieve major accomplishments for themselves and for others.

'paying the price' for seeking to speak 'truth to church power', when challenging issues of patriarchy and homophobia in the Church.

The important challenge that arose from this exercise was the need for ordinary Black people to interpret their own lives in heroic terms. All too often there has been a tendency to give greater weight to the importance of authority figures and the attributes of the so-called 'great and the good'. And, whether it is in terms of the Civil Rights Movement or the Anti-Apartheid struggle in South Africa or the comparatively recent Stephen Lawrence case in the UK, all liberation struggles are only as successful as the ordinary people who make up the so-called 'rank and file'.

This improvised dramatic exercise, a supplement to the opening activity, seeks to demonstrate how ordinary Black people, the group for whom and from whom Black Theology was created, can be enabled to rethink their lived experiences in terms of struggling for liberation and justice for all. And, as a corollary, to believe that they themselves are key agents in this form of prophetic and liberative work, and that such actions are not just for those who are famous or seen as extraordinary.

It is interesting that the grand narrative of the Christian faith as a whole is an account of the great and the good across history. The reading list of most theology courses or theological libraries is an account of the major scholars whose experience and thinking has helped to define theology. The greater preponderance of these persons, until the latter half of the last century, was often 'dead White European men'. Comparatively few were Black people of African origin. Even fewer were poor, ordinary people of faith. To what extent have specific African or, more generally, non-European concepts influenced our theological thinking?[60]

Many of the people with whom I have worked continued to speak of a sense of scepticism that confronted them when they sought to speak truth to power. Many felt they could relate to Moses' encounter with Pharaoh. Many recognized the mocking tone of Pharaoh and gave voice to their own experiences of dealing with predominantly White authority. Moses is viewed with suspicion, bordering on derision. A number of participants recognized that the heart of this encounter spoke to their own struggles with authority. Some spoke of the difficulty of getting White authority to believe their accounts of struggle. One person spoke of the soul-sapping pain of being bullied by a White minister and how it was even more painful to then recount that story to others and for his narrative to be subsequently disbelieved. For many, what they had felt and believed to be true was summarily dismissed as being fabrication or a fantasy.

The critical question that has always been a part of how Black people seek to tell a new story is that of attesting to the truths of their experience.

---

60 See Robert E. Hood, *Must God Remain Greek? Afro-Cultures and God-Talk*, Minneapolis: Fortress, 1994.

To what extent are Black and other minority-ethnic people believed in their religious experience? What criteria are used to determine the truth of any God-talk, particularly if the sources of that discourse are ordinary Black people, often deemed as nobodies?[61]

One of the important subtexts of this exercise is the relationship of revelation and personal experience to the challenges of creating alternative narratives ('telling a new story') for the purposes of fighting for Black liberation. While Black Theology is often characterized as a radical model of faith action and talk that seeks to transform unjust social structures, there is no doubting the sense that it also draws on a liberative model of spirituality, in order to give rise to a more individual form of empowerment and affirmation of Black people.[62] Dwight Hopkins explicates this model of liberative spirituality that is central to Black Theology, arguing that it '[a]rises out of the experiences of social change and the traditions found in several stories – the radical calling in the Christian Bible, African American women's spirituality, and the folk faith of enslaved black workers'.[63]

Black Theology has sought to tell another story by rereading biblical texts and linking that to a liberative spirituality that has emerged from the encounter between the Divine and Black bodies mired for the most part in suffering and struggling for liberation and justice. Ordinary Black people in this later worked example have been encouraged to identify with Moses, and the similar challenges faced by countless Black people across the ages. The critical question has been how one assesses the veracity of one's own experience and the reality that emerges from this? In identifying with Moses, this improvised approach to drama attempts to offer an alternative perspective on a biblical narrative that accords with the troubled realities of Black life in a manner that ultimately seeks to provide new resources for understanding Black life and the struggle to improve it. In effect, it is a Black Theology-inspired approach to telling a new story.

Conclusion

Telling a new story – reinterpreting the meaning of God in Christ for the purposes of Black liberation – is about committing oneself to the struggle for social justice. It is to acknowledge that the Christian faith stands culpable and condemned for colluding in the oppression of 'others', both within and beyond its so-called boundaries. But, thankfully, there is another story to be told. It is one of subversion, liberation and an alternative version of the

---

61 See Reddie, *Nobodies to Somebodies*, pp. 132–40.

62 More will be said on this in Chapter 6 when I look at the role of the Holy Spirit/ Spirit of Liberation in Black Theology.

63 Hopkins, *Heart and Head*, p. 77.

truth. It is a story of another way of seeing the world, indeed another way of viewing the human–divine encounter at the heart of Christian theology.[64]

Telling a new story – reinterpreting the meaning and intent of God – is an ongoing process; it is one that has to face the challenges of this century and not just reflect on the crises of the past. Black Theology must be committed to the wholesale emancipation of all people. It is to conceive of a liberating faith as a broad inclusive terrain that contains many tributaries and possible ways of advancement. In fact, it is to go beyond the claims of Christian faith as the only means of liberation for Black people. The ideological task at the heart of Black Theology of which mention was made in the previous chapter is one of critiquing and challenging existing models of power. It is constantly to ask the critical questions, 'Who is being disadvantaged by this?' 'Who is being left behind?' 'Who will be marginalized or oppressed if we assert this as truth?' These are questions the Church has rarely asked in the past. Perhaps Black Theology can play its part in answering the challenging question W. E. B. Du Bois posed at the beginning of the twentieth century – will we finally gain the courage and nerve to challenge the reality of the colour line? To tell a new story is to gain the necessary strength to assert that very reality as the vision for the twenty-first century.

Questions

1. Given that Christianity has been around for over 2,000 years and has established a long history and tradition through the Church, do you think it is really possible for Black people to 'rethink' and 'reinterpret' it? If so, why, and if not, then why not?
2. What are some of the potential and actual problems in trying to create an alternative perspective on the meaning of the Christian faith for the purposes of Black liberation?
3. The majority of Black people in the world have often rejected Black Theology and its approach to reinterpreting the meaning and activity of God. Can you suggest reasons for why this might be the case?
4. I have named some of the historic and contemporary examples of Black people who have adopted a form of Black Theology in order to fight for social change and justice. What are some of the future challenges a Black Theology-inspired approach to social justice and transformation will have to confront? Is Black Theology up to the task? If yes, then why, and if not, then why not?

---

64 Grant, *White Women's Christ and Black Women's Jesus*, pp. 212–22.

3

Different Ways of Doing Black Theology

So far, we have explored the rationale and the underlying motivations of Black Theology. The previous chapter was concerned with highlighting how Black Theology has sought to tell a new story about God, revealed in Jesus Christ, for the purposes of Black liberation. In this chapter I want to look at a number of different approaches to how Black Theology is done. All forms of theological enterprise have some underlying assumptions and approaches that guide their method for operating. I would like to use two examples from the British context as a means of highlighting alternative methods for doing Black Theology. These two examples will then be placed alongside other significant examples or models in order to show the overall pattern for Black Theology development over the past four decades.

I have chosen to offer two examples from the British context for a number of reasons. In the first instance, I wish to demonstrate the contribution Black Theology in Britain has made to the overall development of the discipline across the world. This focus on Britain does not disguise the overarching strength and leadership that has been provided by African American Black Theology. If one were to name ten Black theologians in the world, then approximately nine of them would be African Americans. This temporary focus on Britain is not seeking to provide some form of alternative hegemony for Black Theology. Rather, it is simply an attempt to acknowledge what my own context has offered to the global enterprise of Black Theology, given the paucity of numbers and material resources in the UK for sustaining this discipline. Second, I have chosen Black Theology in Britain precisely because its own development and identity is less familiar than the more normative African American narrative. I could have chosen to look at Black Theology in South Africa as an alternative context to use as a case-study. What negated this idea was the reality that Black Theology in South Africa is fairly moribund, and so my analysis would be purely historical as opposed to being of a more contemporary nature.

The immediate location of this author leads to another important facet of Black Theology. Black Theology, like other forms of 'theologies of liberation', emerges from specific locations and reflects the concrete experiences of particular groups of people who have been marginalized and oppressed for a number of reasons. All theologies of liberation (indeed all theologies per se) are contextual. By this, I mean that the nature of any theological enterprise is influenced by and responds to the critical issues and experiences of the people in that particular time and space, in their relationship to God. Stephen Bevans is a Euro-American Roman Catholic scholar who has assessed a number of models of contextual theology, essentially illustrating the relationship between religious faith and the cultures and settings in which that faith is located.[1] Of the different models of contextual theology Bevans outlines, the one that most reflects the central concerns of Black Theology is that of the 'praxis model', namely, an approach that emphasizes faithful action for social change.[2]

Given that all forms of theologies of liberation emerge from specific contexts and are committed to the social transformation of that particular setting, I want to identify a specific setting as the basis for looking at the differing approaches to doing Black Theology. All forms of Black Theology represent some particular form of the discipline, depending on the historical experiences, narratives and cultures that have impacted on and shaped the lives of the Black people in that specific context. I will begin by looking at two alternative approaches or methods for doing Black Theology in Britain. What can these two approaches tell us about the more generic methodologies employed by Black theologians in their respective work?

I want to assess the development of Black Theology by way of a comparison with two of its principal exponents in Britain. This analysis explores two differing approaches to the contextual praxis of this discipline. Robert Beckford uses social theory and cultural and social analysis, while my approach utilizes the frameworks of practical theology, in particular Christian education, as a means of undertaking liberative Black theological reflection in the British context. This approach to Black Theology also utilizes elements of social theory, but possesses a clearer methodological intent in bringing such reflections into critical conversation with the Bible.

The above will be concluded by an attempt to put this case-study into the context of the wider concerns of Black Theology, particularly that which has emerged from African American and South African contexts. How does the material in this case-study represent the normative perspectives found in Black Theology and, conversely, in what ways does it present heterodox modes or methods for constructing this work?

Like the previous chapter, the aforementioned will be undertaken via an experiential, participative exercise that seeks to provide a metaphorical point of learning for predominantly Black people. It is important to hold in mind the twin aims of this book – to describe and analyse Black Theology as a scholarly discipline alongside the need to show how it can engage with ordinary Black people as a model of liberative praxis.

---

1 See Stephen B. Bevans, *Models of Contextual Theology*, Maryknoll, NY: Orbis, 2004.

2 Bevans, *Models of Contextual Theology*, pp. 70–87.

Exercise: 'Are we in the story?'

Ask everyone in the group to close their eyes while you read the story of the feeding of the five thousand in John 6.1–15. As you tell the story, ask each person in the group to imagine the scene and to visualize it and the characters in the story. How do they appear? What is each person like? What kind of people are they?

With their eyes still closed, ask the group where they themselves are located in relationship to the action. Are they in the middle of the crowd, or are they standing on the edge, or are they watching the scene on a screen, completely removed from the action?

As the story is well known, participants are asked to imagine the scene in as much detail as possible. What is going on in the story? Who is standing where? Crucially, as they are imagining the story, are there Black people in the story and, if so, where are they standing?

Initial Black Theology reflections

This exercise was created and first used a number of years ago when I first began to develop an approach to the teaching and learning of Black Theology using some of the ideas and methods of Transformative Popular Education.[3] The aim of the exercise was to enable predominantly Black people to reflect critically on the Christian story, seeking to envisage how they locate themselves in relationship to the Christian gospel.

This exercise has been used to help Black people to understand more clearly the need to reflect critically on how they position themselves in relation to the Christian faith. As we saw in the first chapter, Christianity as the religion of European imperialism has often been used as an ideological tool against Black people. In response, Black people have sought to reappropriate the Christian tradition for themselves, seeking to tell a new story based on their own experiences.

When this exercise has been performed, a number of Black people have stated that they have not seen *any Black people in the story*. In many respects, this should not surprise us. A number of Black scholars have written on the processes of mis-education and biased, self-serving teaching strategies that have led many Black people to develop forms of self-negation (denial), in which they relegate or submerge their own self-interests in the belief that they are less in comparison to others.[4]

In the context of this exercise, this can be seen in the inability of 'colonized' people to assert their own worth, or to see themselves reflected positively in

---

3 See Anthony G. Reddie, *Growing into Hope: Vol. 2, Liberation and Change*, Peterborough: Methodist Publishing House, 1998, pp. 7–9.

4 See Carter G. Woodson, *The Mis-Education of the Negro*, Trenton, NJ: Africa World Press, 1990 [1933].

popular stories, myths or historical events that have become central within the narratives that constitute meaning and value. I have witnessed ordinary Black people struggle to locate themselves within the story. It is not so much the case that ordinary Black people do not see themselves as belonging to God, in absolute terms. Rather, it is that they often see the overall backdrop of the narrative as better depicting the cultures and contexts of White European people with power than on terms that speak to their own experiences. As we have seen in a previous chapter, Black Theology has sought to tell a new story for Black people through its reinterpretation of the very meaning and intent of the Christian faith *in the light of Black experiences*.

The aim of this experiential exercise is to describe clearly one of the principal subtexts of Black Theology, namely, the need for oppressed people to reinterpret and appropriate the defining narratives that constitute the story/vision (of the gospel) for their ultimate liberation. While the exercise has raised questions of who is in the story in terms of cultures, ethnicities and nationalities (that is, do Black people have a central role?), the issue that has been of greatest interest to me is where people have located themselves in regard to the story.

What has been at stake in the exercise has been the best way in which to engage with the story. For some, the way in which the story is to be approached is from within it; that is, being right at the heart of the action and attempting to understand it from there. For others, the story is better understood when standing some way back from it and allowing the wider context to shape one's perception of what is going on in the story and how its development is impacted on those witnessing the action.

Clearly, there are advantages and disadvantages to either perspective, or position. For those that are located in the action, they have the advantage of engaging with the story on its own terms as they are in the very heart of the action, seeking to make sense of the events as they unfold around them. In being located right inside the action, some participants have noted the ways in which they could see close at hand what were the salient issues taking place in terms of power relations between the disciples and Jesus. They could also assess the role of the crowd that is present,[5] and the pressures they are exerting on Jesus, to which he must respond.[6] I have described the

---

5 The Indian biblical scholar David Joy has analysed the role of the crowd in Mark's Gospel. He identifies the crowd as subalterns, marginalized, ordinary people from the lower stratum of society and notes how Jesus' engagement with them is reflective of his ministry of liberation and social transformation. See David C. I. Joy, *Mark and Its Subalterns: A Hermeneutical Paradigm for a Postcolonial Context*, Oakwood and London: Equinox, 2008.

6 I have used this text previously, in a very different manner, in which I have identified Jesus' relationship with the crowd and how this is indicative of his ministry of liberation. See Anthony G. Reddie, *Working against the Grain: Re-Imaging Black Theology in the 21st Century*, Oakwood and London: Equinox, 2008, pp. 204–28.

vantage of being located within the story as being one of 'inside looking out'.

Conversely, there have been other participants who have preferred to stand some way back and look on at the story from a distance. For these individuals, being beyond the action, but still in proximity to the events as they are unfolding before them, has its own advantages. Many participants have spoken of being able to see the story in the wider context of the surrounding area and the broader setting in which the events are taking place. This point reminds us that all events or activities or narratives do not exist in a vacuum. Rather, the story events themselves, even if they contain their own internal logic that resides within the activities that are taking place, are nonetheless influenced by and are in relationship to events and factors that may be external to the phenomena that are being discussed.

For some of the participants, being able to stand in an external position to the story does not mean they have no relationship with it. It means, instead, that they have a different perspective and can make different sets of connections and interpretations of what they believe is taking place and can assess what is at stake, when compared to those who are located within.

It is equally the case that, whether located within or external to the story as the group has imagined it, this also carries with it disadvantages. Being located within the story can lead to a kind of myopia or short-sightedness where the participants cannot see beyond the immediacy of the action or the events themselves. There can also exist a form of conservatism, which believes that the only truth is that which can be gleaned from within the story.

Alternatively, being too far removed from the story can lead to a form of disconnection, in which the participants lose sight of what is actually happening within the events and activities in front of them. The dangers of this former position are that one begins to incorporate additional information and ideas from the broader context not realizing that such perspectives either dissipate the essential truth that resides within the story itself or even contaminate it.

When the exercise has been performed with ordinary Black people I think it is fair to say that the bulk of participants, perhaps around two-thirds, have preferred to be within, whereas approximately one-third have opted to be beyond the story.

This enacted metaphor has been used to enable ordinary Black people to reflect on two alternative ways in which Black Theology has been undertaken. One approach has been to interrogate the meaning of the story (a microcosm or scaled-down version of Christianity as a whole) from within. This approach seeks to rethink the meaning of the faith as it is understood and practised by the people within the story; seeking to create meaning and offering this to the context or setting beyond the story itself.

The second approach to undertaking Black Theology in Britain has been to stand away from the story itself and to use the broader setting or context as a means of interpreting the meaning and even critiquing the story. This second move seeks to place Christianity in a broader cultural context and illustrates how linking the inherent meaning of the faith alongside other ideas and theories can also bring about new meaning and forms of liberation for Black people. These two approaches represent the alternative models of Black Theology in Britain from its two principal exponents. The exercise has been helpful in offering a popular, educational way of assisting ordinary Black people in Britain, in the first instance to assess the relative strengths and weaknesses of these approaches to undertaking Black Theology in Britain.

It is unhelpful to see the two approaches as being in opposition. Rather, they are much better understood as two sides of the same coin. What both approaches to Black Theology have in common is the attempt to enable Black people to claim the gospel of Jesus Christ as their own, through the linking of Black cultural perspectives with the central norms of what constitutes the Christian faith. In academic terms, this is often called 'inculturation'. These forms of inculturation are intended (much like the reflections in the previous chapter on 'telling a new story'), to challenge Black people to rethink the Christian faith in the light of their lived experiences for the purposes of proclaiming their liberation from oppression and marginalization.

Defining Black Theology in Britain

When speaking of Black Theology in Britain, I am referring to the specific self-named enterprise of reinterpreting the meaning of God as revealed in Jesus the Christ, in the light of existential Black experience in Britain. This approach to engaging with the Christian tradition is not unlike Black Theology in differing arenas like the *USA, the Caribbean or South Africa*, where one's point of departure is concrete reality of Blackness and the Black experience, in dialogue with the Bible.[7]

Black Theology in Britain, like all theologies of liberation, is governed by the necessity of orthopraxis rather than orthodoxy. This means that one's starting point in talking about God is governed by the necessity to find a basis for acting in response to the lived experiences of struggle and vicissitudes of life, which impinge upon one's daily operations in the attempt to be a human being. The need to respond to the reality of life as it is lived in Britain is one that has challenged many Black British Christians

---

7 See Michael N. Jagessar and Anthony G. Reddie (eds), *Black Theology in Britain: A Reader*, London: Equinox, 2007, p. 1.

to seek in God a means of making sense of situations that seem inherently senseless.[8]

In seeking to make sense of the Black condition in Britain, Black Theology has been inspired by the work of predominantly North American scholars, most notably James Cone, Delores Williams and Jacquelyn Grant.[9]

In seeking to outline the definitional dimensions and parameters of Black Theology in Britain, I am forced to acknowledge my own limitations at this juncture in the proceedings. For while there is a growing wealth of literature that has explored Black Theology from within other religious paradigms, including Rastafari,[10] Hinduism[11] and traditional folk religions,[12] Black Theology in Britain, like her counterparts in South Africa, the USA or the Caribbean, has been dominated by a Christian-inspired gaze. Much of my work has been undertaken as a church-sponsored practical Black liberation theologian based at a church-sponsored theological college (or seminary).[13] My own gaze is indeed a limited one. And yet, in making this confession, I am also forced to acknowledge that most of Black religious expression in Britain (and associated literature and theological reflection) is Christian.

I now want to look at the work of Robert Beckford, the most well-known and visible Black theologian in Britain, in order to assess his method for doing Black Theology in this context.

Theological method in Black Theology in Britain: Robert Beckford

Beckford's perspective on theology has been informed by his relationship with Black British Pentecostalism. His early work, particularly the first two books, owe much to the distinctive emphases of Pentecostalism,[14] echoing many of the relative strengths and weaknesses of that tradition. In all

---

8 These themes are explored by Robert Beckford in *God of the Rahtid*, London: Darton, Longman and Todd, 2003, pp. 1–30.

9 See James H. Cone, *A Black Theology of Liberation*, Maryknoll, NY: Orbis, 1990 [1970]; Delores Williams, *Sisters in the Wilderness: The Challenge of Womanist God-Talk*, Maryknoll, NY: Orbis, 1993; Jacqueline Grant, *White Women's Christ and Black Women's Jesus: Feminist Christology and Womanist Response*, Atlanta, GA: Scholar's Press, 1989.

10 See William David Spencer, *Dread Jesus*, London: SPCK, 1999.

11 Michael N. Jagessar, 'Liberating Cricket: Through the Optic of Ashutosh Gowariker's Lagaan', *Black Theology* 2:2 (2004), pp. 239–49.

12 Kampta Karran, 'Changing Kali: From India to Guyana to Britain', *Black Theology in Britain* 4:1 (2001), pp. 90–102.

13 This was true at the time of writing but is less so in terms of my present location within a secular university and indeed of my future work that is positioned beyond the confines of organized religion.

14 See Robert Beckford, *Jesus Is Dread*, London: Darton, Longman and Todd, 1998, and *Dread and Pentecostal: A Political Theology for the Black Church in Britain*, London: SPCK, 2000.

truth, however, Beckford has never been what one might term a 'traditional' Pentecostal. His theology has always carried much more of an embodied emphasis than that often found within normative Pentecostalism in Britain. The strong focus on Jesus in his work,[15] often focusing on the presence of Jesus within everyday Black cultural life, displays a marked attempt to go beyond the abstract spiritualizing of the central tenets of the Christian faith that is often a marked feature of a great deal of Pentecostal work in the UK.[16]

His later work adopts a much more expansive theological and cultural canvass, which is evidenced in later texts such as God of the Rahtid and God and the Gangs.[17] In the former work, Beckford's persuasive and incisive polemic has enabled many Black people to recognize the ravenous beast that is systemic racism within the context of the Black British experience. In his second book, Dread and Pentecostal, Beckford charts the genealogy of racism within the context of the British Empire and demonstrates the means by which African Caribbean people have sought to respond to the ever-changing force of racial injustice.[18] I would describe Beckford's approach as belonging to the 'outside looking in', typology which was described in the latter part of the opening exercise outlined earlier. As we will see, Beckford's approach is adept at looking at the broader frameworks of African Caribbean cultures, that is, the wider context beyond the story-event (a metaphor for the Christian faith) and showing how one rethinks the former by comparing and contrasting it with the setting that surrounds it.

Beckford's theological method entails the coming together of Jamaican-inspired religious and cultural sources and practices alongside African Caribbean Pentecostal faith and their accompanying religious traditions. Hence, his work seeks to create a link between the so-called worldly and the holy or the sanctified. Whether it is correlating or putting together Bob Marley and Christian theological reflection, or analysing Jesus alongside aspects of Rastafari, Beckford seeks to synthesize elements that have traditionally been seen as oppositional and incompatible. It is this ingenious and interactive construction of disparate theological sources and norms that makes Beckford's work fascinating.

The ingenious and cleverly constructed nature of his work means, however, that it is not without its perennial tensions. Perhaps the ongoing tensions in Beckford's approach to undertaking Black Theology in the British context can be seen in his book Jesus Dub. In this book, the author continues with his radical bringing together of Black religion (African

---

15 See Beckford, Jesus Is Dread, and Jesus Dub, London: Routledge, 2006.

16 See my comments on aspects of this spiritualizing tendency in Reddie, Working against the Grain, pp. 76–8.

17 See Beckford, God of the Rahtid; See Robert Beckford, God and the Gangs, London: Darton, Longman and Todd, 2005.

18 See Beckford, Dread and Pentecostal, pp. 67–130.

Caribbean Pentecostal Christianity) and Black popular culture. *Jesus Dub*, which in many respects is a long-awaited thematic sequel to his first book *Jesus Is Dread*, the first single-authored book on Black Theology in Britain, juxtaposes the 'church hall' and the 'dance hall'. This bringing together of such disparate sources is undertaken in order to rework the political and theological dimensions of Black art and culture and the use of space as constructed by one's belief in the Holy Spirit. In effect, Beckford seeks to provide ways in which Black Pentecostals can link their faith in Jesus to the wider cultural traditions in Britain, in order to establish a relationship between the two. The metaphor for this bringing together of Black religion and Black culture is that of 'Dub'.

The central thesis of this work is that 'Dub is an act of deconstruction, where a reggae musician takes apart the key elements of a music track, and repositions them, transforming the original, enabling new ways of hearing and understanding'.[19] The author argues that, throughout Diasporan African history, Black working-class people have constantly used music and faith as constructs by which they might resist racialized oppression.

Here, Beckford is drawing on music theory and a critical approach to cultural studies in order to create a new way of undertaking Black Theology in Britain. In this approach, Black people are enabled to imagine a new future through their engagement with music and space, either within the dance hall or the church hall. While comparisons can be invidious, it is interesting to note the parallel use of 'dance hall' (often on a Saturday night) and the 'church hall', the classic domain for religious sensibilities on a Sunday morning, with that of James Cone's identification of the blues and the spirituals. The latter framing from African American culture also incorporates a Saturday night–Sunday morning parallel.

In this particular approach to Black Theology, Beckford uses music theory, postcolonial discourse and socio-linguistic analysis, in order to juxtapose two pivotal aspects of Black African Caribbean life, namely, the church hall, which is reflective of the aesthetic dynamics of Caribbean Pentecostalism, and the dance hall, in which the rhythmical cadences and lyrical ingenuity of reggae music and the DJ are key.

As in his previous work, Beckford achieves this ingenious interdisciplinary approach by means of utilizing the correlation method of Paul Tillich,[20] and the notion of 'Revised Critical Correlation', as advocated by the likes of David Tracy.[21] This approach is one in which there is a process of looking at how one undertakes God-talk by means of establishing a mutual relationship

---

19 Beckford, *Jesus Dub*, p. 1. .

20 See Paul Tillich, *Systematic Theology*, vol. 1, Chicago: University of Chicago Press, 1967.

21 See David Tracy, *The Analogical Imagination: Christian Theology and the Culture of Pluralism*, London: SCM, 1981.

between the Christian tradition and the broader world and society in which Christian faith is located. In the first instance, one is attempting to use the ideas of faith as a means of answering critical and crucial questions pertaining to the meaning and value of life in a specific context or cultural setting.

In this approach, Beckford is concerned with the ways in which Black God-talk interacts with our perceptions of human identity and how knowledge of what it means to be a Black human being are constructed and understood. This method is one that uses frameworks of faith alongside the popular cultures in every Black life as a means of constructing a conversation between the two sources. This type of conversation is one that moves from the seemingly sacred to the secular and demonstrates how one can use the ideas of the faith as a means of interpreting the challenges confronted by one's lived experience and existence in a particular context. In effect, the approach that Beckford adopts seeks to use the language and symbolic power of religious faith as a means of reinterpreting the signs and symbols of power and meaning in the wider culture in which Black people live in Britain.

Beckford's approach is one that settles upon the cultural phenomena of dance-hall music and the work of the DJ within African Caribbean life in Britain. Beckford is adept at skilfully identifying issues related to the varied forms of Black cultural production as a means of discerning the liberative dimensions and the presence of God within Black religious and cultural life. For Beckford, truth is not only to be found at within the construct of the story itself, as identified in the opening exercise. Rather, one can stand a distance from of the story-event and use the cultural practices of the surrounding context as a means of reinterpreting the meaning of the Christian narrative, but the same is true in reverse. Namely, the symbols and ideas of truth that exist within the story can be used to reinterpret the wider environment, beyond the story-event itself.

Reflecting further on *Jesus Dub*

In my opinion, *Jesus Dub* represents an important dimension in the attempt to create a new model of Black Theology in the British context. It comes with all the attendant dilemmas and tensions in this particular approach. At its best, *Jesus Dub* provides a compelling case for seeing God's redemptive presence within the urban landscape in the myriad vistas and vantage points that exist beyond the self-defined world of Black Pentecostal churches in Britain. Beckford's Black Theology work draws on cultural performance and practices that lie outside the Church and the often self-defined and sometimes self-referential world of Pentecostal Christianity.

For Beckford, the liberative presence of the divine can be witnessed in the lyrical ingenuity of the DJ and the power of the Holy Spirit can be discerned in the dance hall and not just the sanctified space of the church hall. Beckford's method for undertaking Black Theology moves on from simply working with Paul Tillich's notion of correlation, that is, seeking to bring Christian faith into conversation with the broader environment of human existence in order that the former can provide resources for interpreting the meaning of the latter. Instead, by adopting David Tracy's Revised Correlation, Beckford is arguing that one can use the practices and performances of popular culture as a lens for interrogating the faith perspective of Black African Caribbean Pentecostal believers in Britain.

In other words, the broader cultures and the nature of human existence can provide resources for interrogating Christian theology and the meaning of the faith itself! That, essentially, this coming together of the dance hall and the church hall is not one way, as the frameworks of faith can also inspire a theo-cultural interpretation of African Caribbean cultural performance in Britain. That is, the church hall can also reinterpret the efficacy of the dance hall. Beckford wants to provide an alternative hermeneutical or interpretative framework for understanding African Caribbean urban life in Britain and the role of Christian faith and music as conduits for social protest and change.

How does one speak to the other? How can reading one shape one's reading of the other?

In *Jesus Dub*, Beckford continues to push African Caribbean Pentecostalism beyond its traditional forces of conservatism. These forces are ones that want to deny any serious engagement with the liberative frameworks of faith or to engage with any expansive notions of divine revelation that arise from social locations beyond the biblical text. Beckford is not limited to looking solely at the story-event in and of itself, in isolation from the wider world in which it is set. He seeks to rethink the nature of revelation by inviting Black Pentecostals to discern the liberative impulse of the divine within African Caribbean cultural production, particularly that which emanates from reggae and dance-hall cultures. In effect, one could argue that Beckford is operating as a Black theologian of Black cultural life in Britain and is seeking to liberate God in Christ from the shackles of the Church or from within rigid, literalist readings of the Bible.[22]

This particular approach to doing Black Theology has its obvious strengths. Beckford's entry into the world of broadcast media, seen in his numerous documentaries,[23] is testament to the skills he possesses in mak-

---

22 Elaine Graham, Heather Walton and Francis Ward provide a comprehensive appraisal of differing models of theological reflection. They identify Beckford as a 'theologian of culture'. See Elaine Graham, Heather Walton and Francis Ward, *Theological Reflection: Methods*, London: SCM, 2005, pp. 222–4, and *Theological Reflection: Sources*, London: SCM, 2007, p. 410.

23 Robert Beckford's major documentaries include *Britain's Slave Trade* (Channel 4, 1999), *Black Messiah* (BBC 4, 2001), the BAFTA award-winning *Test of Time* (BBC Education, 2001), *Blood and Fire* (BBC 2, 2002), *Ebony Towers* (BBC 4, 2003), *God Is*

ing links between Black Christian religious ideas and the world of popular culture. The visibility of his work has very few parallels save for that of Michael Eric Dyson.[24]

The strength of Beckford's approach sits in tension with some of its perceived weaknesses. In seeking to utilize a correlation and Revised Correlation method in his constructive theological work, Beckford adopts a method that is *not necessarily* aligned to mainstream Pentecostal sensibilities. It is interesting to note that the author's point of departure in this particular approach to Black Theology (witnessed in *Jesus Dub*) is 'the politics of sound' in the form of reggae music, dance-hall culture and his own formative engagement with and immersion within this complex socio-cultural world.[25] With the exception of Chapter 6,[26] where the author reflects on the praxis (faithful activity) of Jesus as a basis for bringing together a notion of Dub hermeneutics (interpretation) as integral to the gospel, the Bible does not feature prominently nor does it underscore his theological method. In standing at a metaphorical distance in order to interpret the story-event, Beckford does not overly feature the notions of inspired truth such as the Bible that sit at the heart of this phenomenon in the first place. By this I mean that the metaphorical story-event only exists because of what it believes to be true in the revealed truth that sits at the heart of the narrative. By placing the external alongside the lived experience within the story, Beckford appears to be giving both equal weight and importance. But for most people within the story-event, the revealed truths in which they believe are not to be compared with what happens beyond them in the wider context.

Now to be clear, I am not arguing that Beckford's theological method is a flawed one. My critique is simply this. From an analysis of his theological method it is the observation that for one who self-identifies as an African Caribbean Pentecostal Christian, his approach seems at variance with the self-declared constituency with whom he identifies. In effect, Beckford's use of cultural sources from beyond the Christian faith (the story-event) creates a seemingly insoluble impasse between himself and the stance of the people for whom he writes and with whom he declares a sense of solidarity.

Black (Channel 4, 2004), *Who Wrote the Bible?* (Channel 4, 2004), *The Gospel Truth* (Channel 4, 2005), *The Empire Pays Back* (Channel 4, 2005), *The Real Patron Saints* (Channel 4, 2005), *The Passion: Films, Faith and Fury* (Channel 4, 2006). For further information, visit Robert Beckford's website at http://www.robertbeckford.co.uk/.

24 Michael Eric Dyson is a renowned African American religio-cultural commentator who is greatly adept at utilizing the broadcast media for the dissemination of ideas, in addition to the more traditional scholarly mode, by means of writing popular books and monographs. For further details, see http://en.wikipedia.org/wiki/Michael_Eric_Dyson.

25 Beckford, *Jesus Dub*, pp. 15–27.

26 Beckford, *Jesus Dub*, pp. 93–100.

Beckford's approach to doing Black Theology fails to establish any meaningful ground with the self-defined, Bible-inspired Christian frameworks of Black Christians in Britain, in general, and Black Pentecostals, in particular. Black Christianity in Britain, especially Black British Pentecostalism, does not readily acknowledge truth claims that are perceived as emanating from beyond the Bible, which many take to be the *literal* word of God.

In order to expand on the last point, let me share with you, briefly, a true story from a number of years ago. I remember speaking at a major Black church event in London in the late 1990s. I was the designated keynote speaker. On conclusion of my address the majority of the questions sent my way did not pertain to the talk I had just given but were in response to Robert Beckford's allegedly 'controversial'[27] first book *Jesus Is Dread*. I remember spending a spirited 30 minutes or so defending Beckford and his book and arguing that it was an important and indeed vital piece of Black Theology work in Britain. I remember a middle-aged Black woman shaking her fist at me defiantly, as she cried out repeatedly, 'Jesus is Dread?'

For many, at this event, this woman's protestations were the key concern at hand. 'What did Jesus have to do with Dread?' The fact that the latter emerges from Rastafari religious and cultural sensibilities is what was most shocking for many in the audience. For many of them it was simply aberrant to correlate Jesus, the most holy symbol of God's presence in history, alongside the religious and cultural apparel emanating from a still, largely, socially unacceptable 'rebel'-like group, that is, Rastafari. The 'Jesus of faith' might be many things, but Jesus could not be dread, in the minds of many Black Christian people in that room.

It would seem there are clear limits in how one can locate Jesus and divine activity alongside 'non-Christian' cultural sources. When I was pressed by a number in the meeting on how Beckford could attempt to justify placing Jesus within the framework of Rasta-inspired cultural aesthetics, I responded by pointing to the parallels between the 'Jesus of history' as depicted in the Gospels and the 'Christ of faith' who continues to be alongside all marginalized and oppressed peoples in the world. Jesus could be dread because his current status as a Rasta-inspired outsider was entirely consistent with his lived human experience as a marginalized Galilean Jew in first-century Palestine.

Sadly, my attempts to demonstrate the nature of Beckford's use of correlation did not work because the aforementioned explanation could not be imagined from within the realms of biblical literalism. A number of the

---

27 I use this term advisedly, for, as Beckford himself acknowledges, such terms are used as ways of positing the illegitimacy of ideas and approaches that the mainstream, British establishment see as threatening. See http://www.guardian.co.uk/education/2005/may/17/highereducationprofile.academicexperts for further details.

people in the audience asked pointedly, 'Where in the Scriptures does it say that Jesus is Dread?' Clearly, this was an argument I could not win on those specific terms. Beckford's approach was largely dismissed as a transgressive one for the majority of this audience.

As a Black theologian in Britain and colleague of Robert Beckford, I should make my position clear at this juncture, if I have not already done so, by means of the previous story. In the seeming collision between Beckford and aspects of mainstream Black Pentecostalism in Britain, I am clear that, in my own adherence to Black Theology, I stand on the side of Beckford versus the conservative critics of his work.[28] His work remains the only version of Black Pentecostalism in Britain that can be said to be an authentic and viable contribution to Black Theology in the British context.

At this juncture, it is important to assert that my assessment of Beckford's theological method is not intended as a pointed riposte to his iconoclastic status within the developing movement that is Black Theology in Britain. Beckford, to my mind, remains an important thinker and among the most creative Pentecostal theologians in attempting to engage with their Blackness in the world. It is certainly my belief that his work provides the most robust and compelling argument for Black Theology in Britain that operates from within a Pentecostal framework.

Unlike the more conservative offerings of other Black Pentecostal writers in Britain,[29] Beckford provides a more convincing and critical scrutiny of the meeting point between the *seemingly* fixed nature of the Bible[30] and the improvised, ingenious and interactive interpretative qualities of Black people in Britain and across the African Diaspora.

Theological method in Black Theology in Britain: Anthony Reddie

Alongside Robert Beckford, the other major Black theologian in Britain, certainly in terms of scholarly output, has been myself. If you will pardon the immodesty, I want to look at aspects of my own developing approach to Black Theology in Britain in order to discern an alternative direction in which this discipline has been undertaken in this country.

---

28 Unsubstantiated, critical Black evangelical voices have been raised at Beckford's works. See the conclusion of Robert Beckford's entry on Wikipedia. See http://en.wikipedia.org/wiki/Robert_Beckford.

29 See J. D. Aldred, *Respect: Understanding Caribbean British Christianity*, Peterborough: Epworth, 2005. See also Mark Sturge, *Look What the Lord Has Done! An Exploration of Black Christian Faith in Britain*, Milton Keynes: Scripture Union, 2005.

30 I have placed the word 'seemingly' in italics because, as we have seen in a previous chapter, which will be amplified in the penultimate chapter, ideological critical perspectives on the Bible show that it is anything but fixed in terms of its original construction and in how it has been read and interpreted in subsequent years.

As a Black theologian in Britain I have sought to use the theories and practices of liberative approaches to Christian education and conscientization as the basis for my own theological method. This work has seen me adopt, like Beckford, an interdisciplinary approach to undertaking Black Theology in Britain. In this approach, I seek to juxtapose differing ways of discerning truth, in my case, the coming together of Marxist-inspired notions of social and cultural awareness of oppression and change (often described as 'conscientization'), alongside a radical, Black politicized, religious and cultural approach to biblical interpretation. Although I have used this particular method in a great deal of my work over the years, perhaps the best explanation of this approach can be found in *Dramatizing Theologies*.[31]

My own work might be described as an 'inside looking out' approach to doing Black Theology in Britain. Going back to the opening exercise for a moment and the metaphorical perspective of standing inside the story-event or standing back from it – this approach is one that stands within it. What I hope will be clear, in a moment, is that I am making no claims to this approach being 'better' than or more 'authentic' than the one just described. As we will see, there are as many problems, concerns and limitations to my approach as those I have identified with Beckford's method.

This work or approach to undertaking Black Theology has largely been undertaken in workshops in a plethora of local churches across many denominations in Britain. When leading these workshops in local churches and in more formal learning contexts, I have often commented that, for the most part,[32] Black people can be trusted to do two things – namely, 'we'[33] will read the Bible and will also go to church. In a previous piece of work, I argued, along with Michael Jagessar, that the White-dominated complexion of so much religious discourse in Britain was such that no mention was ever made of the burgeoning growth of Black Christianity in Britain. So long as traditionally conceived White notions of Christianity held sway, there was

---

31 See Anthony G. Reddie, *Dramatizing Theologies*, London: Equinox, 2006.

32 I am forced to admit that this is a major generalization, but the recent statistical figures on religious observance in Britain clearly demonstrate the overwhelmingly Christian complexion of Black British communities since 1948. The growing percentage of Black people in historic mainline churches alongside the growth of neo-Pentecostalism is testament to the realization that 'Black Christianity' in Britain is a phenomenon of major import. See Michael N. Jagessar and Anthony G. Reddie (eds), *Postcolonial Black British Theology: New Textures and Themes*, Peterborough: Epworth, 2007. This work is an attempt to speak to the developments of that phenomenon and to demonstrate how Black Theology can be of service in providing the much-needed critical insights of this growth.

33 This work, like all my scholarly research, is undertaken from a subjective insider's perspective, using personal narrative, experience, dialogue and accessible reportage as methods for undertaking Black theological discourse.

or is little or no attempt to acknowledge the vibrancy of Black Christianity in Britain, or what might be learnt from this growing phenomenon.[34]

My particular approach to Black Theology owes much to my previous life, first as a Christian youth worker for two Black-majority Methodist churches in Handsworth (North Birmingham), and then, more recently, as a Christian education worker for the Connexional (National) British Methodist Church. In terms of the latter, I was sponsored by the Methodist Church to undertake a research project that sought to raise the social and political awareness of Black African Caribbean children and young people in Britain by means of an African Caribbean cultural interpretation of the Christian faith.[35] This work attempted to bring transformative Christian education into conversation with Black Theology in order to create an educational approach to the latter for the social transformation of ordinary Black people in Britain.

The central intent of my approach to Black Theology has been the desire to create a practical model of the discipline that engages with ordinary people in their attempts to live out and give expression to their faith. I am concerned that Black Theology should operate at a more interpersonal level, providing a resource that enables people to give expression to the central, basic ideas of this discipline in their everyday lives. Unlike Beckford's more theoretical reflections seeking to bring reggae culture and Black Pentecostal life together, my work is concerned with the more practical task of providing resources for enabling ordinary Black people to reinterpret the meaning and intent of Christian faith by means of an educational approach to Black Theology. The hope is that this work resources ordinary people to become agents of change in their lived engagement with the environment in which they are located.

My formative Black theological work was one that was conscious of the cultures, identities, historical and contemporary experiences and expressions of Christian faith within the socio-political and economic realities of inner-city life in Britain. This work was done between 1995 and 1999 on a research project entitled the 'Birmingham Initiative'.[36] It was an attempt to find a means of providing a culturally appropriate model of Christian nurture and faith formation for Black African Caribbean children in Birmingham,

34 See Jagessar and Reddie (eds), *Postcolonial Black British Theology*, pp. xxi–xxii.

35 Aspects of this work are detailed in Anthony G. Reddie, 'People Matter Too! The Politics and Method of Doing Black Liberation Theology', The Ferguson Lecture, University of Manchester, 18 October 2007, *Practical Theology* 1:1 (2008), pp. 43–64.

36 The 'Birmingham Initiative', was the brainchild of Christopher Hughes Smith, the then General Secretary of the Division of Education and Youth. Having formerly been a Methodist minister and District Chair in Birmingham, he was aware of the deficiencies in the existing Christian education work sponsored by the Methodist Church among Black children. In order to assess the effectiveness of the existing work and to create a mechanism that might attempt to develop a hypothesis for the Christian education of Black children in Britain, funds were obtained to create a research project to that end.

using the insights of Black Theology and transformative pedagogy as educational and theological frameworks for the research.[37]

The work of the Birmingham Initiative was conducted with the support chiefly of the Methodist Church, alongside a number of inner-city churches from other denominations in Birmingham. For the research to progress it was essential that I located a means by which I could 'carry' the number of lay volunteers – Sunday school workers, youth workers, lay preachers – and ordained clergy with me. It was also imperative that they had a sense of ownership and engagement with me in the context of attempting to discover a more theologically contextual and culturally appropriate means of formation and socialization of African Caribbean children and young people into the Christian faith by means of Black Theology.

Analysis of *Dramatizing Theologies*

In *Dramatizing Theologies* (and in other published work also) I have drawn on two key educators in order to assist my attempt at developing an educative approach to undertaking Black Theology in Britain. One of the key dialogue partners in this work has been Thomas Groome, and the other is Paulo Freire. In many respects, I have utilized transformative popular education[38] in order to develop an approach to undertaking Black Theology in Britain that seeks to engage with ordinary Black people of faith.

Thomas Groome is a White Irish American Roman Catholic practical liberation theologian. Groome has created an approach to undertaking liberative theological reflection that seeks to be in dialogue with ordinary Christian believers in North America.[39] Central to Groome's own method for undertaking liberation theology from within the participative frame-

---

37 See Anthony G. Reddie, *Nobodies to Somebodies: A Practical Theology for Education and Liberation*, Peterborough: Epworth, 2003.

38 In using this term I am concerned with an approach to teaching and learning, which proceeds from a critical inquiry into the very basis of what we consider to be truth and the knowledge clams that give rise to so-called 'accepted truths'. In critiquing and challenging such conventions (such ideas of objectivity and neutrality), transformative education hopes to provide tools for the creation of new knowledge and truths, which will ultimately seek to empower ordinary people, particularly those who are marginalized and oppressed. Some key texts in the area of transformative education are the following: James A. Banks (ed.), *Multicultural Education, Transformative Knowledge and Action: Historical and Contemporary Perspectives*, New York: Teachers College Press, 1996; James A. Banks, *Race, Culture and Education: The Selected Works of James A. Banks*, London and New York: Routledge, 2006; Jürgen Habermas, *Knowledge and Human Interests*, Boston: Beacon, 1971.

39 See his two most influential books – Thomas H. Groome, *Christian Religious Education: Sharing Our Story and Vision*, San Francisco: Jossey-Bass, 1999 [1980], and Thomas H. Groome, *Sharing Faith: A Comprehensive Approach to Religious Education and Pastoral Ministry*, San Francisco: HarperSanFrancisco, 1991.

work provided by practical theology[40] has been the towering importance of Paulo Freire. It can be argued that Paulo Freire provides the overall key to understanding transformative approaches to education that underpin my work and that of many others who are seeking to bring theology and education together.

One of Freire's central concepts is that of 'conscientization'. This is a process where poor and oppressed people are enabled to become critically aware of the circumstances in which they live and the ways in which their humanity is infringed upon and blighted by the often dehumanizing contexts that surround them.[41] Allen J. Moore, commenting on this aspect of Freire's work, says:

> Conscientization in Freire's work is apparently both an individual experience and a shared experience of a people who are acting together in history. A way of life is not determined from thinking about the world but is formed from the shared praxis. In this critical approach to the world, basic attitudes, values, and beliefs are formed and a people are humanized or liberated. Conscientization, therefore, leads to a life lived with consciousness of history, a life lived that denounces and transforms this history in order to form a new way of life for those who are oppressed.[42]

In my educational approaches to undertaking Black Theology, the scholarship of Thomas Groome has proved invaluable.[43] I have sought to use his critical thinking in my participative Black Theology work. Groome argues that activity and joint participation are central to the teaching and learning process of Christian education.[44] In *Sharing Faith*, he develops further his notion of critical reflection, which gives rise to committed Christian praxis (faithful action) in the name of the gospel. He incorporates an overarching theory for a practical, radical approach to undertaking liberation theology. In this seminal work, he outlines a participative and practical approach to liberating ordinary people, which he terms 'shared praxis', which he describes as being

---

40 In Groome's work, the overarching framework for his approach to undertaking liberative practical theology work was provided by a highly politicized notion of Christian education.

41 Paulo Freire, *Education for Critical Consciousness*, New York: Continuum, 1990 [1973], pp. 18–20.

42 Allen J. Moore, 'A Social Theory of Religious Education', *Religious Education* 82: 3 (1987), pp. 415–25.

43 See Reddie, *Nobodies to Somebodies*, pp. 87–90.

44 Groome, *Christian Religious Education*, pp. 49–51.

[a] participative and dialogical pedagogy in which people reflect critically on their own historical agency in time and place and on their socio-cultural reality, have access together to Christian story/vision and personally appropriate it in community with the creative intent of renewed praxis in Christian faith towards God's reign for all creation.[45]

Groome details an approach that attempts to link the individual to a process of critical reflection and dialogue. This reflection and dialogue arises through a shared process where individuals are encouraged to enter into dramatic exercises that attempt to address major issues and concerns in the lives of that group of people. This dramatic exercise is, in turn, combined with sacred stories (or narratives), in order that the Christian story/vision, namely, the gospel of Christ, can be better realized.

This process culminates in the final phase of this approach, which is a search for the truth that enables participants to make the contextualized and inculturated story/vision one that they can legitimately own.[46]

Groome argues that participants should be empowered to appropriate the story/vision in order that they can own it, and then remake it, so that they can be set free. Groome's approach is heavily influenced by liberation theology and seeks to speak to the experiences of those who have been marginalized and oppressed. The final act in this liberative cycle is one that calls for 'shared praxis', as the means of realizing and 'making good' the inherent promises of freedom within the gospel of Jesus Christ.[47]

The central characteristic of my work in Black Theology in Britain is the attention to issues of theological method, in particular, how we use the Bible as a means of doing Black liberative theological reflection for the purposes of radical conscientization among ordinary Black people of faith. I would best describe my work as 'participative Black Theology in Britain'. In using this term, I am drawing attention to the need to hold in tension the competing claims of practice and theory in terms of the practical expression of Christian theology and praxis. This approach is one that pays particular attention to Christian action and how and in what ways these forms of 'performance' are resourced, nourished and even impeded by Christian traditions and reflections that have emerged from the latter.

This particular, practical approach to both the articulation and the 'doing' of Black Theology alongside the dissemination of it draws upon my training as a religious educator. In my previous work, I have spoken of my twin interests of Black Theology and Christian education. The latter has been used as a conduit to undertake the former. I have used my interest in

45 Groome, *Sharing Faith*, p. 135.
46 Groome, *Sharing Faith*, pp. 138–51.
47 Groome, *Sharing Faith*, pp. 266–92.

education and experience as an educator to find interactive and participative approaches to doing Black Theology. This approach has been adopted in order to move beyond the intellectual barriers of indifference and mild curiosity that are often thrown at the Black theological educator as a kind of smokescreen to negate any attempt to engage in authentic and transformative learning. In effect, I have attempted to 'get under the skin' of the participants with whom I work in an effort to encourage them to engage with the challenges thrown up by Black Theology.

Like Beckford, and many other Black theologians, my work begins with the primacy of experience and the realities of being Black in a world of overarching and rampant White hegemony. The resultant concentration on experience as a criteria and critical framework for assessing the truth claims of revealed knowledge is one that challenges White participants and Black ones alike in my own work. Central to my approach to Black Theology is the importance of participative models of Black theological reflection. In *Dramatizing Theologies* I argue for a participative approach to Black God-talk that is 'an alternative means of undertaking Black Theology, in which the central ideas of this enterprise are distilled in a dramatic form in order that those who are the "voiceless" can find their voice within an interactive, participative format'.[48] My theological method falls within the wider framework provided by practical theology.

In effect, I am working within the framework of my own practice as a practical Black theologian, who in using the methodological approaches of Christian education is attempting to create a model of Black Theology that is concerned with issues of conscientization and social transformation. I am seeking to place these formative frameworks in conversation with the Bible and Christian tradition in order that the former can rework and reconfigure the latter.

I am working from the standpoint that ecclesial settings remain potent symbols for creative and constructive change, and that transformative ministry can be a conduit for the working out and working through of Martin Luther King Jr's notion of the beloved community.[49] I have described this approach as one that is pragmatic because my point of departure is my recognition of the inherent conservatism of many ordinary Black Christians. This approach is one that attempts to engage in direct fashion with the religious position of ordinary Black people of Christian faith in Britain. So, whereas Beckford's approach assumes the theological justification of correlating Jesus with Rastafari notions of Dread (something with which I agree), my work proceeds from the basis of those elements that are far more familiar and that might be judged as 'more acceptable'. My approach, as I have said previously, is much more of an 'inside looking out' approach. Namely,

---

48 See Reddie, *Dramatizing Theologies*, p. 99.

49 See Donald M. Chinula, *Building King's Beloved Community: Foundation for Pastoral Care and Counselling with the Oppressed*, Cleveland, OH: United Church Press, 1997.

one that stands within the story-event and seeks to rethink and critique its meaning from within, as a means of establishing its truthfulness for the wider context in which it is set.

As a participative Black theologian, working through the approaches and methods provided by Christian education as a means of disseminating and empowering predominantly ordinary Black people, by means of Black Theology, I want to attend to those aspects of Christian practice that directly confront and impinge on the lives of ordinary Black folk.

This approach to doing Black Theology in Britain is a pragmatic one for it seeks to engage with the lived experience and expression of most ordinary Black religious believers, namely, Christians. It seeks to work within the paradigms this religious tradition provides in order to redefine and reassess its central meaning and methodological intent. In many respects, this work is undoubtedly a more conservative one than that found in Beckford's work, for it seeks to operate within the established framework that is 'traditional' Christianity, albeit with the aim of redefining and deconstructing the overall meaning of God's revelation in Jesus Christ.

I have undertaken this approach to Black Theology because, for the most part, ordinary Black Christians are not overly comfortable with juxtaposing or correlating external truth claims beyond the parameters of Christianity. For many Black people wrestling with faith, even younger ones, the salient question remains, 'What has Bob Marley got to do with Christian faith?' What does a Ganja (cannabis)-smoking Rasta say to Black Christians? (A great deal, I would hasten to add, but whether many ordinary Black Christians will hear this is another matter altogether.)

My work does not seek either to defend or to attack the use of alternative forms of knowledge for undertaking constructive and critical Christian theology from a Black theological perspective. I am also using the ideas of Paulo Freire and Thomas Groome, who themselves are influenced by critical ideas of social and political transformation, which can be argued as being external to the Christian traditions. I am not challenging or attacking these methods outright as being deeply flawed, largely because, as can be evidenced in the work of Robert Beckford, I am very much influenced by these self same also. But my work remains within the self-defined hermeneutical framework of reinterpreting the Christian faith, while attempting (in a more disguised fashion) to engage with the tools of social theory as a focusing lens for doing so. My work incorporates the use of theory, particularly that offered by the respective works of Paulo Freire and Thomas Groome, but it does so by juxtaposing such ideas with Christian-inspired knowledge claims in an immediate and relational manner.

Just as Beckford's theological method carries within it the echoes of a dialectical tension between the formative use of non-Christian-generated truth claims, alongside the conservative position of many ordinary Black Pentecostal believers, so my own work carries its own internal contradictions and limitations. The weakness in the theological method I employ is, namely, the over-reliance on potentially self-referential Christian interpretative frameworks for imagining the christological-inspired visions of liberation and freedom. In effect, my approach to undertaking Black Theology in Britain is also confined within the self-defined world of the Church and the perceptions and attitudes of Black Christians themselves. It is worth noting, at this juncture, that the first Black Theology text in the world was *Black Theology and Black Power*, by James H. Cone; in it, Cone seeks dialogue with the Black Power Movement and not necessarily the Church in his articulation of Black liberation theology. (The movement towards the Church occurs in his second book, *A Black Theology of Liberation*.)

In my approach to undertaking Black Theology in Britain, in seeking to 'remake' and 'reinterpret' the basic intent and meaning of Christian faith, I am reliant on the religious frameworks provided by a faith that was the chief tool of mendacious and bloodthirsty Euro-American enslavers. One might well ask: can one dismantle the slave master's house using his own tools?[50] The other failure in my theological method is my limited engagement with Black popular cultures. In many respects, in seeking to limit my gaze to the Black Christian faithful and their engagement with ecclesial settings (namely, churches), my work lacks both the plurality[51] and the breadth[52] of someone like Anthony Pinn, for example.

It could be argued that the essential difference between the respective approaches of Robert Beckford and myself to Black Theology lies in the trajectories of our work. In his use of Black popular culture as his primary resource for undertaking Black Theology, it could be argued that Beckford's point of departure is the plural landscape of urban life and its myriad realities in Britain. His work seeks to bring these wider, contested realities to the immediate purview of the Church. In effect, Beckford is a Black theologian of popular culture in Britain.[53]

---

50 A paraphrase of Audrey Lorde's seminal dictum.

51 Examples of a more plural approach to undertaking Black religious and theological studies can be seen in the scholarly output of Anthony Pinn. Pinn engages with non-Christian sources in his approach to Black religious studies. This can be seen in Anthony B. Pinn, *Varieties of African American Religious Experience*, Minneapolis: Fortress, 1998, and *African American Humanist Principles: Living and Thinking like the Children of Nimrod*, New York: Palgrave Macmillan, 2004.

52 Examples of a more broad and expansionist approach to Black religious and theological studies can once again be seen in the scholarly output of Anthony Pinn, where he engages with sources external to organized religion as a means of discerning the radical impulse of Black spirituality and religiosity. See Anthony B. Pinn (ed.), *Noise and Spirit: The Religious and Spiritual Sensibilities of Rap Music*, New York and London: New York University Press, 2003, and *Embodiment and the New Shape of Black Theological Thought*, New York and London: New York University Press, 2010.

53 For further reflections on this latter point, see Graham, Walton and Ward, *Theological Reflection: Methods*, pp. 222–4, and *Theological Reflection: Sources*, pp. 400–10.

Conversely, it could be argued that my own approach is the opposite of Beckford's, namely, that my point of departure is that of a Church-related practical Black theologian in Britain. My work seeks to reinterpret the meaning of Christian faith from within the context of ecclesial or church practice and attempts to bring such re-contextualized insights into conversation with the broader contexts of urban life in Britain. In effect, Beckford's work is a deductive or 'outside looking in' approach to Black theological method, whereas my own model operates on an inductive or 'inside looking out' procedural basis.

From my perspective, Black Theology in Britain has to wrestle with the Bible, seeking to make sense of the Jesus whom many believe to be the Christ, and to argue for a re-imagined conception of church as a site for liberative praxis and transformative change. Pragmatically, this work has to contend with a self-defined religious tradition in which the norms, knowledge-based frameworks of revealed truth and historical precedent have been circumscribed for some 2000 years. My work is an attempt to deconstruct these building blocks and remake them in a fashion that is consonant with Black experience, which is one of largely struggle and suffering.[54]

As one can deduce from the previous sections of this chapter, my own work has sought to challenge and expand the inhibited and negated consciousness of ordinary Black people in Britain. This work attempts to enable such individuals and communities to critically reread biblical texts and so reconfigure the very meaning of Christian faith for people of African descent. Beckford's work is very much committed to a similar perspective, but he uses a very different approach. Beckford is also concerned with the central task of conscientization in the British context. Like myself, he is also aware of the ways in which Black Christians in Britain have imbibed religious concepts that are often inimical to their own self-esteem and sense of identity.

At the heart of Black Theology in Britain is the desire to rid Black people of the stultifying effects of polite, White middle-class, establishment-friendly forms of religious rhetoric. This form of religiosity is one that often seems geared towards robbing Black Christians of any critical consciousness towards the need for radical social and political change. It has been argued that the overarching framework for imagining Black Theology in Britain is that of a counter-imperial form of discourse and practice that challenges the metropolitan centre from which British Christianity has straddled the world.[55]

---

54 The most systematic outworking of this ongoing thesis can be found in my *Working against the Grain*.

55 See Robert Beckford, '"Doing" Black Theology in the UKKK', *Black Theology in Britain* 4 (2000), pp. 38–60.

In a later work, when addressing the need for Black people to embrace righteous rage and so move beyond the polite blandishments of niceness that seem commonplace within British Christianity, Beckford writes: 'Righteous Black rage is a dimension of the Kingdom of God. This means that Black people struggling with vexation and seeking restitution can find a home within the teachings of Jesus on the Kingdom.'[56]

The two case-studies I have investigated provide differing approaches to undertaking Black Theology in Britain. I am not claiming that either is normative of the discipline in the UK. Robert Beckford and I represent the two most prolific and visible Black theologians in Britain. Our respective approaches represent different sides of the same Black liberation theology coin as it exists in Britain, although there is no doubting the fact that other such coins exist, which are different in shape and size to the one I have highlighted, thus far, in this chapter.[57]

What does this have to say to Black Theology in other parts of the world?

In his use of multiple and eclectic sources for the articulation of Black Theology in Britain, Beckford draws upon the similarly creative work of Black theologians in the USA. In terms of the latter, there are Black religious scholars who have mined cultural sources as a means of undertaking liberative Black God-talk. While Beckford's early work draws extensively upon the style and the substantive content of Cone's work he also utilizes insights and approaches from the likes of Gayraud Wilmore, Henry H. Mitchell, Theophus Smith and Anthony Pinn.[58] Beckford's, use of popular culture as a means of interrogating the liberative dimensions of African Caribbean Christianity in Britain also has parallels with the likes of Michael Eric Dyson in the USA.

Beckford's work, while sitting within the religious-cultural model of Black Theology, nevertheless also avoids any direct categorization one might attempt to make in terms of how his work is discerned and codified. One can

---

56 Beckford, *God of the Rahtid*, p. 44.

57 For alternative approaches to Black Theology in Britain see Jagessar and Reddie (eds), *Postcolonial Black British Theology*, and Jagessar and Reddie (eds), *Black Theology in Britain*.

58 See Gayraud S. Wilmore, *Black Religion and Black Radicalism: An Interpretation of the Religious History of Afro-American People*, 2nd edn, Maryknoll, NY: Orbis, 1983; Henry H. Mitchell and Nicola Copper-Lewter, *Soul Theology: The Heart of American Black Culture*, San Francisco: Harper and Row, 1986; Theophus Smith, *Conjuring Culture: Biblical Formations of Black America*, New York: Oxford University Press, 1994; Anthony Pinn (ed.), *Terror and Triumph: The Nature of Black Religion*, Minneapolis: Fortress, 2003, and *Embodiment and the New Shape of Black Theological Thought*.

see elements of this form of eclecticism when one looks at Beckford's earliest work. *Jesus Is Dread* incorporates cultural analysis and Black christological hermeneutics, plus explorations into Womanist theology, ecclesiology and elements of Church history. Like many of his fellow Black British counterparts, Beckford avoids any straightforward methodological approach to undertaking Black Theology.

Beckford's method for undertaking Black Theology in Britain is one derived from the arena of cultural studies and yet it is so much more than that. In an age when it is becoming important for Black Theology to engage with popular culture and the rapid changes in postmodern societies in the West, Beckford's approach to Black Theology demonstrates an eclectic and creative means of doing so.

My approach to Black Theology is informed by my background as a Christian educator and a former youth worker. I believe my own work seeks to address one of the continuing weaknesses of Black Theology, namely, the difficulty of trying to convert theoretical truth claims into practical service for Black people, the majority of whom reside outside the academy. In this respect, my work is not unlike that first advocated by James H. Harris. Harris asked a number of pertinent questions concerning the efficacy and praxis of Black Theology, particularly in its relationship with the Black church.[59] While Black Theology has, like a number of theological movements, had its formative nurturing within the academy, it would be wrong to doubt the practical dimension of this discipline.

Black Theology has always been more than an effete, elitist academic discipline. A working paper by the Kelly Miller Smith Institute offers a broader conception upon the discipline of theology than that which is usually understood within predominantly academic circles. Theology, they argue, is not purely an academic discipline. It is a natural function of every Christian believer in their existential attempts to conceptualize the nature of God and their relationship with the Ultimate.[60] My work has attempted to combine Black Theology with practical theology in order to create a practical model of the former that can engage with the lived realities of ordinary Black people of faith.

In a previous piece of research, working with Black elders, I was able to use the concrete encounters with these individuals as a means of undertaking a practical approach to the task of doing Black Theology.[61] In the presence

---

59 James H. Harris, 'Black Church and Black Theology: Theory and Practice', in James H. Cone and Gayraud S. Wilmore (eds), *Black Theology: A Documentary History, Vol. 2, 1980–1992*, Maryknoll, NY: Orbis, 1993, pp. 85–98.

60 Kelly Miller Smith Institute Incorporated, 'What Does It Mean to Be Black and Christian', in Cone and Wilmore (eds), *Black Theology*, pp. 164–74.

61 See Anthony G. Reddie, *Faith, Stories and the Experience of Black Elders: Singing the Lord's Song in a Strange Land*, London: Jessica Kingsley, 2001.

of these individuals I witnessed actualized, praxis-orientated examples of Black Theology. Their very narratives were templates for a grounded conception of the Christian faith that was authentic and shorn of pious, esoteric rhetoric. These individuals would have vehemently disavowed any notion of their discourse being the substantive elements of Black Theology. I remain convinced, however, that the substance of these narratives contain within them the antecedents of the liberation struggle of Black people in post-war Britain at the dawn of the new millennium.[62] In this work, parallels can be drawn with the Black Theology work undertaken in the Caribbean, where Marjorie Lewis has undertaken Black Theology work by means of engaging in dialogue with African Caribbean women (Jamaican and British) across a broad age range.[63]

In citing Beckford's work and that of my own, I hope I have been able to offer a snapshot of two differing approaches to undertaking Black Theology. This work can be understood as offering alternative perspectives for undertaking Black Theology. One can be likened to standing a short distance from the main story-event and seeking to rethink it's meaning in the light of the external context in which the activity is located. The other approach can be likened to being located within the activity itself and seeking to rethink its meaning from that particular vantage point.

Black Theology has largely adopted the latter model, often identified as the 'hermeneutical approach'. Given the increasingly plural realities of Black peoples' lives across the world – the fact that we cannot all assume to be Christian (if that were ever really the case) – there must be a question mark about the assumptions surrounding this approach. Is it time to move beyond a reliance on the Black church as the practical expression of Black Theology? Do we need a greater engagement with the broader context in which Black life is lived, which will mean an increasing dialogue with cultural elements like hip hop?

In looking at the two best-known exponents of Black Theology in Britain, I am not suggesting that their work is in any way representative of the discipline across the world. Rather, I am seeking to highlight my home context, offering a case-study of one environment that has produced a particular manifestation of Black Theology. This should not disguise, however, that the bulk of Black Theology work has emerged from the life experiences and scholarship of African Americans. Aspects of this work will be explored in more detail in subsequent chapters.

---

62 See Reddie, *Faith, Stories*, pp. 90–4.

63 See Marjorie Lewis, 'Diaspora Dialogue: Womanist Theology in Engagement with Aspects of the Black British and Jamaican Experience', *Black Theology* 2:1 (2004), pp. 85–109.

Questions

1. What are the merits or otherwise of Beckford's and Reddie's approaches to undertaking Black Theology in Britain?
2. Do you see Christianity as offering a complete framework of truth about the ultimate matters of human existence without the need for insights from other perspectives and sources of truth? If yes, then why? And if not, then why not?
3. To what extent does Black Theology need the Church in order for it to be 'successful' in winning over the hearts and minds of ordinary Black people?
4. Robert Beckford states that 'Theology is never value-free or neutral: because it is human, our language, motives and ambitions affect its expression.'[64] Do you believe this to be true? And, if it is true, then what are the implications for *all* theological enterprises?

---

64 See Beckford, *Jesus is Dread*, p. 14.

4

˙Why So Much About Jesus?

In a previous chapter, I argued that Black Theology in its most traditional mode is essentially a Christ-centred movement, meaning that the focus of much of its reflections centre on Jesus Christ. The focus on Jesus as the central plank in the continued development of Black Theology should not be taken to mean that this movement has a singular or fixed approach to understanding and talking about God. The more recent work of the Womanist theologian Karen Baker-Fletcher, for example, is testimony to a continued level of theological breadth that resides within Black Theology in terms of the exploration of God in trinitarian terms.[1]

Black Theology emerged as an academic discipline in 1960s America as a faith-based response to real issues of suffering and ill treatment meted out to Black people from various quarters of the nation state. Similar movements in South Africa and the Caribbean in the early 1970s were very much predicated on a similar basis. The emphasis in these respective movements was on locating a faith-based means for encountering injustice in order to assert the self-determination and liberation of Black people.

As we have seen, less emphasis is placed on speculative, metaphysical questions for their own sake. Now this is not to say that Black Theology has no interest in speculative questions regarding the nature of God's being or concerns regarding the origins of evil in the world. Rather, it is that these questions are never asked for their own sake. Instead, these questions are posed in order to determine the relationship between these ideas and theories and their impact on Black people in the world. For example, when Black and Womanist theologians have explored the nature of evil and suffering, they have done so less as an exercise in trying to correlate the imponderables between a loving and righteous God and the existence of God's antithesis in the world, but more as a question of determining God's agency. Namely, what are Black people to do in response to the existence and persistence of evil and suffering?[2] How can the liberative resources of Black faith respond

---

1 See Karen Baker-Fletcher, *Dancing with God: The Trinity from a Womanist Perspective*, St Louis: Chalice Press, 2006.

2 Carol Troupe has written an excellent summary of the varying schemas created by Black and Womanist theologians in their attempts to make sense of the pervasive nature

to and counter the pervasive nature of evil and Black suffering in the world? The theological work undertaken by Black theologians has always been essentially praxiological – meaning it is concerned with how Black people can utilize their faith for the practical purposes of fighting for their liberation.

I will not be offering a detailed explication of all the different models of Black Christology that exist in Black Theology. Rather, I want to look at why Black theologians have written so much about Jesus. As a corollary, I believe so much has been written about Jesus because he matters intensely to the material poverty and acute suffering of Black people over the past 500 years. This work attempts to link scholarly reflections with the concerns of Transformative Popular Education and the desire to create critical scholarship for the purposes of social justice and transformation for the poor and marginalized.

Black Theology has been concerned more with who Jesus is for us and how the living Christ continues to live among us in solidarity in the midst of our ongoing suffering. Less emphasis has been placed on the exact identity of 'Jesus the Christ' in his relationship to 'God the Father'. So I will be moving interchangeably from reflecting on the Jesus of history (in his historical identity as a Galilean Jew) to the cosmic Christ of faith (who in the power of the Spirit lives in all contexts of the world and beyond it). So there will be references to simply 'Jesus', 'Christ', or occasionally 'Jesus Christ'. I accept that there are important theological markers and distinctions in how these terms are used and are understood. Given the practical nature of Black Theology, however, and the immediate needs of ordinary Black people and the challenges of their conscientization, these concerns are secondary ones for this work.

So, back to the question, why so much about Jesus in Black Theology? The answer I believe lies in the experiential way in which Black people have identified with Jesus. In the midst of their suffering during the epoch of slavery and beyond, Black people saw Jesus as essentially one of them. This identification with Jesus was not purely a passive affair, however. By this I mean that, in seeing him as one of them, this was not evoked purely for a defensive fashion to help them deal with the reality of their struggles (I termed this as 'passive resistance'). In addition to the passive mode of identification with Jesus, Black people in the midst of their suffering also identified with Jesus as a liberator, as someone who, through his own sacrificial life, ultimately willed their freedom.

It is the immediacy and the power of Jesus that makes name, actions and presence such a potent force within the life experiences of oppressed Black

---

of evil and suffering. See Carol Troupe, 'Human Suffering in Black Theology', *Black Theology* 9:2 (2011), pp. 199–222. For more detailed explorations of this subject in the area of Black Theology, see William R. Jones, *Is God a White Racist? A Preamble to Black Theology*, Boston: Beacon, 1998; James H. Cone, *God of the Oppressed*, New York: Seabury, 1975, pp. 163–94; Anthony B. Pinn, *Why Lord? Suffering and Evil in Black Theology*, New York: Continuum, 1995.

peoples. James Cone, who remains the most important articulator for the intellectual existence of Black Theology and has perhaps written more on Jesus Christ than on any other subject, states that 'Christian theology begins and ends with Jesus Christ'.[3] Cone writes:

> The Black community is an oppressed community primarily because of its blackness, hence the Christological importance of Jesus must be found in his blackness. If he is not black as we are, then the resurrection has little significance for our times. Indeed, if he cannot be what we are, we cannot be who he is. Our being with him is dependent on his being with us in the oppressed black condition, revealing what is necessary for our liberation.[4]

As we will see, a number of Black theologians and Womanist theologians have written a great deal about Jesus, illustrating how the identification with him has been at the heart of the faithful response to Black suffering and oppression. But, as Cone rightly states, it is not simply the Black identification with Jesus that is crucial; perhaps of greater importance is his identification with Black people.

I will introduce an experiential exercise as a means of an enacted metaphor, in order to demonstrate an important facet of Black Theology. Namely, the belief that Jesus' life and death should be understand as the basic grounding for the thrust for Black liberation. That unlike much tradition al Christian doctrine where Jesus' death is for the purposes of achieving our salvation and atoning for human sin, Black Theology rejects this belief and argues for a robust understanding of Jesus' death being linked to the struggle for liberation of all oppressed peoples. To quote the Black British theologian, David Isiorho:

> Jesus died because of our sins, not for them or on behalf of them. God did not demand that his Son be offered as a blood sacrifice but rather that Jesus gave his life as a ransom for many, as a soldier would die for his country. In Jesus as an individual, the universal consequences of sin were annulled through this determination of his human and his divine will combined. His humanity hurt, the wounds were real, and he still bears the scars today. But his divinity was enough to stop the chain of cause and effect, the chain of sin and death, as the new humanity living and embodying the decision to turn to God and to live in love for all, whatever happened. And so our proclamation of his death and our faith in his Resurrection tells us that our powers and our decisions do not have the last word.[5]

---

3 James H. Cone, *A Black Theology of Liberation*, Maryknoll, NY: Orbis, 1990 [1970], p. 110.

4 Cone, *Black Theology of Liberation*, p. 120.

5 David Isiorho, 'Black Identities and Faith Adherence: Social Policy and Penal Substitution in the Epoch of the SS *Empire Windrush*', *Black Theology* 7:3 (2009), pp. 282–99 (298).

As a Transformative Popular Educator, I want to introduce another exercise that has been used to assist people in understanding Black Theology and the rationale on which it has worked as an academic discipline over the past four decades.

Exercise: 'The struggle for liberation'

The group sit on chairs arranged in a circle and link arms. Explain that you will be asking the group to attempt to stand up with arms still linked. Before the group stands up, go round the circle and tell every other person to attempt to stop the group by remaining seated and trying to hold down the people on either side of them. Tell the group to attempt to stand. Let them struggle for a while (make sure no one is in danger of getting hurt!). After a while, tell a seated person to start working with the group to attempt to stand. Start approaching others one at a time and ask them to do the same. Soon the group should be able to stand even if there are still some people attempting to prevent this from happening. Once the whole group is standing they can unlink arms.

How did people feel during the activity (physically and emotionally)? How did they feel once they managed to stand and could unlink arms?

Reflections on the exercise

The exercise was first developed as a means of challenging ordinary people to grasp one of the central dynamics of Black Theology in terms of its identification with Jesus. Namely, it is the sense that Jesus' death and resurrection is the means by which oppressed Black peoples know that God has identified with them. This same Jesus is one who wills their freedom against all 'death-dealing' forces that would deny them their liberation.

When the exercise has been used with different groups, perhaps the most common experience articulated by the group is that of confusion. The confusion arises because of the sheer contradiction that exists between the struggle to be free, which is an integral part of the exercise, and the exhilaration and 'other-wordly' feeling that arises when the physical and psychological pressure is removed from them. When the exercise has been performed with different groups one cannot help but notice the difference in the expressions of the participants in the group.

Individuals and the groups as a whole quickly realize that there is a complex relationship between the efforts exerted by the people in the circle and the resulting freedom from that struggle when it eventually emerges. It might even be said that the one cannot happen without the other. That is, unless there is a struggle, there can be no sense of freedom that will follow. In the Caribbean idiom of Jamaica, there is a saying that evokes this critical struggle for truth from oppression to freedom, which states, 'If you want good, then your nose must run' (with sweat, which denotes the hard work of the struggle).

The exercise has been used on numerous occasions to help oppressed people of faith to realize that the spiritualized version of the resurrection that has often been taught them, one that is removed from the daily realities of one's struggle and oppression, is something that is rejected by Black Theology. In Black Theology, the cross is as much a political statement of God's identification with those who are marginalized and oppressed as it is a spiritual symbol denoting the gateway to everlasting life.

The metaphor of the struggle that is at the heart of the exercise is intended to illustrate the way in which Jesus is thought by many oppressed people of faith to be an inspiring and liberating force. That is, he is someone whose own life and death struggles point the way to the means by which they can be empowered and, in partnership with God, be enabled to fight for their own liberation.

This identification with Jesus' death is one that has challenged many Black people of faith to see their contemporary struggles for justice and equity as bound up in partnership with God, who not only knows their own travails but also participates in them. Jesus is, in effect, the divine co-sufferer with them in the midst of their ongoing struggle to fight for their freedom. The Womanist theologian Jacquelyn Grant states:

> In the experiences of Black people, Jesus was all things. Chief among these, however, was the belief in Jesus as the divine co-sufferer, who empowers them in situations of oppression. For Christian Black women in the past, Jesus was their central frame of reference. They identified with Jesus because they believed that Jesus identified with them. As Jesus was persecuted and made to suffer undeservedly, so were they. His suffering culminated in the crucifixion. Their crucifixion included rape, and babies being sold. But Jesus' suffering was not the suffering of a mere human, for Jesus was understood to be God incarnate.[6]

The inspiration of the resurrection story is one that has propelled myriad people to fight for freedom in the belief that almost certain death does not mean the end and that, in the economy or activity of God, oppression and evil will never have the final word.

People who have taken part in the exercises have often reflected on the contemporary examples of Martin Luther King Jr in the United States or Nelson Mandela in South Africa, as examples of people who have given themselves to the larger struggles for human rights, through the more specific fight for Black liberation. These individuals not only exemplify the inspiring presence of indefatigable Black sacrificial struggle born of love and solidarity for others but

---

6 Jacquelyn Grant, *White Women's Christ and Black Women's Jesus: Feminist Christology and Womanist Response*, Atlanta, GA: Scholars' Press, 1989, p. 212.

also show the emotive power of partnership and solidarity between peoples committed to a common goal.

In the exercise the participants are reminded of the power of collective action as a force for transformative change. While there is a deep temptation for people to believe that their desire to be free necessitates a kind of individual response, the truth is and has always remained that it is the collective thrust for freedom that proves most effective. In the exercise, the participants are united in their common purpose to fight for their freedom, but are enabled and inspired to do so by means of the kind of partnership that is often fuelled by a deep-seated belief that their work is motivated by a source that is willing their freedom. It is in this regard that the resurrection holds its central power over Black liberation struggles.

Consider the following words from Steve de Gruchy from South Africa, written during the final epoch of the apartheid regime in that country:

> We have noted that suffering is the primary datum of life, and indeed the journey of all people ends at the grave. With death at the end, all human effort and achievement have no meaning for us, and we must ultimately face the future in despair. Now, what the resurrection proclaims is that in Jesus Christ God has faced this meaningless future that awaits us all, and has broken its power. Our future lies no longer in the grave but in the resurrected life, and we can therefore face life with hope.[7]

The hope that is imbued in the human spirit as a result of the cross and ultimately the resurrection is one that can give rise to prophetic, faith-based struggles for liberation, as the inspiration of Jesus' actions become the basis for more contemporary battles for justice and equity. The emotive power of Jesus' actions, in solidarity with Black suffering, arises from the belief that God's victory over evil gives expression to the inevitability of the ultimate victory of Black liberation movements. Martin Luther King Jr, in his last speech in Memphis on 3 April 1968, declared:

> I may not get there with you. But I want you to know tonight that we, as a people, will get to the Promised Land. And I'm so happy tonight! I'm not fearing any man! Mine eyes have seen the glory of the coming of the Lord![8]

One could argue that such certainties in the final resolution of God's purposes can lead to a level of passivity. If one believes in that inevitability of God's victory

---

7 Steve de Gruchy, 'Jesus the Christ', in John de Gruchy and C. Villa-Vicencio (eds), *Doing Theology in Context: South African Perspectives*, Cape Town and Johannesburg: David Philip Publishers, 1994, pp. 55–67 (64).

8 Richard S. Reddie, *Martin Luther King Jr: History Maker*, Oxford: Lion, 2011, p. 168.

over evil, as symbolized in the resurrection of Jesus Christ, then it can become the basis for a withdrawal from all forms of politicized, social activism.[9]

As the metaphor in the exercise reminds us, there is the necessity of human activity and participation in the struggle for liberation. While the faith-based claims concerning God's presence in the risen Christ are undoubtedly at the heart of and indeed underpin the Black liberation struggle to which Black Theology bears witness, this struggle will ultimately be of little value unless it is imbued with the commitment of ordinary people to participate within it. And as the death of countless people of faith has shown, whether in the figures of such luminaries as Nanny of the Maroons, Marcus Garvey, Malcolm X, Fannie Lou Hamer, Steve Biko *et al.*, there is always a cost to the struggle for liberation. James Cone's latest book reminds us that the cost of liberation is measured in the cross and the contemporary forms of lynching and the monstrous death that has faced all those who have asserted a fierce 'yes' to life.[10] There is no quick fix to liberation, no short cut to full redemption. Cone writes, 'But we cannot find liberating joy in the cross by spiritualizing it, by taking away its message of justice in the midst of powerlessness, suffering and death.'[11]

Continued Black Theology reflections

Not all Black religious scholars are so convinced of the ultimate promises of victory for Black liberation struggles. Scholars such as William R. Jones and Anthony Pinn have critiqued the certainties entertained by many, if not most, mainstream Black and Womanist theologians. The latter work with convictions that a righteous and loving God identifies with Black suffering and is in solidarity with humanity, in order to bring that suffering to an end.[12] Similarly, not all Black or Womanist scholars necessarily find the cross a helpful motif in encapsulating the Black struggle for liberation. Delores Williams has been the most vocal proponent of a view that rejects the theological utility of the cross and divine suffering as a helpful framework for delineating the meaning and importance of the cross for the overarching purposes of Black redemption.[13]

As a Womanist theologian, Williams has a particular concern for the ways in which Black women's agency was constricted during the epoch of slavery,

---

9 Robert Beckford has noted aspects of this tendency in the actions of some Black churches in Britain. See Robert Beckford, *God and the Gangs*, London: Darton, Longman and Todd, 2004, p. 6.

10 See James H. Cone, *The Cross and the Lynching Tree*, Maryknoll, NY: Orbis, 2011.

11 Cone, *The Cross and the Lynching Tree*, p. 156.

12 See Jones, *Is God a White Racist?* and Pinn, *Why Lord?*

13 See Delores S. Williams, *Sisters in the Wilderness: The Challenge of Womanist God-Talk*, Maryknoll, NY: Orbis, 1993.

when they were often charged with undertaking surrogacy roles for White women and their families who controlled them.[14] For Williams, there is a problematic construct at play when those who are marginalized and denied agency are called upon to work and suffer for others who are powerful and experience great advantage at the expense of the former. Williams is aware of how the cross and Jesus' suffering has been exploited in order to convince Black women that their own suffering has redemptive purposes.[15]

For Williams, it is Jesus' life and the praxis he displays in his relationships with others that provides for the christocentric model of redemption on which Christianity claims a good deal of its uniqueness. This point is made most eloquently when she writes:

> The synoptic gospels (more than Paul's letters) also provide resources for constructing a Christian understanding of redemption that speaks mean-ingfully to Black women, given their historic experience with surrogacy. Jesus' own words in Luke 4 and his ministry of healing the human body, mind and spirit (described in Matthew, Mark and Luke) suggest that Jesus did not come to redeem humans by showing them God's love manifested in the death of God's innocent child on a cross erected by cruel, imperial-istic, patriarchal power. Rather, the texts suggest that the spirit of God in Jesus came to show humans life – to show redemption through a perfect ministerial vision of righting relationships between body (individual and community), mind (of humans and of tradition) and spirit.[16]

This chapter is not intended as an exhaustive exploration of how Jesus Christ has been understood and explicated within Black Theology, as opposed to a critical reflection on why he matters at all, which explains why Black theologians have written so much on this topic. The answer to the question 'why so much about Jesus?' can be found not just in terms of his literal ap-propriation by Black people as a means of dealing with their struggles and ultimately seeking to challenge their experiences of suffering. Instead, the importance of Jesus lies also in the psychological impact his presence exerts on the nature of the Black suffering self.

I believe that a Black Jesus who identifies with Black suffering and oppres-sion has not simply been invoked by Black theologians because it is de rigueur for 'proper' theologians to undertake christological work. Rather, I believe there has been a great deal written on Jesus in Black Theology because many Black theologians have realized the potent force that this figure has for re-imagining the Black self as a figure of worth and value. Conversely, a White Jesus can have the stultifying effect of denigrating the Black self.[17]

---

14 Williams, *Sisters in the Wilderness*, pp. 60–83.
15 Williams, *Sisters in the Wilderness*, pp. 161–9.
16 Williams, *Sisters in the Wilderness*, pp. 164–5.
17 See Josiah Young, 'Envisioning the Son of Man', *Black Theology* 2:1 (2004), pp. 11–17.

As this work is concerned with arguing for the continued importance and vitality of Black Theology, I now want to look at how a Black Jesus is integral to any conception of a Christian-inspired approach to Black liberation.

As a Transformative Popular Educator I have sought to find ways in which I can connect the radicality of Black christological images, often drawn from Black Theology, with the contemporary struggles of ordinary Black people. I believe that the presence of a Black Jesus who is the Christ, God who is with us, remains vital as it provides a means by which ordinary people can be enabled to see and experience another reality and to see beyond the limitations of the material world in which they presently live, move and have their being.

When Black Christologies of authors like Kelly Brown Douglas, James Cone and Robert Beckford are invoked,[18] I believe their continued importance lies in the ways in which they respond to the prevailing challenges of anti-Black rhetoric that remains within the psyche of many Black people. Dianne Stewart, in her ground-breaking work on the African dimensions in the Jamaican/Caribbean religious experience, highlights the continued levels of anti-African thinking (and implied anti-Black for the purposes of this work) in Caribbean religious discourse, even among Caribbean liberation theologians.[19] The denigration of Blackness and the negativity attributed to Black Diasporan African identities is replete within the popular European imagination.[20]

Through the realms of popular education, I have continued to witness to how a Eurocentric interpretation of Christianity has led many Black people to reject the Christian faith on the grounds that it was a religion of exploitation, created for the ultimate benefit of White people by White people. The immediate, experiential appropriation of Jesus by many ordinary Black people often operates at a deep, subliminal level. For many, there exists a dichotomy between what one might acknowledge in a conscious way, when compared to the elemental truths around which their lives are orientated. For many of the participants, the primary importance of a Black Jesus is often found in times of crisis. The Jesus who inspires them to struggle, in terms of the 'passive resistance' described in Chapter 1, is one who is clearly 'one of them' and understands the travails of Black suffering.

---

18 See Kelly Brown Douglas, *The Black Christ*, Maryknoll, NY: Orbis, 2003 [1994]; Cone, *Black Theology of Liberation*; Robert Beckford, *Jesus Is Dread*, London: Darton, Longman and Todd, 1998.

19 See Dianne M. Stewart, *Three Eyes for the Journey: African Dimensions of the Jamaican Religious Experience*, Oxford: Oxford University Press, 2005, pp. 189–98. In Chapter 1, I highlighted, briefly, the alternative naming strategy for a form of Black liberation theology in the Caribbean, known as Caribbean Theology. Many of the leading names I cited in this chapter are also indicted in this claim made by Dianne Stewart.

20 See Robert E. Hood, *Begrimed and Black: Christian Traditions on Blacks and Blackness*, Minneapolis: Fortress, 1994, pp. 115–53. See also Stewart, *Three Eyes for the Journey*, pp. 69–91, for a specific focus on Jamaica.

When using the exercise described at the beginning of this chapter, it was not uncommon to find many Black participants express some unease at the notion of a Black Christ that challenges Black believers to engage with the messiness of the Black struggle for liberation. This messiness can be seen in the work of Kelly Brown Douglas, for example.[21] Douglas argues that the Black Christ within the prophetic Black church tradition has been '[a]t the forefront of Black people's fight for life and liberation against the tyrannies of White racial oppression'.[22]

The inhibitions surrounding a Black Christ have usually manifested themselves when questions of private morality, particularly sexual ethics, have arisen. Many ordinary Black people and the churches they attend are reasonably content to invoke a Black Christ if he is being used to attack racism. But once the question moves to sexism, and particularly the affirmation of gay, lesbian, bi-sexual and transgendered peoples, then the acceptability of the Black Christ dissipates markedly.[23]

In the exercise, it is patently the case that it requires the collective act of will and solidarity of all the participants in the exercise in order to achieve the ultimate breakthrough. The notion that only 'some of the group' should be liberated clearly does not make sense when one considers that all the participants in the group are caught up in the same predicament. A holistic perspective on Black liberation is one that sees the transformation and redemption of all people as essential.[24]

So much has been written about the Black Jesus who identifies with Black suffering because it has been realized that the damages done to Black communities across the African Diaspora and on the continent of Africa cannot be understood solely in terms of material poverty and physical incarceration. Franz Fanon, the renowned Francophone anti-colonialist, spent a great deal of his life investigating the effects of Black self-negation on the psyche of people of African descent.[25]

One of the salient questions that has arisen from the varied performances of the exercise has been the presence of those in the circle who seem intent on preventing the others from standing up and being free. Some have remarked that these figures are clearly 'White oppressors' whose presence is solely to curtail any attempt at Black liberation. But this view has been a minority one, in all truth. For the most part, individuals participating in the exercise have argued that those seeking to prevent the liberation of others have been fellow Black people.

---

21 Douglas, *Black Christ*, pp. 3–6.

22 Douglas, *Black Christ*, pp. 3–4.

23 See Beckford, *Jesus is Dread*, pp. 61–78.

24 Beckford, *Jesus Is Dread*, pp. 72–8.

25 See Franz Fanon, *Black Skin, White Masks*, New York: Grove, 1967; London: MacGibbon & Kee, 1968, and *The Wretched of the Earth*, London: Penguin, 1967.

In the context of reflections on the exercise, this aforementioned realization has emerged from many personal and painful recollections of those who will claim to have been 'stabbed in the back' by fellow Black people.

Putting Black Christologies to work for ordinary people

The claim of the Black Jesus that is evoked within Black Theology is one that seeks to speak to the mis-education and biased, self-serving teaching strategies that have led Black, African people to develop negative self-images. The crucial learning that emerges from the relationship between a Black Jesus and the inhibited and often circumscribed lives of ordinary Black people is believing oneself to be a central character in God's story of redemption, and not a distant player.[26]

My reflections on the seemingly endemic 'in-fighting' between the participants in the exercise have been interpreted, via their own Black experience, as exemplifying the lived realities of such fractures in many Black communities. In the next section, I will provide a worked example of an attempt to address these issues, via a liberative Black Christology.

Confronting the challenge of fragmentation in the many Black communities of the African Diaspora is a necessity, given the importance of solidarity and co-operation needed among Black peoples, in order to thrive. To restate the point made previously, it is only through the active co-operation of the majority of participants in the exercise that they are able to bring about their freedom from the constrictions placed upon them in the exercise. It is my belief that a radical and inclusive Black Jesus is one who will inspire ordinary Black people to a better understanding that the contextual realities of their faith in God demands that they are pulled towards others in love and solidarity, with *all* who are suffering. The quest for liberation is not something that can be reserved for only those who can claim to be Christian like them or the ones who belong to their tradition of the faith.[27]

In the light of the exercise at the outset of the chapter, I now want to present and reflect on a follow-up activity. This exercise will illustrate how the ideas and theories that have been discussed thus far can be used to address some of the practical issues that face ordinary Black people.

The follow-up exercise invites a group of Black people to imagine how the broad, cross-section of people present within a particular biblical narrative can reflect the fractures and dissonances that exist within many Black communities in the UK. The exercise has been used to supplement and speak to

---

26 See Anthony G. Reddie, *Growing into Hope: Vol. 2, Liberation and Change*, Peterborough: Methodist Publishing House, 1998, pp. 8–9.

27 See Michael N. Jagessar, 'Is Jesus the Only Way? Doing Black Christian God-Talk in a Multi-Religious City (Birmingham, UK)', *Black Theology* 7:2 (2009), pp. 200–25.

the previous reflections, in order to demonstrate the continued importance of Black Christologies for the ongoing conscientization of ordinary Black people.

A Black Theology treatment of an inclusive Black Jesus – a Bible study

The following participative exercise has been used in order to enable a group of ordinary Black people to explore the range of diverse identities that exist in many Black communities and how the emerging Black Christologies of the twenty-first century need to recognize this diversity. Given the practical and pragmatic nature of Black Theology, with its central intent of empowering and conscientizing ordinary Black people, I have chosen to use the Bible as an important source for undertaking this work. The Bible, allied to human experience, is an important source and method for undertaking Black Theology, particularly if our concern is to enable the flourishing of greater levels of liberative praxis in the Church and wider society.

This approach to engaging with the Bible uses many of the central ideas of Black Theology. The exercise also draws on the work of Indian biblical scholar David Joy, whose doctoral work investigated the role of the crowd in Mark's Gospel.[28] Joy's work, which is focused through the lens of India and the experiences of the poor, is concerned with the identity of the crowd as 'subalterns' or subordinate peoples who are often denied access to power in their lived experiences.

I am interested in Joy's work because the theme of ordinary people being denied access to power is one that resonates with Black Theology's commitment to liberative praxis. How can Black Theology enable Black people to get access to power? In terms of Christology, this work assumes that Jesus is symbolic of all that might be considered important. Clearly, as someone who was pursued through his ministry by crowds wishing to gain access to him, Jesus can be seen as representing that which is important, but the question is, does he have power? Well, in terms of traditional 'top-down' Christologies, the ones that emphasize his integral relationship with 'God the Father' and the 'Lordship of God', sitting at the right hand of 'the Father', it might be said that Jesus as the Christ has power. The power of the 'Christ of faith', the person who reigns with God, across all space and time, is undoubtedly powerful. But as Jacquelyn Grant has shown, this latter conception of Jesus is not the one that has been spoken of, traditionally, by Black women in the context of their lived experience of struggle and hardship.[29] For many Black women, it is the lived experience of the Jesus of history, who often associated with ordinary women, who is invoked in their daily struggles.

---

28 See C. I. David Joy, *Mark and Its Subalterns: A Hermeneutical Paradigm for a Postcolonial Context*, Oakwood and London: Equinox, 2008.

29 See Grant, *White Women's Christ and Black Women's Jesus*.

In terms of using the Bible in the following exercise, I decided to use Mark's account of the woman who touched the hem of Jesus' cloak in Mark 6.21–34. To make it easier in dividing up the participants into the groups that would play the different characters, I decided to use only the 'first part of the story'. Namely, the point up to which the woman who is haemorrhaging blood is healed.

In this exercise, undertaken in the light of the opening activity described at the beginning of this chapter, I asked a group of ordinary Black people to divide themselves into four groups: Group 1 are Jesus; Group 2 are the disciples; Group 3 are the crowd; Group 4 are the woman. Although no groups were assigned to Jairus and his household, consideration would be given to them in the resultant reflections after the exercise. The different groups were asked to reflect on the passage in the light of the character that had been assigned to their group and to assess who had power in the story in terms of their character. They were also asked to reflect on which characters in the story were seeking to deprive their character of power and access in the story.

The twist in this exercise was to link the range of characters in the exercise with the diversity of Black peoples in the many communities in which Black cultures and their resultant experiences are expressed. The task for the group was to reflect on this passage in the light of the community of which they were a part. So all the participants began by naming the different types of Black people with whom they came into contact and then mapped these concerns onto the text. Where might rich Black entrepreneurs be seen in the text? The disenfranchised youths from the local poor housing estate, where might they be located in the text? What about those who are the aspirant middle-class Black people, who have escaped poverty through education and professional attainment, where are they located?

One of the important subtexts of their subsequent reflections was the realization that the bulk of the people in the crowd, plus the woman herself, would indeed be women. The majority of Black people attending Black churches (in their various guises) and cultural events in the wider society are invariably women.[30]

With this subtext in mind, the initial reflections from the group centred on the role of Black women in the text as they imagined it, focusing particularly on the woman marginalized because of her condition. The group had been introduced to the Christologies of Jacquelyn Grant and Delores Williams in terms of how they see Jesus' message in relationship to Black women. In

30 See Cheryl Townsend Gilkes, *If It Wasn't for the Women: Black Women's Experience and Womanist Culture in Church and Community*, Maryknoll, NY: Orbis, 2001; Rosetta E. Ross, *Witnessing and Testifying: Black Women, Religion and Civil Rights*, Minneapolis: Fortress, 2003; Doreen W. McCalla, *Unsung Sheroes in the Church: Singing the Praises of Black Women Now!*, Bloomington, IN: Authorhouse, 2007, for work by Black women that celebrates the contribution of Black women to the Church and wider society.

this regard, the importance of Womanist theology as a parallel discipline to Black Theology was reaffirmed. As we have seen, Womanist theology is an approach to talking about God in the light of the experience of being a Black woman. That is, in a world governed by White men, to be a Black woman is to struggle with what many scholars have called tri-partite oppression: to be a Black woman is to be *Black*, a *woman* and *poor*. Most of the Black women in the world are indeed *Black*, which is seen as good rather than as a curse, given how 'Blackness' is often perceived. How many positive terms associated with the word 'Black' actually exist? To state the obvious, as Black women they are also *women* (in a sexist world, this is also a curse) and they are *poor* – again another curse. So Womanist theology seeks to read the Bible and rethink religious traditions in the light of these three factors. In terms of biblical studies, it attempts to locate within texts, for example, liberationist themes that can be used in order to liberate and bring self-esteem and dignity to all oppressed peoples. There is a particular concern, of course, for those who are oppressed on the grounds of 'race', gender, poverty and sexuality.

Issues arising from the session

The woman in the passage is interpreted in light of Womanist thought. Patriarchy and power concerns make her invisible. She becomes a cipher through whom and for whom things are done with very little appreciation for how she might have felt. The above can be seen in the fact that she does not have a name. She is defined by her condition and not by who she is as an individual.

Jesus is on his way to deal with a very important official associated with the synagogue. He delays his journey and makes time to deal with this anonymous woman. The woman becomes a 'somebody' because Jesus takes the time to acknowledge her.[31]

The attitude of the disciples from the workshop is a means of 'reading into the text' the concerns of the marginalized and oppressed, which often go unnoticed or unstated in the text. The text does not portray the disciples as oppressive, but by climbing into the experience of the oppressed and marginalized, we can imagine how the disciples might have been perceived by the woman. To what extent do the actions of the disciples mirror the attitude of the Church to oppressed and marginalized people today?

Reading 'into' or 'between' the text, that is, using one's experience to read 'what is not said' in the text, is one of the main ingredients of a Black liberationist approach to reading the Bible. This type of approach is informed by what many scholars call a 'hermeneutic of suspicion'. This means that one reads the Bible in an ideological way, looking with suspicion and thinking

---

31 This Bible study is taken from Anthony G. Reddie, *Nobodies to Somebodies: A Practical Theology for Education and Liberation*, Peterborough: Epworth, 2003.

critically at how the power relations and structures are in evidence in the text. In the exercise, this was undertaken by the participants asking the questions, 'Who has power in this story?' 'Who is disadvantaged?' 'Who benefits or who loses out?' 'How is God's liberative presence displayed in the text?'

It is interesting to note that the woman was healed before Jesus asks who has touched him. In reading this text in the light of Black Theology, it is my belief that Jesus insists that the woman identify herself so that he can acknowledge her in front of all the others. One could argue that Jesus might simply have let the woman go on her way unheeded. From the workshop, the participants witnessed at first hand the diffidence and low self-esteem of the woman. I am sure that the woman did not initially thank Jesus for exposing her in that fashion. By making the woman public and visible, Jesus breaks her anonymity. She is no longer simply a cipher through whom and to whom things are done. She becomes a person in her own right. By healing the woman, Jesus enables her to regain her place within the religious and cultural life of the society, where issues of purity and ritual cleansing are all-important. The woman is liberated from her oppressive condition.[32]

The specific focus on the woman and her relationship to Jesus is one that identified the way in which the latter makes time for the former. This is a model of Christology that is not overly concerned with social niceties and issues of respectability. Many in the group recognized the ways in which this inclusive and sensitive Jesus was often at variance with the powerful and exclusive models that are often portrayed in the many churches attended by these ordinary Black people. In this regard, an authoritarian loving Jesus is used by the Church to establish the status quo, where the concerns for respectability are often upheld at all costs; the Jesus on display condemns those on the margins rather than affirming them. Of particular note was the way in which Jesus seems to turn the obvious socio-political and economic niceties on their head by attending to the woman first before drawing his attention to Jairus, the synagogue leader.

In seeking to focus not so much on Jesus but on the wider groups of people in this biblical narrative, the participants were asked to identify the different types of Black people who might be represented in the text, if this event were transferred into a contemporary Black setting. When asked to focus on Black people drawn from contemporary Black life, who might be represented in the text, attention was focused immediately on the disciples and the crowd. Those in the former group were more likely to be middle class and respectable – the type of people that are often offered up as role models to Black communities, and provided as the 'the best examples of our community' to the outside world. There was some ambivalence expressed towards

---

32 Useful reading matter for this Bible study are Cone, *God of the Oppressed*; Beckford, *God and the Gangs*; Cain Hope Felder (ed.), *Stony the Road We Trod: African American Biblical Interpretation*, Minneapolis: Fortress, 1991.

this group by the ordinary Black people who participated in the exercise. Many spoke of the self-serving nature of some Black middle-class communities and how they seek to inoculate themselves against the seemingly worst excesses of the so-called Black underclass.

When asked to identify a key component of the allegedly Black middle-class disciples who are in effect Jesus' 'officers of the movement', many of the participants spoke of their polite accents that are representative of the assent into the corporate world of White privilege. To be clear, it was not that the participants disliked the allegedly Black middle-class disciples. In fact, many felt proud of them and felt they were to be admired for their hard work, diligence and ability to 'make something of themselves'. Rather, the sense of ambivalence arose through the belief that this group were not necessarily any better than themselves. In other words, they admired the Black middle-class disciples, but did not feel in awe of them and did not feel that they were better examples of Blackness than themselves. It was noted that the disciples largely represent those in hierarchical positions, such as the clergy or deacons or elders, who wield power and control access to Jesus, particularly when pitted against the crowd.

Conversely, the crowd was seen to contain primarily those from a Black working class and perhaps those in the underclass. These people were observed to have a plethora of motives for being present within the narrative. For some, it was a case of opportunism. A few of the participants felt that pickpockets and others from the 'criminal element' would be present within the crowd. But not all of the crowd would be thieves or people with dubious motives for being present. Many would be women, as has already been noted. The women in the crowd would not necessarily be any more sympathetic to the woman at the centre of the narrative than the Black men, who would be the ones predominantly exercising power as the disciples. Nancy Lynne Westfield, a Womanist religious educator, has reflected on the elements of internalized oppression sometimes exhibited by Black women when they are confronted by others with whom they should, notionally, share some sense of solidarity and sisterhood.[33]

There was the sense that aspects of the crowd's behaviour might be considered embarrassing or seen in terms of 'letting the side down'. The latter statement might be equated with the comments of the famed African American comic, Bill Cosby, on the segment of African American communities who have not kept their side of the bargain regarding the social progress of

---

33 See Nancy Lynne Westfield, 'Called Out My Name, or Had I known You Were Somebody: The Pain of Fending Off Stereotypes', in Nancy Lynne Westfield (ed.), *Being Black, Teaching Black: Politics and Pedagogy in Religious Studies*, Nashville, TN: Abingdon, 2008, pp. 61–78.

Black people. Cosby's comments are directed particularly at Black people from predominantly working-class backgrounds.[34]

As with their assessment of the Black middle-class disciples, the participants were asked to name a key characteristic of the predominantly Black working-class crowd. The disciples were seen mainly as Black middle-class professionals who spoke 'well' (however ill-defined, such comments might be well understood in academic terms). Conversely, the crowd were characterized by their speech patterns that used mainly Black cultural idioms, such as Jamaican patois. In short, this predominantly Black working-class crowd was distinguished from their middle-class compatriots by their speech patterns that were perceived to be demonstrably 'Black'. Many of the participants spoke of people in the crowd speaking 'badly' or exhibiting 'poor education'. I shall comment further on this point in a short while.

Black Theology reflections

This exercise was an attempt to get this group of ordinary Black people to read aspects of Black cultural life into a biblical text. In my invitation to the group to reflect on this activity, I wanted to push them to look at the different positions and values adopted by various people within Diasporan Black British communities. I accomplished this task by getting the group to subject this biblical text to the wider socio-cultural contexts in which contemporary Black life is lived. For some of the participants, the crowd could be viewed as representing a type of social gathering at which Jesus was the special guest performer, not unlike a DJ or an MC. In this type of fictional social gathering – party or, in Black Caribbean speak, a 'dance' – a wide variety of Black people and accompanying voices, motivations and behaviours would be present. Such events are common in African Caribbean communities, whether in the Caribbean or in the Caribbean Diaspora across the world. Robert Beckford (whose work was highlighted in the last chapter) has addressed the relationship between the 'church hall' and the 'dance hall' in his critical study of the role of music, movement and space in African Caribbean peoples' fight for social justice.[35] Beckford's work provides a helpful theoretical framework illustrating some of the concerns to which Black Theology must attend.

In much of the early Black Theology work there was a tendency to see Black communities as monolithic. In the twenty-first century Black Theology must work much harder at presenting a more nuanced and holistic view

---

34 See the following link for details on Bill Cosby's comments: http://www.examiner.com/education-in-national/bill-cosby-speaks-bluntly-about-black-people-and-education (accessed 29 February 2012).

35 See Robert Beckford, *Jesus Dub: Theology, Music and Social Change*, London: Routledge, 2006.

of Black cultures and the practices that exist within various Black communities. In highlighting the need for the kind of solidarity and community cohesion necessary for the fight for liberation (as displayed in the opening exercise) Black Theology has underplayed, or even minimized, the differences that exist within Black communities.

In a great deal of this work, issues of sameness or homogeneity have been over-emphasized. Much less effort has been spent looking at questions pertaining to class, gender, sexuality or differences in political outlook, among a few of the concerns in this area. This is particularly the case when scholars have spoken about Black and Black-majority churches.[36] Our tendency to view Black communities as monolithic has meant that the diverse range of experiences and values that exist within the whole tends to be either downplayed or ignored altogether. One of the most pertinent issues in relation to churches, in this regard, is that of providing 'safe space' in which issues of Black self-determination and liberation can be rehearsed. I will return to this at the conclusion of this chapter, because it is a critical issue which Black Theology, and Black Christologies in particular, needs to address.

An uncomfortable truth one can notice in particular types of Black religio-cultural discourse is the existence of a type of hierarchy of 'Blackness'. This often takes its cue from the prevailing concerns in many Black communities themselves, where some people are judged as belonging in a more complete fashion than others. There are many Black people who have been accused of not 'really being Black' or not being 'Black enough'.[37] Scholars such as Michael Eric Dyson, Kobena Mercer and Victor Anderson[38] have challenged us to see beyond the often straightjacketed interpretations we place on Black cultural expression and its accompanying lived experience. Anderson in particular has challenged the way in which Black religious, cultural critics have wanted to acknowledge only the 'positive aspects' of Black life and have often sought to overlook or ignore those elements of which we are not so proud.[39] As Anderson reminds us, we cannot all be saints, heroes and trailblazers.

One of the challenges faced by a number of Black communities in the African Diaspora is the sense of wanting to 'put one's best on show' and to draw a discrete veil over those aspects that cause an element of

---

36 See Peter J. Parris, *The Social Teaching of the Black Churches*, Philadelphia: Fortress, 1985; and Dale P. Andrews, *Practical Theology for Black Churches: Bridging Black Theology and African American Folk Religion*, Louisville, KY: Wesrminster John Knox, 2002.

37 See Isaac Julien, 'Black Is, Black Ain't: Notes on De-Essentializing Black Identities', in Gina Dent (ed.), *Black Popular Culture*, Seattle: Bay Press, 1992, pp. 255–63.

38 Michael Eric Dyson, *Reflecting Black: African American Cultural Criticism*, Minneapolis: University of Minnesota Press, 1993; Kobena Mercer, *Welcome to the Jungle: New Positions in Black Cultural Studies*, London: Routledge, 1994; Victor Anderson, *Beyond Ontological Blackness: An Essay on African American Religious and Cultural Criticism*, New York: Continuum, 1995.

39 Anderson, *Beyond Ontological Blackness*, pp. 118–31.

embarrassment and unease within the community itself. I remember so clearly the sheer visceral shock that first emerged when stories pertaining to the inherent humanity and frailty of the Revd Dr Martin Luther King Jr first began to emerge.[40] I remember a Black community activist, who was my friend at the time, lamenting, 'Why did they have to reveal all this? The man didn't deserve this!' More recently, Michael Eric Dyson's honest account of the life of Martin Luther King is an important example of dealing with the wholeness of human experience, and not just the edited highlights,[41] but this work has still caused anger and disappointment among some.

In a later book, the same author attempts a critical reassessment of the life of deceased rapper Tupac Shakur. Dyson opens up new possibilities for us to see beyond the limitations of 'heroes' and 'villians', 'good people' and 'bad' ones.[42] Life, culture and cultural expression are complex and often contradictory for those kinds of simplistic binaries. In this section I want to look at some specific 'stereotypes' within some African Caribbean communities. I want to look at these different figures in the light of the need to create models of Black Christologies that seek to redeem all of Black life, and not just those elements of which we approve.

One of the strengths of working through a christological framework is that, for many people on the margins of the Church or organized religion, Jesus proves a more compelling figure than those who claim to worship and follow him. Many of us have heard the plaintive words, 'I really hate the Church and all that hypocrisy but I have time for Jesus!' In this later exercise I have noted the occasions when ordinary Black participants have clearly contrasted Jesus' actions in the text with those of the disciples. The latter are seen to represent the Church and are identified as officious, bureaucratic, petty, jealous and insecure, wanting to 'keep Jesus to themselves'. These are characteristics many have also levelled at the Church. Jesus, in contrast, was seen as inclusive, relaxed, caring and 'down to earth'.

Mark's Gospel, in particular, has been highlighted as representing something of the gap between how Jesus viewed his own ministry and the somewhat confused perspectives held by the disciples, as they followed him on his ministerial journey. In effect, for some, Jesus can be seen separately from the dictates of the Church. There are, however, a number of specific and distinctive truth claims about Jesus, in terms of who he himself claimed to be, in addition to those that the Church has given an account for over 2000 years. But, as we have seen, Black Theology is less concerned with the

---

40 See Ralph D. Abernathy, *And the Walls Came Tumbling Down*, New York: Harper and Row, 1989.

41 Michael Eric Dyson, *I May Not Get There with You: The True Martin Luther King, Jr*, New York: Simon and Schuster, 1999.

42 Michael Eric Dyson, *Holler If You Hear Me: Searching for Tupac Shakur*, Pittsburgh: University of Pennsylvania Press, 2002.

strictures of such debates when there are much more elemental challenges facing us, such as how we live with others and show the kind of respect and concern for those on the margins that Jesus himself did.

In creating the range of stereotypes in this exercise, I wanted the participants to read their perspectives and prejudices through the lens of Black Theology. I wanted also to challenge Black Theology to undertake a more honest appraisal of how Black communities engage with the broad cross-section of people, and how they are assessed for meaning. Sadly, it is all too common to witness in churches the ways in which a rigid conformity to the status quo and the respectable prevents those on the margins of society from being enabled to find love and healing within the Church. Church sometimes becomes a place for the self-righteous to look down and disparage those who are not considered as good as them!

Black Theology must seek to represent all those on the margins, and not just those who can wear the right metaphorical or literal clothes of respectability, and mimic the patterns and practices of the aspirant middle class. It must find ways of taking seriously the range of characters on display within this Black religio-cultural reading of this biblical text.

Some of us will be familiar with a number of stereotypes outlined by the participants. The question that challenges Black Theology is one of developing a more inclusive mechanism for recognizing and addressing all aspects of Black communities in the ongoing work of Black liberation praxis.

In more recent times the scope of Black religious scholarship has expanded the gaze on Black communities in ways that are attempting to capture the complex diversity at the heart of Black living in the twenty-first century. An important figure in this development has been Anthony Pinn. Pinn, as a critical dialogue partner with Black Theology, has pushed the movement to go beyond the traditional hinterland of the Church and Black church history, in order to engage with Black popular culture. In looking at issues pertaining to hip-hop, Black body aesthetics and film studies, Pinn's work has challenged Black theological thought to give greater consideration to the complexities and nuances in Black communities, principally, in the USA.[43] In a similar vein, important and crucial work has been undertaken looking at the phenomenon of Black televangelism, which surely cannot be ignored in the global age of the mass media. This is especially the case, given the popularity of the 'God channel', for many ordinary Black people.[44]

---

43 For the more recent developments in Pinn's work, see Anthony B. Pinn (ed.), *Noise and Spirit: The Religious and Spiritual Sensibilities of Rap Music*, New York and London: New York University Press, 2003; *Black Religion and Aesthetics: Religious Thought and Life in Africa and the African Diaspora*, New York: Palgrave Macmillan, 2009; *Embodiment and the New Shape of Black Theological Thought*, New York and London: New York University Press, 2010.

44 See Jonathan L. Walton, *Watch This! The Ethics and Aesthetics of Black Televangelism*, New York and London: New York University Press, 2009.

It is not my claim that all the aforementioned works are necessarily Black Theology; it is that they express a range of ideas and concerns with which Black Theology should be engaged. In a moment, I will show how an inclusive model of Christology in Black Theology can be reclaimed, in order to address some of the concerns to which I am making reference in this section of the work.

In the exercise, the participants are clear that some of the people in the crowd would be speaking in a variety of linguistic forms that are reflective of African Caribbean cultures that are important signifiers of their sense of identity. Scholars such as Willis, Tomlin and Callender[45] have all explored the importance of Black idioms to the identity construction of African Caribbean people in Britain. The linguistic traits of African Caribbean people are hugely important for the distancing effect they have exerted on White people. Basically, if people cannot follow what you are saying, then it becomes easier to sustain one's own self-determined identity and, to a lesser extent, one's destiny.[46]

In more recent times, research undertaken by Lynnette Mullings in the British context has explored, further, issues pertaining to the legitimacy of 'Black language', in this case Jamaican patois. Mullings explores Jamaican patois as a legitimate idiom for Black God-talk, particularly that which engages with the 'the Word of God'.[47] Mullings's work, which sits at the intersections of Black biblical studies and Black Theology in Britain, is important for the purposes of this discussion for a number of reasons. Its importance lies in the fact that it addresses the class issues at play in how middle-class Jamaicans will look down on and disparage their more working-class counterparts. The latter are disparaged for speaking in an idiom that is often attacked as being crude, and is often seen as a sign of poor education, also indicating inferior forms of socialization. And yet, as Beckford and others have shown, this language is also the idiom of social protest![48]

Mullings's work explores the gains that would be accrued if Jesus could be envisaged by ordinary, poor, marginalized Black people in Jamaica as a militant patois-speaker like them. In effect, Jesus would be a social outcast

---

45 Lerleen Willis, 'All Things to All Men? Or What Has Language to Do with Gender and Resistance in the Black Majority Church in Britain', *Black Theology in Britain* 4:2 (2002), pp. 195–213; Carol Tomlin, *Black Language Style in Sacred and Secular Contexts*, New York: Caribbean Diaspora Press, 1999; Christine Callender, *Education for Empowerment: The Practice and Philosophies of Black Teachers*, Stoke–On-Trent: Trentham, 1997, pp. 65–95.

46 See Reddie, *Nobodies to Somebodies*, pp. 97–9, 105–6.

47 See Lynnette Mullings, 'Teaching Black Biblical Studies in the UK: Special Issues for Consideration and Suggested Hermeneutical Approaches', *Discourse* 8:2 (2009), pp. 81–126. This article is a part of a doctoral studies project looking at the sociocultural, religious and political issues at play in the Jamaica Bible Society's translation of the Bible into patois (or the Jamaican language, as is their preferred nomenclature). For more information on the latter see http://www.biblesociety.org.uk/products/1273/49/first_patois_bible_gospel_of_luke/ (accessed 29 February 2012).

48 See Robert Beckford, *God of the Rahtid: Redeeming Rage*, London: Darton, Longman and Todd, 2001, pp. 53–65.

of so-called 'bad breeding', not from the comfortable middle-class communities that constitute the leadership of the Church in Jamaica.[49] Some of the characters imagined in this exercise are not the ones who are going to win any prizes for societal achievement, nor are they the ones we hold up as exemplars for the so-called progress and development of the 'Black community'. And yet, as the opening exercise reminded us, it is essential that such common cause and a sense of solidarity are found among all people in order for Black liberation to be achieved.

How can this be achieved?

One of the polarizing elements in some approaches to Christian theology is the determination to view the perspectives of truth through a very fixed, tightly focused christological lens. This is summed up in the belief that (a) the only way to be saved is through faith in Jesus Christ, (b) that same Jesus Christ belongs to the 'the Church' (understood in very exclusive terms), and (c) this Jesus Christ can be reached via the strict and unyielding doctrinal formulas created by the Church over the past 2000 years. This Jesus is the 'Christ of faith', who rules history and all peoples, across all space and time. This Jesus is the 'Only Way'.

Often, when one reads Black religious discourse there is the assumption that all Black people are Christians and that 'Jesus is the Only Way'. Michael Jagessar has critiqued this assumption in looking at the development of Black Theology in Britain, which often assumes a normative christological point of departure.[50] I am aware that my own work has often exuded a kind of uncritical Jesus-only focus in the past, and indeed this chapter could be seen in that vein.

More recently, Jawanza Eric Clark has sought to develop an alternative perspective on Jesus as a saviour, one in which the salvific figure is shorn of the exclusivist Christian tag that has often proved problematic when dealing with the plurality of Black religious communities.[51] Clark's work is helpful for the purposes of this book because he does not assume that the Christ figure has to be located purely within the realms of doctrinal Christianity. His work reminds us that African people have not always been 'Christian'.

In the final part of this chapter, I want to outline how one can reinterpret the case for and cause of a Black Jesus from a more expansive and inclusive perspective. This more expansive position is one that does not use Christology

---

49 Mullings, 'Teaching Black Biblical Studies in the UK'.

50 See Jagessar, 'Is Jesus the Only Way?'

51 See Jawanza Eric Clark, 'Reconceiving the Doctrine of Jesus as Savior in Terms of the African Understanding of an Ancestor: A Model for the Black Church', *Black Theology* 8:2 (2010), pp. 140–59.

as a means of dictating who is in and who is out. Such an inclusive model also rejects such binary opposites, for example, 'who is saved' and 'who is not saved'. I want to approach this work by using the ideas of Trevor Eppehimer as a means of reflecting further on this issue.[52] Eppehimer seeks to chart a constructive 'middle way' between James Cone and Victor Anderson.

In the first instance, Eppehimer investigates the militant, Christ-centred Black Theology approach to liberation of James Cone. In this work, as we have seen, Cone assumes an 'essence of experience' of Black people that is focused on the reality of Black suffering and oppression. He believes that God, in the form of Christ, is revealed in and through that Black experience. Cone spends little time reflecting on the diversity within 'the Black experience' when linking that experience to Jesus for the purposes of Black liberation. The opposite position is held by Victor Anderson who argues that Cone's perspective is too monolithic and does not take sufficient credence of the plurality of Black experiences and that suffering and oppression are not the sole markers or metaphors for discussing Black experiences (which are plural and not singular).

Using Cone's position, one is able to achieve the kind of unity that one would hope to see at work in the exercise that was illustrated at the beginning of the chapter. But is this unity and solidarity achieved at the expense of a failure to take seriously the kind of diversity and difference we see exemplified in the follow-up exercise I presented a short while ago? Conversely, Anderson's project seems much better at dealing with the wide range of characters and perspectives in many Black communities in the follow-up activity. In emphasizing this difference, more than the sameness and shared perspectives that do exist, can his approach achieve the kind of unity and solidarity, often illustrated by means of the 'Black church', as a pre-requisite for solidarity and a collective Black liberation?

Eppehimer's proposal is to argue for a 'strategic essentialism'. This is a looser form of coalition that is sufficiently strong to enable Black people to coalesce around notions of Black liberation and struggle, but is not too rigid or tightly bound so as to constrict those within or to exclude those outside the alliance.

So how can a strategic essentialism help us get at a practical, more expansive notion of Black Christology? A more inclusive model that takes seriously the fact that the realities of Blackness are now more complex than when Black Theology was first created? You will notice I am still arguing for a christological focus in the first place! Why am I doing that when Jesus can often seem to be the problem? Well, I am still pushing for the category of Christology because of the embodied and practical role that Jesus can play as an inspiration for radical Black action for the sake of liberation. The Jesus that is modelled in this strategic essentialist

---

52 See Trevor Eppehimer, 'Victor Anderson's Beyond Ontological Blackness and James Cone's Black Theology: A Discussion', *Black Theology* 4:1 (2006), pp. 87–106.

model of Black Theology is one who remains a potent inspirer of revolutionary change, but he does so while not claiming any absolutism for his own self that has often been claimed on his behalf by his followers, including the Black ones!

An expansive Black Christology needs to take account of the reality of the increasing pluralism of so many contexts within the African Diaspora. In the USA, the work of Delroy Reid-Salmon has offered an important critique of African American Black Theology for its failure to take account of the Caribbean Diaspora within its midst.[53] Within the UK, William Ackah has explored the growing diversity among the African Diaspora in this context. He has argued that Black Theology in Britain, wedded as it is to a Conean model of liberation, has taken insufficient cognizance of the growing importance of African Christianity.[54] This latter phenomenon is one that sees its identity not in terms of the transatlantic slave trade and the trope of exile and forced removal, but rather as one of economic migration and colonialism. In the Caribbean, however, religious and cultural pluralism has abounded for centuries and it has never been a simple matter of defining what constitutes Blackness.[55] In this context, Caribbean theology, which is the contextual model of Black Theology for that region, one needs to be reminded of the constructed pluralism in which Blackness has always existed.[56] By this, I mean that Jesus cannot be seen solely as belonging to the Church.

At the centre of many Black Christian households is the Bible as the unimpeachable depositor of the Christian faith. The Bible, and the Gospels in particular, give us a direct and, for many, an inviolate picture of Jesus, who remains the bedrock for notions of absolute, religious truth. I know that was the case in the household in which I was nurtured. In more recent times, the unswerving fidelity to the Bible and an exclusive model of Jesus, which characterized my youth, has been replaced with a more critical, striving and restlessness of spirit and intellectual struggle. As a Black theologian and a Transformative Popular Educator, I have asked a series of ongoing, nagging questions regarding the relationship of the Bible and the inherited Christianity of empire to my life and that of other Black people.[57] As someone who is committed to taking seriously the growing levels of diversity in many Black communities, I have

---

53 See Delroy A. Reid-Salmon, *Home away from Home: The Caribbean Diasporan Church in the Black Atlantic Tradition*, Oakwood and London: Equinox, 2008.

54 William Ackah, 'Back to Black or Diversity in the Diaspora? Re-Imagining Pan-African Christian Identity in the Twenty-First Century', *Black Theology* 8:3 (2010), pp. 341–56.

55 See Ennis B. Edmonds and Michelle A. Gonzalez, *Caribbean Religious History: An Introduction*, New York: New York University Press, 2010.

56 See Michael St Aubin Miller, 'He Said I Was out of Pocket: On Being a Caribbean Contextual Theologian in a Non-Caribbean Context', *Black Theology* 9:2 (2011), pp. 223–45.

57 I have raised this question in a number of places, most recently in Anthony G. Reddie, *Is God Colour Blind? Insights from Black Theology for Christian Ministry*, London: SPCK, 2009, pp. 53–7.

continued to wrestle with the challenges posed by the oftentimes anti-Black Christian faith I imbibed as a child. I have often wondered why Black people continue to show their allegiance to this faith after so many years of Christian-inspired violence (physical and psychological) perpetrated against them.[58]

The critical question for me is 'can Christianity be remade so as to shed its col-lusive relationship with oppression, domination and exploitation?' For many or-dinary Black people who adhere to the Christian faith as their particular mode of spiritual orientation, there is the challenge of dealing with the exclusivity of Jesus. Literalist readings of John 14.6 have been used to make Jesus such an exclusive figure that there can be no co-operation or rapprochement with others of a dif-ferent faith or even no faith. And yet, going back to the exercise at the beginning of this chapter, one cannot even assume that all the people in the circle belong to the same faith or even have a faith. Does this matter? Surely, the realities of their oppression are more important than the exactitudes of their faith adherence?

The challenge for any model of Black Christology is to find some kind of mediation between the desire to be faithful to God, as revealed in the person of Jesus, and the need to hold an expansive and generous faith that seeks co-operation with others. In the many diverse contexts that are represented in the African Diaspora, perhaps the sharpest challenge that faces us is often unyielding the exclusivity of the Christian faith.[59] Yet, Black Christianity sits in negotiation with indigenous religious traditions and spiritualities, and this ongoing nexus for mutuality and co-operation remains a live issue in many religio-cultural set-tings across the world. Recent work from the International Association for Black Religions and Spiritualities[60] has sought to illuminate how one can juxtapose 'traditional' models of post-Constantinian Christian faith alongside other forms of religious expression and spiritualities. This work shows what can be done even in contexts where Christianity has been the less than benign harbinger for the acceptance of indigenous religions and spiritualities.[61]

Many Black Christians, particularly in Britain and the USA, remain located within contexts in which the Christian faith was and is an inviolate guarantor for the normativity of what might be described as authentic religious expres-sion. In other words, to talk about a person of faith is to be a Christian.[62] The

---

58 This question has been raised by Kelly Brown Douglas in *What's Faith Got to Do with It? Black Bodies/Christian Souls*, Maryknoll, NY: Orbis, 2005, pp. ix–xix.

59 This has been addressed by Michael Jagessar who asks, 'Is Jesus the only way?' The seemingly didactic absolutism of John 14.6 has often been used as a kind of one-verse microcosm for the seemingly inviolate meaning for the whole Christian tradition. Jagessar has argued that Jesus cannot be the only way for postcolonial subjects in Britain. See Jagessar, 'Is Jesus the Only Way?'

60 Details about this organization can be found by going to http://www.iabrs.org/.

61 See Dwight N. Hopkins and Marjorie Lewis (eds), *Another World Is Possible: Spiritualities and Religions of Global Darker Peoples*, London: Equinox, 2009.

62 In an otherwise fine book, Curtis Evans explores the development and nature of 'Black Religion' in the USA, but he limits his gaze to that of Christianity alone. The

religious frameworks in which I was socialized did not permit any sense of dialogue with that which was considered to be the 'other', whether in terms of 'non-belief' or heterodox belief. White, western evangelical Christianity of empire and colonialism was seen as undoubtedly true and its supposed superiority was not to be questioned.

In creating a critical coming together between what might be considered orthodox or heterodox, normative or aberrant, conventional or transgressive, I want to argue that an expansive and inclusive Black Christology must steer us beyond unreconstructed binaries that are located within the fading horizons of the past. The Christianity of the evangelical revival that has influenced my upbringing remains a powerful means of describing Black Christianity across the world. The undoubted gains of this tradition that are often expressed in terms of a very personal Jesus of the Bible nevertheless need to be updated and expanded. This critical struggle for truth is one that seeks to hold in check fidelity to that in which many Black Christians have been formed and shaped, and the realization that the challenges of the future cannot be met by such strictures and limitations.

I know that my own religiously orientated background continues to oscillate between the basic Baptist-inspired Christian faith of my mother that dominated my formative years and the alternative and creative theological musings of my onset middle age. The sharp divide between the perspectives held by Cone or those of Victor Anderson can be bridged not only by Eppehimer's 'strategic essentialism' but also by the notion of a 'limbo space' third way.[63] The latter phrase, borrowed from Michael Jagessar, draws on the metaphor of Caribbean cultural space in which plural and heterodox notions of identities reject the fixed binaries often imposed on ordinary Black people by traditional models of Christianity that have been inherited from the imperial past.

Problems with the traditional notion of the 'Black church' as 'safe space'

In the past I have argued for the primacy of a Black Jesus supporting and affirming Black people in their own self-determined spaces.[64] I argued for

---

complexity of religious expression is reduced to only one mode of religious orientation. See Curtis J. Evans, *The Burden of Black Religion*, New York and London: Oxford University Press, 2008. A much more plural text in this regard is Anthony B. Pinn, *Varieties of African American Religious Experience*, Minneapolis: Fortress, 1998.

63 This term emanates from Michael Jagessar, who argues that hybridized Black and Asian Christian subjects in Britain should embrace the 'limbo spaces' in which they can 'play' and manoeuvre between varying forms of religious identities. This form of movement is one that rejects fixed notions of religious identity that often speak to the totalizing camp mentality of modernity. See Jagessar, 'Is Jesus the Only Way?', p. 221.

64 See Anthony G. Reddie, *Faith, Stories and the Experience of Black Elders: Singing the Lord's Song in a Strange Land*, London: Jessica Kingsley, 2001.

this because I believe that for Black people to fight for liberation within religio-cultural spaces that were dominated by White people, for example, would lead to a phenomenon called 'cultural dissonance'.[65] In *Nobodies to Somebodies* I described cultural dissonance as part of the experiential, religious and cultural repertoire of Black Christians living in Britain.[66] Cultural dissonance is the emotional and psychological breach that exists between different expressions of being a human being, where the individual subject feels out of place and experiences a sense of discord in their engagement with an environment that is not considered entirely safe.

In this earlier work I understood my own struggle for truth with the evangelical Christianity in which I had been nurtured as one that carried with it all the hallmarks of this cultural dissonance.[67] Cultural dissonance was a conceptual framework that helped to explain my ongoing antipathy and suspicion at the fixity of the doctrinal certitude with which I was taught that 'Jesus is Lord!' In short, growing up in a conservative, White-majority church, the all-powerful White Jesus who was Lord did not sit easily with the powerless, Black working-class realities that represented my life.

What has proved helpful in this later rethinking is the sense that cultural dissonance can be assessed as a kind of 'limbo-spaced' third way. Namely, that cultural dissonance provides a means by which one can critique not only the vestiges of traditional, evangelical Christianity, but also asks critical questions of the very notion that there is secure ground on which any Black person can stand. Because, as many Black Christians have found in their retreat into so called 'Black space' and the trappings of an African-influenced religious-cultural repertoire, the residual stains of internalized racism and the restrictions on who belongs and who does not are no less apparent in these settings than in the White European ones. And yet the discourse of Black 'safe space' and 'White space' has often been used to attack those Black people who happen to belong to the latter.[68] The use of this kind of discourse has created a critical distance between the Black people who worship in Black churches and those who worship in White-majority ones.

---

65 Reddie, *Nobodies to Somebodies*, pp. 97–106.

66 Reddie *Nobodies to Somebodies*, pp. 97–106.

67 I have described my struggle to love my Blackness having been nurtured in a White evangelical Methodist church in a previous piece of work. See Anthony G. Reddie, *Black Theology in Transatlantic Dialogue*, New York: Palgrave Macmillan, 2006, pp. 7–13.

68 Michael Battle, a Black Anglican (Episcopalian) has argued for a more plural understanding of the Black church in America and any resultant spirituality of Black people in that context. As someone who belongs to a White-majority church in the USA (the worldwide Anglican Communion now has a greater majority of people of African descent/people of colour within its ranks), he wants to locate Black spirituality as not only residing in traditions like Baptists, Methodists and Pentecostals. See Michael Battle, *The Black Church in America: African American Christian Spirituality*, New Malden, MA, and Oxford: Blackwell, 2006.

In my own work I have favoured the discourse around Black people worshipping in Black-majority spaces. In my previous work I argued in favour of such binaries as 'Black majority' cultural contexts and the notion of 'safe space' versus those social settings that represent the antithesis of the former. I am now of the view that the relationship between these differing ways of engaging with church are much more closely aligned. Namely, that Black churches that are very traditional in how they 'police' Black respectability, as seen in the second exercise described a short while ago, can be as 'unsafe' to 'some' Black people who are not considered 'respectable enough', as the White ones! We are all 'at home' and feel 'alienated' in a variety of social settings! So even within Black-majority settings a sense of cultural dissonance may still find expression, and experiences of negation and even alienation from notions of Blackness may still come to fruition. The notion of Black 'safe space' does not always take account of LGBT people, for example! How safe are Black churches for Black people whose sexual identities would be described in these terms?[69] Black Theology must continue to press for a more critical appraisal of the varied complexities and subjectivities of Black people within the African Diaspora. It must take account of the realization that not all Black people have been welcomed or have felt at ease within Black religio-cultural settings.

The challenge begins with ourselves. How do we read ourselves for meaning?[70] What does it mean, in my case, to be a Black subject in postcolonial Britain who is at once an outsider in terms of ethnicity and constructions of 'race' in terms of my Blackness, and yet is a privileged subject in terms of my gender, as a male; in more specific terms, a heterosexual male?[71]

While the early models of Black Theology, like other theologies of liberation, have provided us with much-needed models of social analysis,[72] often grounded in the apparent boundaries of identity politics, they have, nevertheless, been less successful at engaging with the contested, multiple subjectivities of the end of the last century and the early part of this one. This new era is one when people are no longer defined by any singular notion of what it means to be Black.

---

69 See Horace Griffin, *Their Own Receive Them Not: African American Lesbians and Gays in Black Churches*, Cleveland, OH: Pilgrim Press, 2006.

70 I have argued for ways of interrogating and 'reading' (could also be understood as 'interpreting') oneself for meaning, in terms of how we engage with those with whom we meet. As all of us are social beings, our lives are lived at the intersection of our engagement with others. See Reddie, *Is God Colour Blind?*, pp. 37–52.

71 I address the issue of interlocking systems of oppression, power, privilege and normativity in one of my more recent books. See Reddie, *Is God Colour Blind?*, pp. 37–52.

72 Emmanuel Lartey offers a most helpful dissection of the methodological heart of Theologies of Liberation through the prism of 'practical theology'. See Emmanuel Lartey, 'Practical Theology as a Theological Form', in James Woodward and Stephen Pattison (eds), *The Blackwell Reader in Pastoral and Practical Theology*, Oxford: Blackwell, 2000, pp. 128–34.

One of the unfortunate residues of Christendom has been the temptation to construct theological discourse in terms of fidelity to doctrinal absolutism. Michael Jagessar has argued that fixed notions of what constitutes religious fidelity are unhelpful because they rarely accord with the religious pluralism that abounds in the lived experiences of many people, particularly those of African and Asian descent.[73] Jagessar is particularly wary of the blandishments of conversion[74] and baptism (in the name of Christ) as means of creating totalizing ways of viewing the old self and the new self in terms of religious identity.[75]

We live in an era where there is a growing reality of diversity and difference, where narratives of identity are complex and blurred. There needs to be a growing awareness that, for many their familial religious affiliations have not always been Christian. In this context, a more expansive Black Christology should remind us that people who worship God within alternative religious frameworks are not outside the orbit of God's love and grace. This love of God can still be reflected in the figure of a Black Jesus who can remain an inclusive symbol for all people who are committed, in an act of solidarity, to fight with others to overthrow oppression and so achieve their liberation. In short, that is why Black theologians have written so much, and indeed have so much to say, about Jesus!

Questions

1. Is a Black Jesus *really* essential for Black faith expression and liberation? If yes, then why, and if not, then why not?
2. To what extent is Jesus' importance as a universal symbol for love and the reconciliation of people compromised by depicting him as Black?
3. What are the strengths and weaknesses of an overly christological or Jesus-centred approach to faith and thinking about God?
4. What are the pluses and minuses in suggesting that Jesus can be understood as *solely* an inspirational figure for justice and liberation separated from the truth claims of him being 'Lord' or the 'Son of God'? Does this matter?

---

73 See Michael N. Jagessar, 'A Brief Con-version: A Caribbean and Black British Post-colonial Scrutiny of Christian Conversion', *Black Theology* 7:3 (2009), pp. 300–24.

74 Jagessar, 'A Brief Con-version', p. 321.

75 Michael Jagessar, writing with Stephen Burns, a former colleague from the Queen's Foundation for Ecumenical Theological Education, provides a compelling scrutiny of Christian worship using the refracting optics of postcolonial discourse. They argue that much that is understood as Christian worship in many churches across the world often re-inscribes the totalizing, hegemonic tendencies of colonially inspired theology that echoes to the epoch of Christendom. They are particularly concerned with the symbolism and patriarchal conscription of the priestly led symbolic-liturgical models of Baptism that seek to obliterate the former 'old' self at the behest of the church-legitimized notion of the 'new'. See Michael N. Jagessar and Stephen Burns, *Christian Worship: Postcolonial Perspectives*, London: Equinox, 2011, pp. 105–12.

5

Why So Little About the Holy Spirit?

In the last chapter, we looked at why so much has been written about Jesus in Black Theology and why this matters. Now I want to address the corresponding issue on why comparatively little has been written on the Holy Spirit in that same time period?

This chapter will seek to offer an explanation for this, but not simply in terms of the reasons for this apparent oversight, but, of greater import, why this matters. What are the consequences of this, not simply for the discipline of Black Theology, but more importantly for the oppressed and marginalized peoples it purports to represent and support? In locating this work within the frameworks provided by Transformative Popular Education, it is my intention to show how greater attention to the Spirit can provide a helpful means for enabling Black Theology to better engage with the lived realities of ordinary Black people. I intend to demonstrate how renewed attention to the role of the Holy Spirit (or, to borrow Dwight Hopkins' phrase, 'the Spirit of Liberation'[1]) can better enable Black Theology to become the praxis-based, mass movement it was always intended to become.

On the face of it, how can it not seem puzzling that comparatively so little has been written about the Holy Spirit in Black Theology, given the importance of the Spirit in Diasporan Black life. Reading James Cone's *A Black Theology of Liberation*, one will notice that while there are chapters entitled 'God in Black Theology', 'The Human Being in Black Theology' and 'Jesus Christ in Black Theology', there is no corresponding chapter on the Holy Spirit. One can also see this omission in James H. Evans's work on African American systematic theology, *We Have Been Believers*.[2]

A number of Black religious and cultural commentators have looked at the role of the Spirit in Black life, and have demonstrated the extent to which people of African descent have invariably found ways of engaging

---

1 This phrase and how it differs from traditional notions of the Holy Spirit, the Third Person of the Trinity, will be addressed at a later point in the chapter. See Dwight N. Hopkins, *Heart and Head: Black Theology – Past, Present and Future*, New York and Basingstoke: Palgrave Macmillan, 2002, pp. 77–90.

2 See James H. Evans Jr, *We Have Been Believers: An African American Systematic Theology*, Minneapolis: Fortress, 1992.

with the non-material dimensions of life, as a means of profoundly influencing the material basis of their existence.

It is not my intention to suggest that *nothing* has been written by Black theologians on the Holy Spirit or that there is nothing in the literature of Black Theology pertaining to this subject. My contention is that it is an under-appreciated and under-resourced subject area when compared to the work on Christology or the Church, for example. In terms of the latter, this comparative dearth becomes all the more apparent when one considers the central importance of the Spirit to the very birth of the Christian Church itself as depicted in Acts 2. I want to acknowledge the wealth of material that *has been* written by Black religious scholars detailing the relationship of Black people (particularly African Americans) to the work of the Spirit and Black spirituality.[3] It should be noted, however, that even here, there is comparatively little that can be said to be an exhaustive treatment of the nature of the Person of the Holy Spirit in Black life. Part of the reason for the latter, I believe, is down to the very nature and identity of Black Theology itself. Black Theology, taking its cue from the early work of James Cone, defined itself as a practical religious, faith-based response to the ongoing realities of racialized oppression in the Black

---

3 See, for example, Hans A. Baer, *The Black Spiritual Movement: A Religious Response to Racism*, Knoxville: University of Tennessee Press, 1984; Karen Baker-Fletcher, *Dancing with God: The Trinity from a Womanist Perspective*, St Louis: Chalice Press, 2006; Robert Beckford, *Dread and Pentecostal: A Political Theology for the Black Church in Britain*, London: SPCK, 2000; James H. Cone, *The Spirituals and the Blues: An interpretation*, New York: Seabury, NY: Orbis, 1972; Carol B. Duncan, *This Spot of Ground: Spiritual Baptists in Toronto*, Waterloo, Ontario: Wilfred Laurier University Press, 2008; Ennis B. Edmonds and Michelle A. Gonzalez, *Religious History: An Introduction*, New York and London: New York University Press, 2010; Michelle A. Gonzalez, *Afro-Cuban Theology: Religion, Race, Culture, and Identity*, Gainesville: University of Florida Press, 2006; Hemchand Gossai and Nathaniel Samuel Murrell (eds), *Religion, Culture and Tradition in the Caribbean*, Basingstoke and London: Macmillan, 2000; Robert E. Hood, *Must God Remain Greek?: Afro-Cultures and God-Talk*, Minneapolis: Fortress, 1994; Stephanie Y. Mitchem, *Name It and Claim It: Prosperity Teaching in the Black Church*, Cleveland OH: Pilgrim Press, 2007; Peter J. Paris, *The Spirituality of African Peoples: The Search for a Common Moral Discourse*, Minneapolis: Fortress, 1995; Archive Smith Jr, *Navigating the Deep River: Spirituality in African American Families*, Cleveland, OH: United Church Press, 1997; Theophus H. Smith, *Conjuring Culture: Biblical Formations of Black America*, New York and Oxford: Oxford University Press, 1994; Yolanda Y. Smith, *Reclaiming the Spirituals: New Possibilities for African American Christian Education*, Cleveland, OH: Pilgrim Press, 2004; Dianne M. Stewart, *Three Eyes for the Journey: African Dimensions of the Jamaican Religious Experience*, New York and Oxford: Oxford University Press, 2005; Carlyle Fielding Stewart III, *Black Spirituality and Black Consciousness*, Trenton, NJ: Africa World Press, 1999; Linda E. Thomas, *Under the Canopy: Ritual Process and Spiritual Resilience in South Africa*, Columbia, SC: University of South Carolina Press, 1999; Gayraud S. Wilmore, *Pragmatic Spirituality: The Christian Faith through an Africentric Lens*, New York and London: New York University Press, 2004.

experience. For Cone, Black Theology is rooted in the social existence of a people who have suffered and continue to suffer. He describes Black Theology thus:

> The goal of Black Theology is to prepare the minds of blacks for freedom so that they are ready to give all for it. Black Theology must speak *to* and *for* black people as they seek to remove the structures of white power which hover over their being, stripping it of its blackness . . . because Black Theology has as its starting point the black condition, this does not mean that it denies the absolute revelation of God in Christ. Rather, it means that Black Theology firmly believes that God's revelation in Christ can be made supreme only by affirming Christ as he is alive in black people today.[4]

This sense of Black Theology being committed to speaking to the lived realities of Black people and not arcane and abstract philosophizing for its own sake is reiterated by Gayraud Wilmore. Wilmore argues that there are two types of Black Theology, which are related to one another.[5] In the first instance, Black Theology is an academic discipline, one which attempts to reflect on the meaning of God, in Christ, in the light of Black social existence.[6] In terms of this first meaning, he writes:

> To use the term *black theology* to describe a way of thinking about the Bible and Jesus Christ that emphasizes this doctrine as the essence of the faith as it relates to our existence as a people ought not to be as threatening to intelligent white men and women as it appears to be – even though they may not be persuaded by the academic credibility of our argument.[7]

This second definition of Black Theology relates to the lived expression of faith of Black people as they seek to harness their belief in God as a means of facing the vicissitudes of life in predominantly poor, inner-city contexts in America (and across the African Diaspora).[8] In both definitions, Black Theology is concerned with how faith and theological reflection relate to Black life as it is lived in all its grim peculiarities and variations in the world. In both definitions there is little time for arid speculation for its own sake. So perhaps it is this concern for the practicalities of life, as it is lived and experienced by Black people, that has led Black Theology to display little time for abstract speculation on the Third Person of the Trinity and the relationship of the Third Person to the Father and the Son?

---

4 James H. Cone, *Black Theology and Black Power*, Maryknoll, NY: Orbis, 1989 [1969], p. 118.

5 See Wilmore, *Pragmatic Spirituality*, pp. 155–66.

6 Wilmore, *Pragmatic Spirituality*, pp. 155–7.

7 Wilmore, *Pragmatic Spirituality*, p. 157.

8 Wilmore, *Pragmatic Spirituality*, pp. 159–63.

It can be argued that this attention to more practical issues pertaining to lived experience has led to two perennial weaknesses in Black Theology. First, Black Theology can be accused of being much closer to anthropology than theology, and, second, it becomes a self-consciously biased form of ideological construction as opposed to a universal revelatory faith-based movement. By emphasizing the Black lived experience as being its point of departure, some ordinary Black people have wondered if Black Theology is more concerned with human realities than divine possibilities. In offering such a positioned perspective, the universal dimensions of the faith, such as a universal saviour, are seemingly abandoned for a more specific and arguably limited and impoverished faith.

I would reject both of these contentions, but it would be naive not to acknowledge these critical issues when reading the remainder of this chapter, because they are very relevant to the following discussion. Some ordinary Black people with whom I have worked have cited the comparative lack of engagement with the 'Holy Spirit' as illustrative of the weaknesses and failures to which I have just drawn attention.

The following exercise has been used to help ordinary Black people to understand the ways in which the Holy Spirit/the Spirit of Liberation has been understood within Black Theology.

Exercise: 'The Spirit of change and transformation'

Each person has a lump of plasticine or clay. The lumps should be quite shapeless and non-descript. What are the group's impressions of the clay?

Now ask everyone to mould their clay into a human face with as much detail as they can manage. Each face should be as individual as possible. When the faces are finished, display them on a table.

Ask the group to look at the variation in design and details – no two faces are exactly the same. The plain, ordinary modelling clay they began with has been changed into something much more interesting.

Black Theology reflections

When the exercise has been used with groups of ordinary Black people, two immediate outcomes are *always* discernible. First, *all* the faces are different from one another. No two people have produced the same face. The second observational outcome is that the faces are very different from the piece of clay each individual received in the first instance.

Individuals are invited to reflect on the nature of the exercise. Why did they create the face they did? What inspiration encouraged them to create it in this fashion? The exercise, like the others used in this work, is drawn from the discipline of Transformative Popular Education. It has been used as a means of creating accessible teaching and learning materials, which in this book operate as enacted metaphors for articulating and illustrating central ideas of Black Theology. It is hoped that these activities connect with the lived experiences of ordinary people.

In this exercise participants are asked to reflect initially on the lump of clay they have been given and to appreciate it in its own right *before* they attempt to change it. It is important that the participants are asked to do this, because one of the unfortunate consequences of not stressing this point is that one gives the impression that the clay had no intrinsic worth before it was changed. This is not true. The clay is valuable in its own right. This is not to say that the change is not beneficial or does not bring about pleasing results, but to assume that only the altered clay is of merit or consideration is to suggest that, metaphorically, the pre-transformed Black self has no meaning or merit in and of itself.

One of the weaknesses of some forms of charismatic Christianity in which Black people reside is that they often emphasize a kind of 'before' and 'after' syndrome.[9] One of the consequences of this kind of binary 'before' and 'after' is that it can have a disparaging view on the merits of the 'pre-changed self', often denigrating the former as being 'not of God' or being 'un-civilized'. Michael Jagessar has argued against the limitations of such binaries, particularly given the fact that for many African and Asian people the religious expressions of our forebears have not always been Christian.[10] A number of emerging Black theologians have begun to explore religious traditions beyond Christianity, particularly those that have their origins in West Africa and represent the 'pre-converted African self', as frameworks for talking about Black liberation,[11] building on the ground-breaking work of Anthony Pinn from the late 1990s.[12]

Black Theology, while often adopting a dominant Christian perspective, nevertheless does not hold to a literalist reading as often depicted in John

---

9 See Ashon T. Crawley, "Let's Get It On": Performance Theory and Black Pentecostalism', *Black Theology* 6:3 (2008), pp. 308–29, for an excellent distillation of the perfomative elements of Black Pentecostalism and how this can be construed in terms of notions of change and transformation.

10 See Michael N. Jagessar, 'A Brief Con-version: A Caribbean and Black British Postcolonial Scrutiny of Christian Conversion', *Black Theology* 7:3 (2009), pp. 300–24. See also his previous work, where he expands the basis of Black Theology in Britain by arguing for a movement away from a purely Christocentric conception of Black religious identities. Michael N. Jagessar, "Is Jesus the Only Way?" Doing Black Christian God-Talk in a Multi-Religious City (Birmingham, UK)', *Black Theology* 7:2 (2009), pp. 200–25.

11 See Marcus Louis Harvey, 'Engaging the Orisha: An Exploration of the Yoruba Concepts of *Ibeji* and *Olokun* as Theological Principles in Black Theology', *Black Theology* 6:1 (2008), pp. 61–82; Jawanza Eric Clark, 'Reconceiving the Doctrine as Jesus as Savior in Terms of the African Understanding of an Ancestor: A Model for the Black Church', *Black Theology* 8:2 (2009), pp. 140–59.

12 See Anthony B. Pinn, *Varieties of African American Religious Experience*, Minneapolis: Fortress, 1998.

14.6, which asserts that 'Jesus is the Only Way'. The old self is not to be disparaged, especially if that old self does not self-identify as 'Christian'.

Having stressed the importance of the 'pre-changed' clay as a metaphor for according respect to the 'pre-transformed' Black self, Black Theology, however, still wants to assert the dynamic and dramatic possibilities of being transformed by the Spirit. In the exercise we see how the clay is transformed into something that is beyond its previous appearance. In the new shape, there is a specific intention and design to the clay and it has attained a greater level of individuality than what existed formerly, even if one wishes to affirm the previous existence of the clay. The new shape and design is one that enhances and completes the former existence; it does not deny or disparage it.

Oftentimes, when the participants have reflected on this metaphor in terms of the life experiences and struggles of Black people they have remarked on the process of such transformation and the challenges presented in such encounters and events. The clay, in being changed into an individual face, now attains a kind of individuality and identity that can be challenging when compared to the more amorphous shape that existed previously. The change and transformation of the clay represents something wholly different from what has gone before. Many of the participants have noted that a seemingly anonymous and nondescript piece of clay rarely possesses the capacity to shock, disturb or upset, but conversely all of these things might be found in the newly created face. In effect, change and transformation are not always seen in a positive light.

Of particular import is the nature of the face that has been created by the various participants. The participants are encouraged to create something that is significant and personal to them. At times I have witnessed the creation of faces that have not always pleased other people in the group. The importance of what has now been created as a result of the transformation of the clay can be seen in two ways. First, the new face might not be deemed acceptable by others. Some may consider it ugly, or it might transgress acceptable notions of beauty. Second, given that this exercise is concerned with assisting people to understand Black Theology, it should come as no surprise that many of the participants create faces that are depictions of people of African descent. Some choose to create historic faces, of people of African descent, possibly those who have a link with ancient biblical narratives, likes those described in the Pentecost narrative in Acts 2.[13] Others, conversely, decide to create contemporary images of Black people; some even decide on self-portraits. While there is no stipulation on what faces

---

13 One can see some of these images in Carol Troupe's Popular Educational Black Theology material related to Pentecost in her 'Living Out Faith' website. See the following links for some of these images: http://www.livingoutfaith.org.uk/index.php?op=mo dload&name=knowledge&file=index&viewCat=15 and http://www.livingoutfaith.org. uk/index.php?op=modload&name=knowledge&file=index&viewCat=16.

they can create, as the facilitator I have often reminded ordinary Black people of the deeply political nature of their Black depictions.

More recently, Black and Womanist theologians have written at length on the nature and theo-political importance and substance of the Black body. While a good deal of early Black Theology work concentrated on the damage racist and anti-Black rhetoric and racialized teachings had exerted on the Black mind, causing significant levels self-hatred,[14] later Black scholars have focused on the theological significance of the visible Black body. Of particular note is the work of Anthony Pinn and Shawn Copeland[15].

If one considers the violence unleashed on such innocent figures as Emmet Till in the USA in 1955 or on Stephen Lawrence in Britain in 1993, for the apparent crime of simply being 'Black', one is reminded of the continued political charge of being a human being in a Black body and, for the context of this exercise, with a Black face. In the creation of Black faces in the exercise, the participants, most often ordinary Black people, are engaging in a deeply political and subversive activity, for it still remains the case that 'too much Black visibility' of the Black countenance remains unacceptable, in terms of marketing and subsequent profit margins.[16]

The critical subtext of the exercise is the politicization of Black transformations. The work on Black embodiment by Black and Womanist scholars, particularly, within the context of change and transformation, is crucial because it locates the possibilities of redemption within a specific religio-cultural context. Namely, while there is no doubting that all people can

---

14 Vincent Harding, 'Black Power and the American Christ', in Gayraud S. Wilmore and James H. Cone (eds), *Black Theology: A Documentary History, 1966–1979*, Maryknoll, NY: Orbis, 1979, pp. 35–42. See also Cone, *Black Theology and Black Power*, pp. 5–30; Walter Rodney, *The Groundings with My Brothers*, London: Bogle-L-Ouverture Publications, 1990 [1969].

15 See Anthony B. Pinn and Dwight N. Hopkins (eds), *Loving the Body: Black Religious Studies and the Erotic*, New York: Palgrave, 2004; Anthony B. Pinn, *Terror and Triumph: The Nature of Black Religion*, Minneapolis: Fortress, 2003; 'Sweaty Bodies in a Circle: Thoughts on the Subtle Dimensions of Black Religion as Protest', *Black Theology* 4:1 (2006), pp. 11–26, and, *Embodiment and the New Shape of Black Theological Thought*, New York and London: New York University Press, 2010. See M. Shawn Copeland, *Enfleshing Freedom: Body, Race and Being*, Minneapolis: Fortress, 2010.

16 It is interesting to note the arguments that have been made by White editors of popular White-owned magazines in the areas of fashion, beauty or the media, that placing a Black face on the cover often lowers the sales for that particular issue. This point has particular piquancy when applied to the cut-throat arena of high fashion. See http://bitchmagazine.org/article/when-tyra-met-naomi for an interesting insight into this issue. Note also the controversy that has arisen from George Lucas claiming that he was forced to self-finance *Red Tails*, the story of Tuskegee Airmen, as Hollywood did not want to fund a film that consisted of an all-Black cast. See http://www.huffingtonpost.com/2012/01/10/george-lucas-hollywood-di_n_1197227.html.

be the subject of these kinds of critical changes in the very essence of what it means to be a human being, the fact that this notion of transformative change is located in Black bodies and within Black experiences and cultures in history is of great importance. As Eze has shown, within the epoch of the Enlightenment, the so called age of reason, one still finds conceptualizations of Black people predicated on the notion that they represent lower forms of humanity and so are incapable of the kinds of creative transformations that are considered the preserve of White Europeans.[17]

In Black Theology, transformation in the Spirit is not just about ecstatic utterances for their own sake or privatized notions of emotional experiences. Rather, as James Cone states, 'To be possessed by God's spirit means that the believer is willing to be obedient unto death, becoming the means through which God makes his will known and the vehicle of the activity of God himself.'[18] In short, the critical transformation of the Black self is a social movement, in which Black people are charged and changed in order to affect those around them and the social contexts in which they are immersed.

The politicization of this kind of transformation is all too rarely articulated in a good deal of theological literature. Spiritual transformations can and have been distorted, to the point where the prevailing negativity surrounding such activities can lead to a level of disengagement at best, and downright hostility at worst, from radical liberationist thinkers.

It is this notion of transformation that is complicated by a number of factors, which perhaps explains the under-reporting of this theme in Black Theology, as has been explained previously. But before we get to the potential problems pertaining to *particular* Christian accounts for Christian transformation (often termed as 'sanctification' and 'holiness'), it is perhaps helpful to outline the social implications of this for Black people, given that this is central to Black Theology.

The literature in Black Theology has often pointed to significant people who, it is argued, having been transformed and energized by the Spirit, are then enabled to undertake pioneering and prophetic work in the fight for Black liberation. In highlighting these individuals, the emphasis has been less on trying to discern the specifics of their transformation in detailed theological terms. Rather, it has been the analysis of their praxis – their faith-inspired actions – that has attracted the greater interest.

Carol Troupe, a Black British woman educator and theologian, has explored the significance of 'heralded' Black women and men and the ways in which religious faith has inspired them to fight for justice and equity for

---

17 See Emmanuel C. Eze (ed.), *Race and the Enlightenment*, New Malden, MA, and Oxford: Wiley-Blackwell, 2008.

18 Cone, *Black Theology and Black Power*, p. 59.

all people.[19] Troupe's work seeks to explicate the importance of faith and how notions of the spirit provide a kind of catalyst and energizing force for enabling seemingly ordinary people to undertake extraordinary feats of bravery and commitment in order to confront injustice and oppression, often in situations that seem insoluble.

In many respects, the most iconic of figures one can highlight is that of the Revd Dr Martin Luther King Jr. A plethora of work has been produced that celebrates King's legacy and analyses the way in which faith and a liberative spirituality transformed his life and provided the basis for his prophetic revolutionary actions.[20] Black Theology believes that life and activism of someone like King exemplifies the embodied nature of the praxis of liberative spirituality that has fuelled the faith-inspired struggle for Black liberation.

This radical expression of the work and presence of the Spirit in Black experience is what animates Black Theology from a dry intellectual exercise into a form of dynamic praxis that seeks to change the world. In this regard, Christology and pneumatology (the study of the Holy Spirit) are very much connected. In a previous chapter I spoke about how Black Theology envisions the telling of a new story, one that seeks to give agency to Black experience and the desire for a new reality in the world. This, in turn, has often taken shape and found a thematic framework in the person of Jesus. The inspiration in belonging to and, perhaps of greater import, following Jesus is itself often made manifest in the power and inspiration of the Spirit, which provides the strength and the determination to continue the fight for liberation when the task seems insurmountable.

Black Theology critique of traditional evangelical piety

While Black spirituality is indeed varied and complex, much of the prevailing theological literature tends to locate the Christian origins of what is often seen as the progenitor for Black Theology within the Second Great

---

19 See Carol Troupe's work on the 'Living Out Faith' website. The section detailing this work can be found at http://www.livingoutfaith.org.uk/index.php?op=modload&name=knowledge&file=index&viewCat=2.

20 Lewis V. Baldwin, *Towards the Beloved Community: Martin Luther King Jr and South Africa*, Cleveland, OH: Pilgrim Press, 1995; Donald M. Chinula, *Building King's Beloved Community: Foundations for Pastoral Care and Counselling with the Oppressed*, Cleveland, OH: United Church Press, 1997; James Echols (ed.), *I have a Dream: Martin Luther King Jr. and the Future of Multicultural America*, Minneapolis: Fortress, 2004; Vincent Harding, *Martin Luther King: The Inconvenient Hero*, Maryknoll, NY: Orbis, 2008 [1996]; Johnny Bernard Hill, *The Theology of Martin Luther King, Jr. and Desmond Mpilo Tutu*, New York: Palgrave Macmillan, 2007; Michael G. Long, *Martin Luther King Jr. on Creative Living*, St Louis: Chalice Press, 2004; J. Deotis Roberts, *Bonhoeffer and King: Speaking Truth to Power*, Louisville, KY: Westminster John Knox, 2005.

Awakening of the early to mid-nineteenth century.[21] In the evangelical schema of faith, the role of personal experience is invested with immense importance. It is through personal experience of the risen Christ that the Christian believer is able to gain a sense of their assurance of salvation. This has been part of the bedrock of Black faith that has enabled many radical, Black activists to fight for social justice, firm in the belief that the security of 'everlasting life' meant they had nothing to lose in fighting for justice in the 'here and now'.[22]

In the wider context of Black religious experience, the birth of Black Christianity in the African Diaspora finds very many echoes in the dramatic persona of individual conversation. For the majority of Black Christians, who converted to Christianity as the 'religion of choice', it was the outpouring of the Spirit that gave substance to their sense of being changed. This was replicated among African peoples, largely within evangelical Protestant churches, in North America and the Caribbean.[23]

One of the ironies of Black Theology as a largely Christian[24] movement committed to radical, liberative change is that, while its central reworking of Christian faith and doctrine is radical in thought and practice, this work has still largely operated from within conventional Christian-inspired frameworks.[25] This dichotomy can be seen in classic expression in James H. Cone's early work. Cone's approach to undertaking Black Theology is very much a biblically orientated one that uses the existing frameworks of the Judaeo-Christian tradition as a basis for arguing for Black freedom here on earth.[26] Frederick Ware, talking of Cone's biblical approach to Black Theology, says: 'For him, the meaning of liberation, is best expressed primarily within the context of the Bible. In other words, the Bible provides his model of liberation.'[27]

---

21 See Henry H. Mitchell, *Black Church Beginnings: The Long-Hidden Realities of the First Years*, Grand Rapids, MI: Eerdmans, 2004; Edmonds and Gonzalez, *Caribbean Religious History*, pp. 45–154.

22 For a good example of this form of social activism arising from pietistic evangelical Black Pentecostal roots in Britain, see the conversation with Pastor Ira Brooks in Anita Jackson, *Catching Both Sides of the Wind: Conversations with Five Black Pastors*, London: British Council of Churches, 1985, pp. 1–32.

23 See Noel Leo Erskine, *Decolonizing Theology: A Caribbean Perspective*, Maryknoll, NY: Orbis, 1981, pp. 73–85. See also Anne H. Pinn and Anthony B. Pinn, *Fortress Introduction to Black Church History*, Minneapolis: Fortress, 2002, pp. 8–17.

24 Not all Black Theology is indeed Christian or undertaken by those who would profess to be Christian. A notable example can be seen in Pinn, *Varieties of African American Religious Experience*.

25 See Frederick L. Ware, *Methodologies of Black Theology*, Cleveland, OH: Pilgrim Press, 2002, pp. 28–65.

26 Perhaps the explicit rendering of this work can be seen in Cone's classic *God of the Oppressed*, New York: Seabury, 1975.

27 Ware, *Methodologies of Black Theology*, p. 35.

This traditional aspect of Black Theology is in some ways both its strength and its weakness. The strength of Black Theology lies in the fact that as an essentially practical Christian discipline it can find a means of connecting to the experiences and needs of ordinary suffering Black people the world over. The fact that Black Theology has utilized the personalized faith formation of Protestant evangelical piety is testament to the fact that this movement can and should be a practical resource for both personal and systemic change. In effect, it should be a resource for ordinary Black people of faith to understand themselves better and to empower them in their attempts to be a sign of transformative change within White normative societies, across the world and within their respective churches.

Going back to the exercise for one moment, one can read the transformative change in the clay in terms of 'conversion'. This sense of the individual encountering God in such a way that this leads to a personal decision to believe in God, through the person and work of Jesus, *in the power* of the Holy Spirit, is an important facet of Black evangelical faith. The notion of personal change arising from conversion is easier to discern in Black religious experience, in many respects, than a sense of commitment to collective social action. Perhaps this is one of the reasons why Black Theology has sometimes remained a little cautious in spending too much time reflecting on the Holy Spirit?

Looking at the growth of Black neo-Pentecostalism around the world, one sees much greater evidence of the former than the latter. Namely, one witnesses more of the individual's personal encounter with the Spirit and the settling for that in and of itself than on a committed and determined stance to use that sense of transformation for the purposes of radical, social change. The assurance of a very personal salvation and the ensuing change is an important characteristic of this evangelical Protestant-inspired model of Christian Black Theology.[28] Central to this particular religious framework is the essential work of the Holy Spirit as the initiator and guarantor of conversion and individual change.

In reflecting on the development of Black Theology in the light of the spiritual drama of personal conversion in the context of Black experience it is interesting to note that the sense of the work of the Holy Spirit in Black Theology has been largely implicit. The transformation that arises from this spiritual change is one that enables Black people to see and interpret their wider experience and reality in an alternative, liberative fashion.

---

28 See Beckford, *Dread and Pentecostal*, p. 40. See also See Clarence E. Hardy III, *James Baldwin's God: Sex, Hope, and Crisis in Black Holiness Culture*, Knoxville, TN: University of Tennessee Press, 2003, p. 34. It should be noted that while Black Theology has utilized the religious frameworks of evangelical Protestant theology, it has nonetheless moved beyond the creedal and doctrinal building blocks of this mode of Christian religious expression.

One may argue that it is in Pentecostalism that Black Theology has been able to 'resurrect' an explicit rendering of the work and Person of the Holy Spirit, as witnessed, for example, in the scholarship of Robert Beckford, to which I will return shortly. Particularly, in his second book, *Dread and Pentecostal*, Beckford offers a pneumatologically inspired version of Black Theology in which the work of the Spirit is explicitly referred to, and through whom notions of individual, collective, corporate and systemic change is made possible.[29]

To reiterate the important caveat I made previously, regarding this chapter, it is that I am arguing for an under-assessment of the role of the Spirit in Black Theology, not suggesting that nothing of note has been written on this subject. For example, one can cite Black Theology work that has addressed the Holy Spirit,[30] but the point I am making is that one has to hunt far and wide for such explicit reflections. For the most part, Black Theology has fought shy of offering an extensive treatment for the role of the Spirit in its liberative and transformative religious ideology. This, however, is despite its attachment to the overall frameworks provided by the formative roots within North American and Caribbean eighteenth- and nineteenth-century evangelical Protestant theology. Many Black and Womanist theologians will talk about the 'Spirit of Liberation' or 'spirituality', but comparatively little addresses the Holy Spirit and the work of the Holy Spirit in explicit terms.

I wonder whether one of the reasons for the more implicit role given to the Spirit within Black Theology writings is the need to counter the worst excesses of the privatized and spiritualized notion of personal experience within evangelical Protestantism. It is easy to see how the often dramatic accounts of personal conversion can be read in very negative terms by Black theologians. I have witnessed many accounts of personal conversion in the lives of Black people in Britain, when such discourse has not been allied to the wider struggle for social justice[31] for the largely urban poor in Britain. As one who

---

29 See Beckford, *Dread and Pentecostal*, pp. 160–220.

30 A very good recent example can be found in Baker-Fletcher, *Dancing with God*, although it is worth noting that her text does not use a classic 'trinitarian' approach to the subject: namely, there is nothing in the work that specifically draws attention to the named Third Person of the Trinity and how 'she' plays an active part in the construction of Black religious experience. As I am not a systematic theologian, it is not my place to mount any substantive critique at scholars for not doing what I myself have neither been trained nor ever had any inclination to do – namely, trying to figure out the inner workings of the mystery that is God. Baker-Fletcher's work rejects the classical or traditional modes of operation favoured by White Euro-American systematic theology. Her approach to the Trinity is more concerned with the human capacity for seeking to make community, which is inspired by the Trinity, as opposed to an all-out exhaustive investigation of the trinitarian quality of God as an abstract, metaphysical puzzle.

31 I have sometimes dubbed this the 'Me and myself and I' gospel.

was brought up in the Methodist tradition, I know, for example, that John Wesley's own conversion led to the development of a movement that sought to locate her missiological intent among the poor of eighteenth-century England. Aspects of Wesley's comparative radicalism can be seen in his thoughts on slavery, which for their time read remarkably prescient,[32] particularly in terms of Black Theology's continued commitment to racial justice.[33]

While Wesley's underlying source for truth and knowledge concerning enslaved Africans at the time can be critiqued,[34] he nonetheless was able to ally his personal encounter with the Holy Spirit alongside a determination that the spiritual freedom he had gained in Christ should be translated into material and spiritual freedom for all downtrodden and marginalized peoples.

Sadly, Wesley's commitment to spiritual and social change was not matched by all his eighteenth-century contemporaries. Kelly Brown Douglas has shown how, within the context and framework of North American evangelical Protestantism, the bulk of White Euro-Americans saw little or no contradiction between being personally saved by grace, through faith, and yet denying even the most basic of material or spiritual freedoms to Black people.[35]

Black Theology has resolutely turned its face away from the spiritualizing and individualized conception of Christianity in the past. This was particularly the case during the era of slavery and then colonialism, because the constant approach of this mode of religious activity was one that sought to promote White inertia, passivity and even racism in the face of Black suffering and struggle. Black theologians are rightly critical and suspicious of the kind of religious rhetoric of 'born again' White conservative evangelicals. They are rightly suspicious of those who often used the spiritual declarations evoked by the language of personal experience and conversion alongside their refusal to live out their allegedly transformed and saved Christian selves in their daily encounters with Black folk. One can witness the most hypocritical examples of such protestations during the epoch of slavery. As James Cone has demonstrated, the dichotomy between White religious zeal and social-based discrimination against Blacks at the hands of the former did not dissipate at the ending of slavery.[36] One can see the reasons for this

---

32 See John Wesley, *Thoughts Upon Slavery*, first published in 1774, republished by the Racial Justice Office of the Methodist Church for the Bicentenary of the Abolition of the Slave Trade Act (1807), London: Methodist Church, 2006.

33 See Inderjit Bhogal, *A Table for All*, Sheffield: Penistone, 2000, for a Black Theology in Britain example of the thrust towards inclusivity and racial justice.

34 See Michael N. Jagessar, 'Review Article: Critical Reflections on John Wesley, Thoughts Upon Slavery', *Black Theology* 5:2 (2007), pp. 250–5.

35 See Kelly Brown Douglas, *What's Faith Got to Do with It? Black Bodies and Christian Souls*, Maryknoll, NY: Orbis, 2005.

36 See James H. Cone, *The Cross and the Lynching Tree*, Maryknoll, NY: Orbis, 2011.

scepticism, especially in terms of the language of conversion and religious change during the evangelical revivals of the eighteenth and nineteenth centuries, and the inability of most White Christians to link personal faith to social holiness. Dwight Hopkins states:

> AntiBlack racism or White supremacy or the reflex that African Americans are secondary and come last in all spheres of life in the United States required a full spiritual concentration and effort on the part of White Christians. They could not serve two masters; they could either advocate White power over Black life or pursue God's spirit of liberation for the poor and vulnerable in society. The sermons from White Christians that Black workers received under slavery had nothing to do with the joy of the spirit.[37]

The fact that White slave owners and those who colluded with slavery could claim some semblance of God's re-orientating power in the form of the Spirit and yet show no discernible change in outward behaviour, conduct or ethics has been a significant reason for Black Theology to distance itself from the formal frameworks of this form of religious discourse. For many Black theologians, myself included, our efforts have been directed at the tangible struggles that face Black people, suffering on a daily basis, and not the 'yet-to-be-proved' rhetoric of spiritual change that seems to offer no amelioration to Black oppression in the 'here and now'.

Black Theology and Spirit-filled liberative praxis

It is the practical and radical commitment to demonstrable change in the present that has made Black Theology suspicious of, but not wholly distant from, nor disrespectful of, the religious activity of dramatic change, as exemplified in the exercise. Despite the ways in which this particular religious facet has been abused and misused, Black Theology and the theologians who work within this tradition still acknowledge the power of personal experience and conversion and the intimate encounter with the Spirit. One cannot ignore the dramatic account of spiritualized change and transformation one finds repeated in the lives of countless Black people down through the centuries. It is this form of embodied, radical change that the exercise at the beginning of this chapter tries to reflect, albeit in metaphorical terms.

But this form of dramatic change and transformation in the power of the Spirit does not and cannot exist in a vacuum. This form of dramatic change must be allied to practical models of collective living and communitarian

---

37 Hopkins, *Heart and Head*, p. 87.

action that seek to harness the emotive power of religious change within the broader framework of freedom for all people, irrespective of faith or none.

It is this second element that has often been lacking when one looks at the rhetoric and the literature pertaining to the Holy Spirit in some forms of religious discourse. Black Theology, as stated previously, argues for an embodied, radical and collective understanding of such change, for the wider purposes of struggling for Black liberation and social justice for all marginalized people.

In more recent times, the work of Black practical theologians, such as Tribble, Andrews and Smith, building on the pioneering work of James H. Harris,[38] has sought to offer practical theological models by which the liberative impulse of Black Theology can be made operational within Black churches. Harris, in his landmark book, sought to provide, through the lens of pastoral theology, a mechanism by which the liberative impulse of Black Theology could be made operative in the many ministries of the Black church in the USA. Writing on the subject of worship and the work of the Spirit as a means for holistic change, Harris writes:

> Conversion should manifest itself by making us different spiritually, socially, and politically. This will mean that our conversion or transformation, springing forth from the structured worship in church, will become the basis of our efforts to transform society into a more egalitarian community where justice and righteousness will be more reality than myth. Conversion, to be born again, or to receive salvation is a process of becoming more attuned to understanding the meaning of the kingdom of God here and now. When we become saved, we will understand that social and political justice are intimately connected to salvation and a born-again status. Individual salvation has as a necessary correlate the salvation of the community.[39]

Harris's words provide the broader socio-cultural and political framework for the conversion experiences of the Black people with whom I worked. Harris's social and politicized approach to the concept of spiritualized change and transformation, what he terms conversion, is a practical outworking of Black Theology for Black liberation. This notion of conversion is one that finds echoes in the lives of millions of Black people and is something to which Black Theology bears witness in its belief in the spiritually empowering basis of individual *and* collective change.

---

38 See Jeffrey L. Tribble Sr, *Transformative Pastoral Leadership in the Black Church*, New York: Palgrave Macmillan, 2005; Dale P. Andrews, *Practical Theology for Black Churches: Bridging Black Theology and African American Folk Religion*, Louisville, KY: Westminster John Knox, 2002; Robert L. Smith Jr, *From Strength to Strength: Shaping a Black Practical Theology for the 21st Century*, New York: Peter Lang, 2007; James H. Harris, *Pastoral Theology: A Black-Church Perspective*, Minneapolis: Fortress, 1991.

39 Harris, *Pastoral Theology*, pp. 92–3.

These initial reflections on the language of dramatic change and transformation show that it is one that can be used as a resource for helping Black people to see a holistic, liberative spirituality as the basis for their commitment to systemic transformation.[40]

In looking to ally personal, individual spiritual change with the challenge of forging this into a movement of liberative praxis I want to look for a few moments at the work of Robert Beckford. In *Dread and Pentecostal*, Robert Beckford has created one of the most incisive and compelling accounts of merging the dynamic spiritualized power of change, often associated with Black Pentecostalism, and the liberative praxis of Black Theology. As we saw in a previous chapter, when looking at different methodological approaches to undertaking Black Theology, Robert Beckford has been at the forefront of linking the analysis of Black cultural expression with the ideas, concepts and themes that have emerged from Christianity. He has undertaken this form of 'correlation' in order to provide an approach to Black Theology that can be located not simply within the Church but, rather, can be linked symbolically with the material cultures developed and practised by African Caribbean people in Britain.[41]

At the heart of this work is Beckford's merging of Rasta sensibilities with African Caribbean Pentecostalism. While this is a constant thematic thread in all his major work, I think it is fair to say that it finds its most eloquent expression in *Dread and Pentecostal*. The model of Black Theology that Beckford employs in this work is not without some flaws. For example, unlike his previous book, *Jesus Is Dread*,[42] where Beckford acknowledges the contribution of Black Christians who belong to traditions other than Pentecostalism, in this text there is an assumption of the representative nature of Black Pentecostalism for all Black Christian people.

What is important for the nature of this discussion, however, is the way in which Beckford argues for a Spirit-filled approach to radical, liberative action that utilizes the insights of Rasta, as a means of analysing the wider socio-political context of Black faith in Britain.[43] For example, Beckford's treatment of Black Pentecostalism in Britain is able to address issues of gender inequality in a manner that is completely absent in a much more recent publication that seeks to engage with issues that are pertinent to the Black church in Britain in the twenty-first century.[44]

---

40 Hopkins, *Heart and Head*, pp. 77–90.

41 For a concise distillation of Robert Beckford's major works, see 'Dread and Rahtid: Robert Beckford's Canon', in Michael N. Jagessar and Anthony G. Reddie (eds), *Black Theology in Britain: A Reader*, Oakwood and London: Equinox, 2007, pp. 81–108.

42 See Robert Beckford, *Jesus Is Dread: Black Theology and Black Culture in Britain*, London: Darton, Longman and Todd, 1998.

43 Beckford, *Dread and Pentecostal*, pp. 150–86.

44 Joe Aldred and Keno Ogbo (eds), *The Black Church in the 21st Century*, London: Darton, Longman and Todd, 2010, does not mention the issue of gender in a book that

Given the growing importance of Black Pentecostalism in world Christianity in general and among Black Christian communities in particular, *Dread and Pentecostal* provides a holistic model of transformative change that combines two important facets of Spirit-filled, personal, Black religious experience. In the first instance there is the nature of that personal experience itself. As we have seen in previous chapters, for many, perhaps the majority of ordinary Black people, their experience of God is not an abstract or a distant one. God, often revealed in the person of Jesus, is a part of the immediacy of their lives and supports them daily in their struggles.

The role of the Holy Spirit is that of the force and power of God that enables many ordinary Black Christians to live out the inherent promises of the gospel and to seek to make a difference in the world. In terms of 'passive radicalism' as explained in a previous chapter, sometimes the role of faith is to be defiant and to 'keep on keeping on' in the face of seemingly insurmountable odds. This form of faith is itself a form of resistance, even if it does not move beyond the immediacy of the individual and their attempts to survive.[45] But Beckford realizes that often the best of 'passive radicalism' can manifest itself in the worst excesses of a form of 'selfish faith'. Selfish faith for Beckford is one in which the benefits of Spirit-filled forms of dramatic change result in nothing further than the recipient claiming their material blessings from God, solely for themselves. In this unfortunate corruption of the strengths of Spirit-filled forms of religious change, the thrust for the collective well-being of the whole community is disregarded, as individuals think purely in terms of their own self-interest.[46] Beckford's challenge is to link the growing tendency towards individualism within the growing traditions of charismatic forms of Black Christianity with the traditional collectivism of the Black church. He advocates this in order to provide the necessary force that will propel Black Theology forwards as a grass-roots movement for radical, social change.

Black Theology, the Spirit and transformative worship

In the next section of this chapter, I want to locate these initial reflections on the Black Theology critique of seemingly 'traditional' individualized and privatized notions of spiritual change and show how this can be rethought in the

---

purports to address the 'key' challenges facing Black-majority churches in Britain in the twenty-first century.

45 For an explanation of 'passive radicalism', see Valentina Alexander, 'Passive and Active Radicalism in Black-Led Churches', in Jagessar and Reddie (eds), *Black Theology in Britain*, pp. 52–69.

46 See Robert Beckford, 'Theology in the Age of Crack: Crack Age, Prosperity Doctrine and "Being There"', *Black Theology in Britain* 4:1 (2001), pp. 9–24.

practical task of collective and communitarian living. I have sought to locate this work in terms of the practice of worship. My reason for looking at worship in terms of the liberative praxis of Black Theology is its immediacy and utility within what might be described as 'normal' church activity. By this I mean that what remains central to all church traditions within what might be described as the 'Black experience' is the centrality of worship. Worshipping God in the power of the Spirit is an important factor in Black religious expression.

So in this section I want to locate the previous discussion within a contemporary, practical concern, in order that the ideas and concerns that have been discussed previously can be utilized for the benefit of ordinary Black people.

Now to be clear, I am not assuming any specific or particular characteristic of Black worship. I am not claiming that all Black people are charismatic, for example, as is sometimes the approach of some Black religious commentators.[47]

Worship within much that can be construed as Black Christianity takes its cue from the Bible. In John 8.12, Jesus states that 'I am the light of the World'.[48] It is not my intention to attempt any detailed examination of this statement. I want to look at this passage in the context of worship – that which lies at the heart of the churches' existence. Although Christians, both individually and corporately, are called to do many things, nothing is more important than loving God, with all of one's heart, soul, mind and strength (Matt. 22.37). The interconnectedness of this love (that is, it is more than a simple vertical relationship between the individual and God) is found in the following verse, where we are called to love our neighbour in the same way that we love ourselves (Matt. 22.38).

It can be argued that these two commandments of Jesus provide a foundational reason for the corporate, gathered presence of people to worship God. Such coming together is both vertical (with God) and horizontal (with one another). The limits of space prevent a detailed exploration of the roots of our Christian worship, or the biblical and theological justification for

---

47 Joe Aldred, 'The Holy Spirit and the Black Church', in Aldred and Ogbo (eds), *Black Church in the 21st Century*, pp. 45–62.

48 Michael Jagessar and Stephen Burns have sought to problematize and question the usefulness and the efficacy of juxtaposing terms of 'light' (as being good) and 'dark' as being bad, in their exploration of Christian worship from the context of postcolonial theory. See Michael N. Jagessar and Stephen Burns, 'Liturgical Studies and Christian Worship: The Postcolonial Challenge', *Black Theology* 5:1 (2007), pp. 39–62. Postcolonialism in its broader sense can be understood as a theory that 'is not about the demise of colonialism as "post" since it embodies both "after" and "beyond". It is not about historical chronologies, but more about a critical stance, oppositional tactic or subversive reading strategy.' See Michael N. Jagessar and Anthony G. Reddie (ed.), *Postcolonial Black British Theology: New Textures and Themes*, Peterborough: Epworth, 2007, p. xvi.

undertaking this habitual act (weekly at the very least). While there is not the space to undertake a detailed discussion, it seems important, nevertheless, that we at least begin to ask a most basic question: namely, what is worship for?

Black Theology seeks to bear witness to and offer testimony of a God that is revealed in Jesus Christ who enters into human history. The presence of Jesus, in the power of the Spirit, works within those who are seekers of truth, justice and peace attempting to live in solidarity one with another. Jesus seeks to be alongside those who need Jesus' presence the most.[49]

It is not uncommon that worship can become something of a battleground for the different wings of the Church as they attempt to parade their ecclesial hobby horses and vent their respective liturgical spleens. Worship can often appear to be more trouble than it is worth, so why should Black Theology be concerned with it? Despite its oftentimes problematic nature, I still want to locate this work within the framework of worship, because it represents the collective, spiritual domain in which many people experience a sense of cathartic freedom and liberation. Robert Beckford outlines some of the transformative power of Black Pentecostal worship in Britain. He believes there is power in this form of worship, particularly when it is allied to the wider cause of systemic liberation and individual transformation.[50]

Worship should be a crucial arena in which the work of Black Theology seeks to anchor itself for, if the Church is to do nothing else, it must worship God, in whose image we are created, through whom salvation (however that is understood) is possible and from whom all possibilities derive.

We come to worship because we are mandated to do so by a loving God who has created us in order that we can live life to its fullest in a covenantal relationship with God, in Christ, through the power of the Spirit.[51] Without wishing to become trapped in caricature and stereotypes, there is a broad coalition within the Church, from 'low' evangelicals to 'high' Catholics, who will argue, not only upon the primacy of worship but on the necessity of it also. This primary role of worship is that it foregrounds all other activities such as evangelism, social action, involvement in education etc. That is, worship is the inspiration and the source for all the subsequent action undertaken by the Church. At its best, authentic worship empowers us to be more effective in all the other things we are called to be and do in the name of Christ.

I want to assert the importance of worship, particularly that which empowers us to be an active, prophetic presence in a world in need of dramatic change. Creative and participative worship is that which inspires us to see

---

49 See Delroy A. Reid-Salmon, *Home away from Home: The Caribbean Diasporan Church in the Black Atlantic Tradition*, London: Equinox, 2008, pp. 88–91.

50 Beckford, *Dread and Pentecostal*, pp. 168–76.

51 See Jagessar and Reddie (eds), *Black Theology in Britain*, pp. 228–9.

God as active in the world, in solidarity with the oppressed and the marginalized. Worship that precludes those on the margins from bringing their authentic, bruised and battered selves into God's presence is that which fails to understand what God most desires.[52]

As a participative Black theologian I want to argue that transformative worship should be one of the key settings in which ordinary Black people are empowered in order that they can catch sight of a new vision of the future. This new vision is one in which God, in Christ, in the power of the Spirit, is inviting us all to participate.

Why transformative worship matters

Using the insights and central ideas of Black Theology in the everyday activities of ministry can help to transform worship and the lives and outlook of ordinary Black people in churches and in other communities of faith. Black Theology is of vital importance because it is the sacred reflection that emerges from the concrete life experiences of Black people of faith as they attempt to make sense of their continuing struggles and hardships in the world. The experiential-based nature of Black Theology, as we have seen previously, lies in the very essence of the discipline itself. Right from the outset of its development, Black Theology was attempting to be more than just intellectual conversation for its own sake. It represents a committed and rational response to the challenges of being a Black human being in a world run by White people with power for the benefit of others like themselves.[53]

Christians believe that they have been created by God. God has created all people. An important part of being human is the need to express oneself. People need to express emotions as they respond to the vicissitudes of life – to put it very simply, we all need to cry, laugh, dance, sing, connect with one another etc. This is all part of what it means to be human. Transformative

---

52 Black theologians have cited the prophetic literature within Scripture as 'proof texts' for the belief in a God who prefers praxis (reflective and prayerful action) and whose essential being is revealed in the desire to liberate all people as opposed to rigid conformity to religious norms, official teaching and empty piety. Such themes can be found in the following: (1) Acts 17.26; Gen. 1.27–8; 3.4; Rom. 3.9–21. (2) A God who acts for justice – Ps. 76.7–9; Gen. 4.9–12; Ex. 3.7–11.20; 14.8. (3) Christ died to free all creation – Rom. 8.21; 8.19–22; John 3.16; Matt. 25; Luke 4.18–19. (4) Christ died to create a single humanity – Eph. 2.11–12; Matt. 12.48–50; 1 Pet. 2.9–10; Gal. 3.26–9; Eph. 2.11–16; Col. 3. (5) The Kingdom of God is . . . Justice – Rom. 14.17; Matt. 7.15–24; Eph. 6.10; John 3.18; James 2.1–13; 5.1–6; Isa. 1.15–16; Amos 5.21–24. (6) The future Kingdom – Heb. 11.13–16; Matt. 5. 6, 10; Rev. 7.9; 21.1; Acts 10.34–35; Rev. 7.15–17; 2.3–4.

53 See Hopkins, *Heart and Head*, pp. 127–54.

worship is a means of enabling people to respond to the most basic of impulses in terms of what it means to be a human being.

A number of writers have argued that an important part of being human is the need to worship. There is a need to give thanks – to mark moments of celebration and expression in order to respond to events, circumstances or situations that have meant a great deal to us. Oftentimes, worship contains important 'rites of passage' moments when human beings mark special events in the collective and corporate life of communities, such as births, baptisms, coming of age, weddings, deaths and so on. Black Theology has often sought to identify rites of passage as recognition of the communion with God and humans within a specific ritualized moment of encounter.[54] Humans often express the need and the desire to respond to events and situations in which they have been moved. I am sure we can all think back to some of the events that moved us and forced us to connect with something or someone beyond ourselves.

Often, how people react to the sense that there is something larger and beyond us is itself a form of worship. In the Bible, there are many stories and events when people respond to situations and experiences in particular ways. Often, people have made a particular response to their immediate circumstances and context because they have felt God is close at hand. God may have intervened directly in the lives of these people, and one of the ways in which they have reacted and responded is by worshipping God. Many Black theologians point to the celebratory aspects of Black spirituality as evidence of the transformative power of Black celebration in the light of our gratitude for God's goodness and providence.[55]

Worship can be described as showing our love, loyalty, enthusiasm, thankfulness, commitment and our whole selves (or whole being) to God. Humans offer all that they have to and in recognition that without God we would not exist. God is worthy of our total love, respect, devotion and commitment. God has created us to react and respond in love to God in recognition of the love that God has shown us, in and through the life of Jesus Christ. In biblical terms one can cite a number of texts in which the challenge to respond to the presence of the 'Other' in our midst is palpable. For example, in Luke 1.26–55 (particularly, vv. 46–55) Mary the mother of Jesus is given a dramatic, life-changing piece of news.

In moments when the presence of the 'Other' confronts us with knowledge of that which is beyond us, then the individuals or peoples concerned

---

54 See Marjorie Lewis-Cooper, 'Some Jamaican Rites of Passages: Reflections for the Twenty-First Century', *Black Theology in Britain* 6 (2001), pp. 53–71.

55 See Larry Murphy, 'Piety and Liberation: A Historical Exploration of African American Religion and Social Justice', in Iva E. Carruthers, Frederick D. Haynes III and Jeremiah A. Wright Jr (eds), *Blow the Trumpet in Zion: Global Vision and Action for the 21st Century Black Church*, Minneapolis: Fortress, 2005, pp. 35–58.

are forced to respond and act – indifference is not an option. If one considers the experience of Mary the mother of Jesus, for example, one can imagine the sense in which this event has a transformative impact upon her life from that moment onwards. Her life is literally changed forever. Her emotional response to the presence of the 'Other' finds expression in the *Magnificat* in Luke 1.46–56.

One can see similar biblical expressions of spiritually charged reactions to the 'Other' in our midst, if one considers the language of the psalmists. These ancient poetic texts express the thoughts and feelings of the authors about significant moments and events in their individual lives or the communal life of their people. The contexts in which the psalms are written vary greatly in circumstance. Many of the psalms express a wide range of emotions and perspectives. These pieces contain a number of approaches. They all address God in a variety of ways. Some are hymns of praise, and would originally have been sung. Others are prayers, pleading for God's help. Some are prayers thanking God. Some are written to express great confidence in God and what God will do for the writer. Still others are dramatic denunciations of God, as the writer seeks to make sense of God's apparent absence from their life.

The psalms offer us a window into the mind of the ancient followers of God in the Jewish tradition, demonstrating how people have approached and responded to God for a whole number of reasons and in a variety of ways. Crucially, not all the psalms are happy or joyous accounts of human responses to the 'Living God'.

In the context of transformative worship as a source for liberative praxis, it is of crucial importance that we remember it is not mandatory to be happy when worshipping God. Worship should not be an environment in which people are made to feel guilty if they have feelings of hurt or have extreme emotions of profound sadness or a sense of brokenness and feel unable to 'celebrate'.

In a previous work, I argue that part of my concern for particular models of charismatic Christianity is that they have lost the important spiritual facet of lament, when confronted with situations of unremitting pain and suffering.[56] James Cone in his early work juxtaposed the tensions between the Saturday night experience of the blues with the Sunday morning lament of the spirituals. He argued that these idioms in the African American religio-cultural landscape were differing dimensions of the same unitary Black experience and were not in opposition. Rather, they were two sides of the same coin.[57]

I am sure there are many ordinary Black people who will have experienced that sharp sense of embarrassment when they have felt beleaguered

---

56 See Anthony G. Reddie, *Re-Imaging Black Theology in the 21st Century*, London, Equinox, 2008, pp. 175–7.

57 See Cone, *The Spirituals and the Blues*.

and dispirited and have become estranged from the wider worshipping community because others could not handle their palpable sense of pain and
brokenness! On such occasions, worship can be anything but transformative or liberating. Spirituality and worship should be about bringing people
into the very heart of God's presence in which they are confronted with the
raw emotions and the realness of the world. It should not become a hasty
retreat from the numbing pain of reality that confronts many people. Black
Theology has always been concerned with enabling Black people to claim
full life within history as opposed to an escape into eternity before many of
us have even died![58]

In the psalms, we see that people have come to God and in doing so have
expressed all their frustrations and disappointments with God. It is my belief that the psalms offer us a rich menu of emotional expression in order to
highlight the wide and differing contexts in which humankind has sought to
establish communion with God as a response to the most basic and foundational of human concerns.

If we respond to God in worship through the vast panoply of human
expression, then what can we say of God's response in return? An insight
into the response of God to human pain and suffering, and to the passionate
and strident human encounter with God, can be seen in the book of Job. In
this book, we see how Job, a very influential and important man, is brought
low, losing everything he has except for his life. At one point Job even begins to express his rage at God. Through looking at Job and at the Psalms,
which come immediately after the book of Job, we are shown a great many
examples of how people have responded to God. For many ordinary Black
people these texts have become exemplars for how people across the ages
have expressed their loyalty, commitment, anger, frustration, joy, happi-
ness and many other emotions to God. People have expressed these differing ranges of emotion in recognition that God is worth all that they have,
and that same God who created us knows that we have been created, and
indeed have a fundamental need to respond. If we look at Mary the mother
of Jesus, or look to the plight of Job, or examine the psalms, or the writings
in Lamentations and the Song of Songs, we are shown the many different
ways in which people have sought to give God a sense of worth, by bringing their whole selves to God – to worship God. God can be worshipped in
a transformative manner through songs, prayer, meditation, through our

---

58 This issue is addressed extensively in *Black Theology* (http://www.equinoxjour
nals.com/ojs/index.php/BT) by Michael Jagessar. Jagessar's doctoral work addresses the
theological legacy of Philip Potter, the first Black General Secretary of the World Council
of Churches. The central theme in Potter's theology is the notion of 'Full Life for All'. See
Michael N. Jagessar, *Full Life for All: The Work and Theology of Philip A. Potter – a
Historical Survey and Systematic Analysis of Major Themes*, Zoetermeer: Boekencentrum, 1997.

actions, our commitment to justice, even through our silence, and even in the act of being still.

Expressing one's utmost to God in the context of transformative worship should command one's entire self. Whether people are in moments of exhilarating joy or in the depth of despair, God receives our all with grace and loving kindness. Whether in anger or in joy, when we are in the context of transformative worship, the power of one's connectedness to one another and to God's very own self should be of profound significance that opens up opportunities for people to bring their whole selves before God. When we look at the Psalms or at other sections of the Bible where people are responding to God, we rarely if ever see indifference or an absence of feeling. Transformative worship should create within us a need to respond to God in a sense of passion. God is not a supine and passionless being who demands our quiet acquiescence and emotionally repressed conformity.

I believe that creative attempts to see worship as the grounding and inspired source for liberative praxis in the Black Theology tradition can provide the practical framework for the Black liberation struggle. For Black Theology to succeed as a mass movement in the Church it must harness the emotive power of Black worship as a means of engaging with the passionate intent and anger of ordinary Black people who are trying to find a way of surviving. The work of the Trinity United Church of Christ, in Chicago, is an important example in this regard. The former pastor Jeremiah Wright has sought to build and develop the church along the lines of the principles and ethics found in Black Theology.[59] Speaking on the relationship of Black Theology, spirituality and worship, Wright states:

> For twenty years, we have had a Black Liberation Workshop once a month at the church . . . In spite of all the negatives, however, we still have had (and continue to have) our share of successes. One example is our Rites of Passage Programs – *Isuthu* for African American males and *Intonjane* for African American females. Another is our *Umojo Karamu* service which is now packed like an Easter Sunday service or a Freddy Hayes's revival where the sanctuary is standing room only.[60]

What Wright attempted to do at Trinity United Church of Christ was to capture the raw intensity of Black struggle and to link that with the power of the Spirit. This work has been undertaken in order that ordinary Black people can be enabled to reinterpret their lived experiences and reality; in effect, to be inspired, to tell a new story! Worship and the engagement with

---

59 See Jeremiah A. Wright Jr, 'Doing Black Theology in the Black Church', in Linda E. Thomas (ed.), *Living Stones in the Household of God: The Legacy and Future of Black Theology*, Minneapolis: Fortress, 2004, pp. 13–23.

60 Wright, 'Doing Black Theology in the Black Church', p. 21.

African cultures and practices is one way in which worship can harness the movement of the Spirit in order to energize ordinary Black people for the Black liberation struggle. Transformative worship that is informed by the Spirit of Liberation can enable the Church to catch sight of the social challenges and concerns of the wider society, to which it needs to respond, in the belief that God is already at work in these contested environments.

One can see something of the passionate presence of the Living God revealed in Jesus Christ in the early writings of Black theologians in 1960s' America. These authors sought to align their work with the liberative presence of the Divine in their midst. In this context, Black theologians sought to respond to the militant thrust from Black America for 'Black Power' and an end to White, Christian ethnocentric-inspired racism.[61] The passion of early Black Theology advocates as they sought to respond to the transformative spirit of God in their midst can be seen in the following quotation from Vincent Harding who, writing on the need to repudiate a White supremacist Christ, states:

> For a growing edge of bold young black people all that is past. They fling out their declaration: 'No White Christ shall shame us again. We are glad to be black. We rejoice in the darkness of our skin, we celebrate the natural texture of our hair, we extol the rhythm and vigor of our songs and shouts and dances. And if your American Christ doesn't like that, you know what you can do with him.'[62]

In terms of engaging with the Spirit of Liberation, Black Theology must not forget to look to the Bible in order to remember the different ways in which people have responded to God. The plethora of ways in which people give themselves to God is often reflective of their commitment to God who is worthy of worship. That commitment to engage with God, in Spirit-filled ways, arises from the very passion and desire of Godself to engage with human beings, particularly those who are marginalized and oppressed.

In effect, worship should be transformative and expressive of all that Black people are and can and should be within the presence of God and others. It should never be the case that one is 'forced' to pretend to be something one is not while in the context of worship. One should never have to simply 'go along with the flow' in worship, whether in church or in any other communitarian setting. I do not believe that we need to be afraid to be passionate and committed when engaged in worshipping God.

Transformative worship should provide the means by which ordinary Black people are enabled to respond to the emotive force of the Spirit.

---

61 See Wilmore and Cone (eds), *Black Theology*, pp. 15–134.

62 Vincent Harding, 'Black Power and the American Christ'. See also Wilmore and Cone (eds), *Black Theology*, p. 37.

Through seeing worship as the Spirit-filled response to a liberative God, ordinary Black people can be enabled to connect the social and political with the religious and the spiritual. The convergence of the personal and collective, of which Beckford speaks, can be achieved through the context of weekly worship in the church.

Transformative worship, in which the frameworks of dramatic change are re-hearsed on a habitual basis, through reading the Bible, through bread and wine, through the collective singing of the faith, through prayer and testimony, is one that seeks to connect us with the force of the Living God. Black Theology seeks to bear witness to the God who is alive and who loves suffering humankind with a fierce passion. This fierce love of God challenges ordinary Black people to express that same love in their ongoing commitment to serve others. The link between the Spirit and faithful action for change lies in Jesus' solidarity with ordinary people by means of his life and the challenge of the cross. The Spirit of Liberation is one that enables ordinary people to feel committed to following Jesus in according respect and dignity to all those who are the 'least of these' (Matt. 25.31–46).[63] The fusing of the dynamics of transformative change within the context of worship is one that can create the space for the authentic expression of the Black self – a self so often troubled and assaulted by a world in which, often, Black flesh simply does not matter.

The transformative worship of which I speak is fuelled to my mind by the passionate energy of Black Theology. This practical model of Black Theology is one that seeks to give expression and commitment to bringing one's radical, real self before God and not the polite conformist versions often demanded by the paternalistic and passionless models, bequeathed to Black people by imperial, mission theology.[64] In this respect, I am clear that God is not colour blind. God is not blind to the material realities of struggle and marginalization that afflict the bulk of Black peoples across the world.[65]

To follow the framework of Black Theology as the key to reinterpreting the meaning of the Christian faith is to commit oneself to a passionate, no-holds-barred decision to follow the way of the radical Christ. This radical Christ is one who stands against all forms of complacency, self-satisfaction, corporate greed and vested self-interest.[66]

It can be argued that in its attempt to offer a radical, politicized agenda for transformative change, Black Theology has not always offered sufficient

---

63   This phrase is used extensively by the Womanist theologian Jacquelyn Grant, who argues that Jesus is in solidarity with the 'least of these'. See Jacquelyn Grant, *White Women's Christ and Black Women's Jesus: Feminist Christology and Womanist Response*, Atlanta, GA: Scholar's Press, 1989, pp. 216–18.

64   James Cone argues against the notion of a passionless, neutral and indifferent God in one of his classic early texts. See Cone, *Black Theology of Liberation*, pp. 1–20.

65   See Anthony G. Reddie, *Is God Colour Blind? Insights from Black Theology for Christian Ministry*, London: SPCK, 2009.

66   Cone, *Black Theology of Liberation*, pp. 17–20.

resources for enabling ordinary Black people to live this out. It has not provided sufficient resources to indicate how this prophetic movement could
be harnessed within the realities of their lived experiences. In this chapter, I
have sought to demonstrate that Black Theology must engage in a renewed
understanding of the Holy Spirit, the Spirit of Liberation and Justice.[67] As
we have seen, there are reasons for the under-explored relationship of the
Spirit, within Black Theology. I believe also that there remains an ongoing
synergy within the lives of ordinary Black people that can be harnessed
within the context of worship in order that the radical intent of this movement can be activated.

Questions

1. Do you think some of the suspicions Black Theology has developed in
   response to the Holy Spirit/Spirit of Liberation are justified? If yes,
   then why, and if not, then why not?
2. Does Black Theology need spirituality in order to become a grass-roots
   movement that harnesses the creative energy of ordinary Black people? If yes, then why, and if not, then why not?
3. In this chapter, I have moved interchangeably between traditional
   terms like 'the Holy Spirit', 'the Spirit' and 'the Spirit of Liberation'.
   Do you see these terms as interchangeable and so denoting the same
   thing, or are they different? Does it matter?
4. On a scale of 1–20, where 1 represents extreme individualism and 20
   extreme collective activity, where do you place your spirituality and
   why? (You cannot choose any number between 9 and 12, to stop people
   simply going for the middle numbers!)

---

67 See Hopkins, *Heart and Head*, pp. 77–90.

6

Black Theology and Social Analysis

In this chapter, I want to look at the ways in which Black Theology has sought to provide a public role for analysing society and a critical perspective on the continued oppression of marginalized, poor people in any given setting. As we have seen from previous chapters, Black Theology is essentially a socially related movement that seeks to articulate the reality of Black struggle and oppression. It is not overly concerned with abstract theorizing for its own sake, especially if this is divorced from the daily struggles of ordinary, poor Black people. This is not to say that Black Theology has necessarily fulfilled this role adequately, but it is important that *the reason it exists is to undertake this task.*

I want to reflect on an extended activity that serves as a metaphor in helping us understand why Black Theology has attempted to provide critical, interpretive tools to find out why particular groups of people are oppressed. In terms of identifying groups of people who are oppressed, the principle gaze has been directed to ordinary, poor people of African descent. Within this large and sometimes amorphous group, there are subgroups, which include women, LGBT communities, disabled people and children, all of whom are treated less favourably than many others. This work is important, because all knowledge is contested and represents some vested interest in and perspective on the world, and religion is no different. Black Theology has always contained a twin focus in its critical opposition to all forms of social control that seek to limit the independence and freedom of human beings. One focus has been the need to challenge the broader society in which any religious tradition and social institutions that are linked exist. All religion has a social basis to it.

Right from the outset, when Black church leaders in the USA were issuing the rallying call for the need for Black Theology in the mid 1960s, they were responding to what were social conditions of the time.[1] To quote from the preamble to the historic statement issued by the National Committee of Negro Churchmen, it reads:

---

[1] See 'Black Power: Statement by the National Committee of Negro Churchmen, July 31, 1966', in Gayraud S. Wilmore and James H. Cone (eds), *Black Theology: A Documentary History, 1966–1979*, Maryknoll, NY: Orbis, 1979, pp. 23–30.

We, an informal group of Negro churchmen in America, are deeply disturbed about the crisis brought upon our country by historic distortions of important human realities in the controversy about 'black power'. What we see shining through the variety of rhetoric is not anything new but the same old problem of power and race which has faced our beloved country since 1619.[2]

Similarly, in the British situation, Clarice Nelson outlines the social context in which Black Theology was birthed and articulates the (then) contextual challenges to which this movement had to respond.[3] One can cite similar reflections in the Caribbean[4] and South Africa,[5] for example. In short, Black Theology emerged as a response to pressing socio-political issues that were impacting on Black people. In terms of the last context, South Africa, it is worth noting the words of Louise Kretzschmar who, in writing about the broader socio-political context of South Africa, states:

As already indicated, black South African Christians have long been interested in the Africanisation of Christianity, and in its application to the realities of their socio-economic and political existence. Concern for Africanisation, Black Consciousness and Liberation thus all occur in South Africa. But before Black Consciousness and Liberation are examined, it is necessary to discuss the African Independent Churches, since they are a good example of the practical workings of Africanisation, and they also reflect a degree of socio-political consciousness.[6]

But the second focus of Black Theology is equally important, namely, its critique of organized religion, particularly Christianity. We have seen how a particular version of Christianity, slave-holding Christianity,[7] functioned as

---

2 'Black Power: Statement', p. 23.

3 See Clarice Tracey Nelson, 'The Churches, Racism and the Inner-Cities', in Raj Patel and Paul Grant (eds), *A Time to Speak: Perspectives of Black Christians in Britain*, Birmingham: A joint publication of Racial Justice and the Black Theology Working Group, CCRU/ECRJ, 1990, pp. 3–10.

4 See Noel L. Erskine, *Decolonizing Theology: A Caribbean Perspective*, Maryknoll, NY: Orbis, 1981, pp. 2–26. See also George Mulrain, 'The Caribbean', in John Parratt (ed.), *An Introduction to Third World Theologies*, Cambridge: Cambridge University Press, 2004, pp. 163–81.

5 See Allan A. Boesak, *Farewell to Innocence: A Soci-Ethical Study on Black Theology and Black Power*, Maryknoll, NY: Orbis, 1977, pp. 9–45.

6 Louise Kretzschmar, *The Voice of Black Theology in South Africa*, Johannesburg: Raven Press, 1986, p. 39.

7 For an excellent dissection of the basic tenets of the form of Christianity practised by the slave-holding planter class of the Americas, see Albert J. Raboteau, *Slave Religion: The 'Invisible Institution' in the Antebellum South*, Oxford and New York: Oxford

the overarching framework that colluded with Black oppression and was the beneficiary of European colonialism.[8] James Cone argues that the underlying meaning of the Christian faith is one of liberation for those who are oppressed.[9] Cone sees Christianity as a socially situated phenomenon, in which God is an agent and driver for transformation of the poor and the oppressed, within history.[10]

The internal critique of the meaning and intent of Christian theology lies in the attention it has given to issues pertaining to racism and White supremacy.[11] The evasion of White Euro-American Christian theology to acknowledge the assumptions of its perceived normality and universality has been remarked upon by other Black theologians.[12]

The relationship between empire and colonialism in many respects remains the unacknowledged 'elephant in the room'. Empire and colonialism found much of its intellectual underscoring on the basis of White, Eurocentric supremacy, which marked the clear divide between notions of civilized and acceptable against uncivilized and transgressive. There are no prizes for guessing on which side of the divide Black people found themselves relegated. Robert Beckford remarks on the unacknowledged weight of invisible Whiteness and its damnable offspring, White supremacy:

I would say that theology is the last bastion of White supremacy in Britain. Most disciplines have woken up to the need to engage with critical theory. They've engaged with diversity at the core, thinking more critically and constructively about how they shape things. Sociology students here at Goldsmith's take courses in 'critical Whiteness'. In theology circles they'd think you were dealing with table cloths they have at different times of the year![13]

University Press, 1978, pp. 95–150; Dwight N. Hopkins, *Down, Up and Over: Slave Religion and Black Theology*, Minneapolis: Fortress, 2000, pp. 13–49.

8 See R. S. Sugirtharajah, *Postcolonial Reconfigurations: An Alternative Way of Reading the Bible and Doing Theology*, London: SCM, 2003, pp. 143–61.

9 See James H. Cone, *A Black Theology of Liberation*, Maryknoll, NY: Orbis, 1990 [1970], pp. 1–20.

10 James H. Cone, *God of the Oppressed*, New York: Seabury, 1975, pp. 39–83.

11 See James H. Cone, 'Theology's Great Sin: Silence in the Face of White Supremacy', *Black Theology* 2:2 (2004), pp. 139–52. See also James H. Cone, *The Cross and the Lynching Tree*, Maryknoll, NY: Orbis, 2011.

12 See Michael N. Jagessar and Anthony G. Reddie (eds.), *Postcolonial Black British Theology: New Textures and Themes*, Peterborough: Epworth, 2007, pp. xi–xxiv. See also Dwight N. Hopkins, *Being Human: Race, Culture and Religion*, Minneapolis: Fortress, 2005, pp. 13–35.

13 Interview with Robert Beckford in *Reform* (June 2010), p. 12.

There are relatively few texts written by White British authors seeking to explore the relationship between empire, colonialism, Whiteness and racism.[14] The almost complete absence of literature pertaining to the collusion between imperial mission Christianity and Black people of faith remains one of the significant challenges facing Black and Asian theologians in the British context.

So Black Theology has always sought to hold in tension these twin aims. Namely, critiquing the social conditions and contexts in which Black life is lived, and the issues that impinge and prevent human flourishing, alongside the desire to critique the meaning and intent of Christianity as the 'religion of empire'.[15] This chapter offers some reflections on the way in which Black Theology attempts to accomplish this task, by means of an extended reflection on an enacted exercise. This serves as a popular educational metaphor for empowering ordinary Black people.

Exercise: 'Who are the poor in the world and why?'

For this exercise every participant should be given a copy of the diagram below. In the diagram, *Person 1* is in the crouched position and has the least amount of power. They are looked down upon. In fact you cannot even see their face. *Person 2* is in the rising position, beginning to climb to their full height. This person is better off than *Person 1*. *Person 3* is standing tall with arms aloft. This person is in the best position of all three. The participants have to decide who are the people in the diagram.

To guide them, individuals should consider the following in the first instance:

Who is *more likely* to be *Person 1* in terms of being:

- male or female
- White-European-American or a person belonging to an Afro-Asiatic or Hispanic community

---

14 To the best of my knowledge these texts include Kenneth Leech, *Struggle in Babylon*, London: Sheldon Press, 1988, and *Race: Changing Society and the Churches*, London: SPCK, 2005; David Haslam, *Race for the Millennium: A Challenge to Church and Society*, London: Church House for the Churches' Commission on Racial Justice (CCRJ), 1996, and *The Churches and 'Race': A Pastoral Approach*, Cambridge: Grove, 2001; John L. Wilkinson, *Church in Black and White: The Black Christian Tradition in 'Mainstream' Churches in England: A White Response and Testimony*, Edinburgh: St Andrew Press, 1993; Timothy J. Gorringe, *Furthering Humanity: A Theology of Culture*, Aldershot: Ashgate, 2004. In the American context, see James W. Perkinson, *White Theology: Outing Supremacy in Modernity*, New York: Palgrave Macmillan, 2004, and *Shamanism, Racism and Hip-Hop Culture: Essays on White Supremacy and Black Subversion*, New York: Palgrave Macmillan, 2005. See also Laurie M. Cassidy and Alex Mikilich (eds), *Interrupting White Privilege: Catholic Theologians Break the Silence*, Maryknoll, NY: Orbis, 2007.

15 See R. S. Sugirtharajah, *The Bible and Empire: Postcolonial Considerations*, Cambridge and New York: Cambridge University Press, 2005.

- From the Global North or the South
- formally educated or not formally educated
- able-bodied or disabled
- heterosexual or lesbian–gay–bisexual–transgendered
- Christian or someone belonging to another world faith?

Jenue Morrison

Black Theology reflections

The aim of the exercise is to see how the various participants ascribe value and recognize power among differing groups of people in society. In the exercise the group quickly have to engage with their inherent prejudices as they seek to 'interpret' the three figures for meaning and then apply these perspectives to the 'types' of individuals on the list.

In the first instance the various participants have to wrestle with their basic conflict between what they would like to believe is true and what 'may' appear to be the reality. I have inserted the word 'may', for, as we will see, what human beings assume to be fact is often an illusion, born of inbuilt prejudices and false information or data.

Many of the groups with whom I have worked have argued vociferously about the *Person 1* in the crouched position. When asked to decide between this person being 'White' or a 'Black' or 'Asian' or 'Hispanic' person, groups tend to be divided between those who want to see things in more idealistic or less politicized ways and those who take the contrary view.

For those who see it in terms of the former they often point to the reality of the world. They will concede that 'in theory' it is perfectly possible for the person in the crouched position *not* to be a person of colour. Yet, when one looks at the indices in most western societies, they will clearly demonstrate that those at the bottom of the socio-economic ladder are people who come from such marginalized and disadvantaged backgrounds.[16]

Conversely, when asked to reflect on *Person 3*, the polarities of the conversation were very much reversed. By this, I mean that for some there was the strong belief that this person *could* be a Black person or someone from a non-European background. For others, however, while not denying this possibility (or even desirability), it was also clear that, given the ways in which political, economic and cultural systems operate, it was most unlikely. The challenge for participants was to come to some kind of understanding of their 'gut reactions'. Why did some feel that these figures could and perhaps should be interpreted in racialized and gendered ways? (Interesting to note that most participants see *Person 1* as most likely to be a Black, African woman and *Person 3* most likely to be White American man.)

The challenge for all the participants was not simply to try and decide on the identity of each of the figures but, more importantly, to deduce how and for what reasons they are in that specific position. As we will see, Black Theology has long been adept at looking beyond the obvious conclusions

---

16 For the purposes of this chapter we are going ignore *Person 2*, until the final part of the chapter when we will look more closely at global economics and what might constitute the 'development' and growth of *Person 2* from the crouching position of *Person 1* to the triumphant position of *Person 3*.

for why societies are structured in particular ways, and their resultant impact upon people.

In the exercise, those who have been conscientized by Black Theology from the previous activities that have been described in this book have been able to critique the assumptions we might employ when seeking to interpret the three figures for meaning and truth. It is often assumed that the essential difference between *Person 1* and *Person 3* is one of entitlement. Namely, issues of poverty and economic struggle that are likely to be the contextual experience of *Person 3* are linked to 'her' inherent laziness or lack of character or moral fibre.[17]

In a previous chapter we looked at how Black Theology incorporates an inherent 'hermeneutic of suspicion' in questioning how knowledge and truth are constructed and for whose purposes. An excellent example of this can be seen in Emilie Townes's analysis of the work of the media in shaping our perceptions of what is understood as truth.[18] Of particular importance for the purpose of this introductory text is Townes's analysis of the ways in which the media (which represents the systemic, covert cultural production of evil) subverts particular narratives, while propagating myths, half-truths and distortions, in order to portray very biased and pointed notions of convenient 'truths'.[19] Townes writes: 'Exploring evil as a cultural production highlights the systematic construction of truncated narratives designed to support and perpetuate structural inequalities and forms of social oppression.'[20]

Black Theology has been concerned to offer critical forms of analysis that challenge the biased assumptions for why *Person 1* and *Person 3* are in their relative positions. It has been interesting to note the occasions when those participating in the exercise have offered theological reasons for the relative positions of the three characters. Some have speculated on whether notions of God's blessing and choice have determined why one person appears triumphant and powerful and the other not. Black Theology does not hold to the view that God is in the business of offering blessing and gifts upon one set of humanity at the expense of another.[21]

The question of whether the respective figures deserve to be in their respective positions is often one that consumes the thoughts of people who have participated in the exercise. This point is a variation on the previous

---

17 Interestingly one often hears participants make these kinds of assumptions about the person in the crouched position. This is based on no evidence and is a response to the ways in which the media often portray economically poor people.

18 See Emilie M. Townes, *Womanist Ethics and the Cultural Production of Evil*, New York: Palgrave Macmillan, 2006.

19 Townes, *Womanist Ethics*, pp. 11–55.

20 Townes, *Womanist Ethics*, p. 4.

21 See Anthony G. Reddie, *Working against the Grain: Re-Imaging Black Theology in the 21st Century*, London: Equinox, 2008, pp. 172–5.

concern, namely, has God blessed and cursed some people, which explains why they are in either *Person 1* or *Person 3*. One can observe the comments and reflections of conservative evangelical commentators who put forward the belief that poor nations, such as Haiti, for example, remain so because of the 'unholy' alliances they have made with 'non-Christian' spirits and deities.[22] These arguments are ones that seek to ignore material structural and systemic causes of poverty, which emanate from within history, in favour of spiritual and theological reasons whose causes are linked to divine punishment, which come from beyond history.

Black Theology has always been concerned to provide sharp analyses for explaining 'who are the poor and why'. It has recognized that quite often the spiritualized reasons offered for the relative success and failure of the different people in the picture are nothing but a smokescreen for disguising the callous and greedy forces of western capitalism. The latter has always benefited from the material poverty of the Black majority of the world. The demonization of particular groups of people, most often Black people of the African continent, is often undertaken on the basis of seeking to mask the intent of global capitalism that exploits the natural resources of Africa, for example, while condemning Africans for being lazy and corrupt.[23]

In terms of the latter, some Black theologians have used the insights of social forms of analysis in order to scrutinize western capitalism and the overall profit motive that diminishes the basic humanity of poor people.[24] The poor are the pawns in such industrialized and mechanized processes because they do not have an inherent stake in the ongoing production for which their labour is an essential source. In more recent times, African theologians are seeking to develop a more culturally orientated approach of African Theology (which is often seen as the natural inheritor of Black Theology),[25] as they have sought to analyse the ways in which the era of colonialization sowed the seeds for Africa's present malaise. Jonathan Gichaara, for example, is critical of the 'civilizing' role played by Christianity and the missionaries in seeking to displace traditional notions of African culture and its accompanying religious heritage in order to impose a western form of Christian hegemony upon the continent.[26] Gichaara states:

---

22 See Ronald Charles, 'Interpreting the Book of Revelation in the Haitian Context', *Black Theology* 9:2 (2011), pp. 177–98.

23 See Munyaradzi Feliz Murove, 'Perceptions of Greed in Western Economic and Religious Traditions: An African Communitarian Response', *Black Theology* 5:2 (2007), pp. 220–43.

24 See Itumeleng J. Mosala, *Biblical Hermeneutics and Black Theology in South Africa*, Grand Rapids, MI: Eerdmans, 1989; Itumeleng J. Mosala and Buti Tlhagale (eds), *The Unquestionable Right to Be Free: Black Theology from South Africa*, Maryknoll, NY: Orbis, 1986.

25 See Mokgethi Mothlabi, *African Theology/Black Theology in South Africa: Looking Back, Moving On*, Pretoria: University of South Africa Press, 2008, pp. 42–9.

26 See Jonathan Gichaara, 'Issues in African Liberation Theology', *Black Theology* 3:1 (2005), pp. 75–85.

African theology of liberation is called, daily, to reflect on the fact that Africa's poverty and the concomitant powerlessness are not just 'home-grown'. There are international players whose actions are more subtle than the local immediate agents of poverty, human degradation and squalor. Whereas neo-colonialism replaced the departing colonial powers in the grand scheme of exploiting Africa's raw material and human resources, globalization is the 'new kid on the block' in this economic power game.[27]

Lewin Williams, who was one of the leading Caribbean theologians, like Gichaara, has adopted a socio-political form of analysis to assess the ways in which the 'missionary Christianity' of the European colonial powers sought to create passivity and inertia in the minds of Caribbean peoples.[28] Caribbean theology, as a theology of liberation, has found it necessary to critique the relationship between the status-quo tendencies of the Church and the accompanying reactionary politics that seek to control the destiny of the poor. Lewin states:

> In contemporary times the affinity between right wing politics and the conservative church is highly suggestive of the perfect grasp of the idea in the rough and tumble of the political arena. As long as humanity can be successfully steered towards the portals of heaven it becomes so pre-occupied with the heavenly demands that it looks away from the human condition of here and now.[29]

It is interesting to note the ways in which African American Black and Womanist theologians have analysed the experiences of Black people living in the richest and most powerful country in the world. For example, when a range of seemingly simplistic and biased/racialized perspectives were offered seeking to explain the catastrophe of Hurricane Katrina and the resulting devastation of New Orleans, Black and Womanist theologians provided alternative perspectives to those which emanated from the mainstream news media.[30] Diana L. Hayes, in her analysis of the disaster, writes:

> The events that transpired in New Orleans should not have come as a surprise to anyone; it had long been predicted but at the same time ignored. Efforts by parishes (counties) and the Corps of Engineers to rebuild, shore up, or in other ways strengthen and stabilize the levee system protecting the city has been underfunded for years, coincidentally the years of the

---

27 Gichaara, 'Issues in African Liberation Theology', p. 81.
28 Lewin L. Williams, *Caribbean Theology*, New York: Peter Lang, 1994, pp. 31–53.
29 Williams, *Caribbean Theology*, p. 45.
30 See Cheryl A. Kirk-Duggan (ed.), *The Sky Is Crying: Race, Class and Natural Disaster*, Nashville, TN: Abingdon, 2006.

Bush administration and the wars in Iraq and Afghanistan. Local politicians even admitted, as did New Orleans Times-Picayune, that over several years, from 2001 to 2005, funds intended for the city's protection had been cut and redirected to these wars as well as to supporting the tax cuts and other gifts to the wealthy that the heavily Republican Congress supported.[31]

Hayes's analysis of the causes of the Katrina disaster and its disproportionately negative impact on poor Black women brings to mind some of the reflections of the participants in the exercise at the beginning of this chapter. When reflecting on the three figures in the picture, for many, *Person 1* was most representative of Black women. It was noted on several occasions that Black women are often at the bottom of the socio-economic ladder in many societies and that they bear the brunt of the hardship in trying to keep families together in times of national emergency and economic disasters.[32]

In this chapter, we have been concerned with Black Theology's commitment to analysing the underlying reasons for why disproportionate numbers of Black people in the world are poor. The use of the opening exercise is intended to act as a metaphor for enabling ordinary Black people to begin to think critically on what might be the underlying reasons for particular groups of people being represented as *Person 1* or *Person 3*.

As we have seen, Black religious scholars have analysed the underlying reasons that give rise to particular groups of people being located at the bottom of the socio-economic ladder. Black Theology rejects pseudo-spiritual reasons (like being cursed by God)[33] for Black marginalization,

---

31 Diana L. Hayes, 'We, Too, Are America: Black Women's Burden of Race and Class', in Kirk-Duggan (ed.), *The Sky Is Crying*, pp. 69–79 (72).

32 See Isabel Apawo Phiri and Sarojini Nadar (eds), *African Women, Religion and Health: Essays in Honor of Mercy Amba Ewudziwa Oduyoye*, Maryknoll, NY: Orbis, 2006. See also Mercy Amba Oduyoye, *Beads and Strands: Reflections of an African Woman on Christianity*, Maryknoll, NY: Orbis, 2004; Elizabeth Amoah, '"Poverty is madness": Some Insights from Traditional African Spirituality and Mental Health', in Dwight N. Hopkins and Marjorie Lewis (eds), *Another World Is Possible: Spiritualities and Religions of Global Darker Peoples*, Oakwood and London: Equinox, 2009, pp. 207–18.

33 One of the enduring and persistent myths regarding Black people's poor representation in socio-economic statistics across the world has been the notion of them being cursed. The 'Curse of Ham' is drawn from the Genesis account of Noah's interactions with his sons, one of whom (Ham) is believed to have seen him naked and is cursed (Gen. 9.18–25). This text is often cited as the underlying reason for Black suffering. The 'cursed' Ham is seen as the progenitor for all Black people of African descent. Similarly, 'the Mark of Cain', drawn from Gen. 4.8–16, is also seen as a foundational 'proof text' to explain Black poverty and oppression, as the 'mark' on Cain, which results from his expulsion from human society for killing his brother Abel is believed to be the 'curse' of Black skin. Needless to say, there is no exegetical basis for either of these racialized myths. For further

suffering and oppression, in favour of critical analyses of social structures and systems.

One can see the kind of spiritualized notions of being cursed that Black Theology rejects when looking at the current situation of the Caribbean island of Haiti. This type of demonization is very clearly in view when we consider the comments of the right-wing, White American Christian spokesperson and sometime politician Pat Robertson.[34] Robertson's use of spiritualized reasons for the struggles of the predominantly Black people of Haiti is yet another form of conservative, obfuscated demonization that seeks to mask the real reasons for Haiti's struggles. These have everything to do with 200 years of racism and neo-colonialism. Robertson's claims that the Black people of Haiti have made 'pacts with the devil' are crude attempts to obscure socio-political reasons for Haiti's plight. Rather than address the 200 years of systematic destabilizing of Haiti by most of the major European powers and the USA, instead we get unfounded and quite plainly preposterous claims by a right-wing Christian spokesperson. His approach is one that is clearly intent on blaming one of the poorest people in the world for their own plight.[35]

As we have seen, Black Theology also rejects any sense that it is the moral failings or lack of discipline or civilizing cultures that account for Black failings, in many societies in the West and on the continent of Africa.[36] In seeking to apportion blame for Black oppression at the hands of systemic and structural forms, it can be argued that Black Theology has adopted a largely 'left-of-centre' perspective in terms of its social analysis. It has moved clearly from any notion that the victims of oppression are somehow to be blamed for the conditions in which they find themselves. Jacquelyn Grant expresses the central concern of Black and Womanist theologies like this:

> Part of the tendency to negate the humanity of some peoples may be
> seen in the corresponding tendency to locate blame for their situation on

---

information, see Sylvester A. Johnson, *The Myth of Ham in Nineteenth-Century American Christianity: Race, Heathens, and the People of God*, New York: Palgrave Macmillan, 2004; Stephen R. Haynes, *Noah's Curse: The Biblical Justification of American Slavery*, Oxford and New York: Oxford University Press, 2002; David M. Goldenberg, *The Curse of Ham: Race and Slavery in Early Judaism, Christianity and Islam*, Princeton, NJ: Princeton University Press, 2005.

34 See http://www.facebook.com/l.php?u=http%3A%2F%2Fwww.youtube.com%2Fwatch%3Fv%3DaQ4dA6kZsEs&h=QAQGN7mMf for Pat Robertson's spiritualized tirade against Haiti.

35 For an alternative understanding of Haiti's context of racism and colonial and postcolonial struggle, see Ronald Charles, 'Interpreting the Book of Revelation in the Haitian Context', *Black Theology* 9:2 (2011), pp. 177–98.

36 See Michael N. Jagessar, 'Early Methodism in the Caribbean: Through the Imaginary Optics of Gilbert's Slave Women – Another Reading', *Black Theology* 5:2 (2007), pp. 153–70. See also Gichaara, 'Issues in African Liberation Theology'.

those who have been dehumanized. Hence, we hear the familiar question: What is wrong with blacks, or women or youth? What is their problem? Although these questions often have been asked, they are inappropriate questions. These victims are blamed for situations and conditions over which they have no control.[37]

The structural leftist position of Black Theology has certainly been called into question by some Black religious scholars who will argue that this position fails to take into account questions pertaining to morality and religious observance.[38] It may be argued, even further, that one of the reasons that Black Theology has failed to gain any significant foothold in Black churches, among ordinary Black people, has been its links to the political left and the perception that it is 'too close' to socialism and Marxism. One has to take account of the inherent suspicion that many churches have held towards socialist and Marxist thought (often viewing them as 'anti-Christian' and incompatible with Christ). This may explain why often, inherently conservative ordinary Black people might feel that Black Theology, like other 'theologies of liberation', is too 'extreme' in its analysis of the social ills that befall various societies. Yet, as was demonstrated in the exercise in Chapter 1, any assertion for what is understood as knowledge or truth (described in academic terms as 'epistemology') is itself a particular, biased position, linked often to specific vested interests.

It can be argued that the arena in which Black Theology has expressed its most clearly 'biased' or 'positioned' perspective on the structural and systemic reasons for Black marginalization and oppression is in its analysis of the world system.

Black Theology and its critique of world systems

Black Theology has played a pivotal role in calling into question the workings and ethics of the 'global economy'. In using this term, I am concerned with the interconnected means by which countries undertake their economic activity. This can be seen in terms of how multi- and transnational companies operate. Quite often the activities of multinational corporations take advantage of being located within large global markets, where they seek to maximize their profits, using the framework of technological capitalism.[39]

---

37 Jacquelyn Grant, 'A Theological Framework', in Charles R. Foster and Grant S. Shockley (eds), *Working with Black Youth: Opportunities for Christian Ministry*, Nashville, TN: Abingdon, 1989, pp. 55–76 (66).

38 See J. D. Aldred, *Respect: Understanding Caribbean British Christianity*, Peterborough: Epworth, 2005; Garth Kasimu Baker-Fletcher, *Bible Witness in Black Churches*, New York: Palgrave Macmillan, 2009.

39 Perhaps the best explanation for this phenomenon in terms of Black and Womanist

The existence of the global economy emerged in the nineteenth century, but perhaps came into its own in the last century. In the twenty-first century it is no less commonplace. In fact it is so much a part of the economic landscape that it is hard for us to remember a time when people did not trade across national boundaries, or that companies did not belong to, or have their primary allegiance to, one country. The national boundaries of so-called sovereign nations have been ignored and are now often overrun by multinational companies whose primary commitment is making profit for their shareholders.[40] Black Theology has observed the ways in which profit and the corporate concerns of multinational companies do not seem to care about the needs of ordinary people. The mechanisms of the global economy often work hand in hand with neo-liberal models of political ideology. In using this term, I am talking about models of economic activity that have minimum regulation or interference by the state. In these specific models of economic activity there is a wholesale distaste of government intervention. This is often accompanied by the sense that the levers of control of major corporations and the development of economic production are better controlled by the few as opposed to the many. Black Theology has offered a largely, left-of-centre critique of world economic systems, arguing that these models of corporate, global capitalism are the primary reasons for the lowly position of *Person 1* in the exercise at the beginning of this chapter.

Black Theology opposes global capitalism

As we have seen, Black Theology burst into academic life[41] within the crucible of the Black Power Movement in 1960s America. It has always represented the overly political or politicized version of Black Christianity in the world. In its critique of the world economic system, one built on free-market capitalism (as described above), Black Theology has offered an undeniably pointed, critical explanation for world poverty. It has critiqued the negative impact of this model of economic activity on ordinary Black people. It is this form of pointed, left-of-centre approach that has seen Black Theology

---

theologies can be found in Keri Day, 'Global Economics and U.S. Public Policy: Human Liberation for the Global Poor', *Black Theology* 9:1 (2011), pp. 9–33.

40 See Tissa Balasuriya, 'Liberation of the Affluent', *Black Theology* 1:1 (2002), pp. 83–113.

41 Some African American Black Theologians have argued that, prior to the academic conceptualization of Black Theology, one could detect elements of this nascent practice in the actions and writings of enslaved Africans living in the USA. Slave narratives, in particular, are seen as a foundational source for determining the historical trajectory of Black Theology in the USA, from the eighteenth and nineteenth century through to the present day. For further information, see Hopkins, *Down, Up and Over*.

attacked in many quarters.[42] As we have seen in the broad survey of Black Theology, via significant themes like 'telling one's story' or looking at Jesus, this intellectual movement is an international one. One of its strengths has been the way in which it has engaged with a broad range of theological movements from across the world – often called 'Third World theologies' or theologies from the 'underside' of history.[43] Black Theology, for example, has been an important contributor to the work of EATWOT.[44]

Right from the outset, Black Theology has been concerned with the issue of global poverty. Black theologians have argued against the self-serving workings of the fundamentalist, free-market capitalist system of world trade. Black Theology, in seeking to explain why *Person 1* is in that position has identified the workings of the so-called 'free-trade' system. Although this system pretends to carry the trappings of Christianity and offers a generous form of support for all peoples, it is in actual fact an exploitative framework that ignores the needs of the poor.[45]

In this last part of this chapter I will try and show how Black Theology has adopted a number of perspectives in its critique of the world economic system. As I undertake this work, I will highlight the ways in which this world system exploits the poor and leaves predominantly ordinary Black people as the impoverished objects at the bottom of the economic barrel, much like *Person 1* in the exercise. I make no pretence that the position Black Theology has largely adopted is a 'fair one'. On the contrary, as I will demonstrate in the final chapter (and identified in the exercise in the first),

---

42 See Thabita M. Anyabwile, *The Decline of African American Theology: From Biblical Faith to Cultural Captivity*, Downers Grove, IL: IVP Academic, 2007, where the author questions the 'orthodox' theological credibility of Black Theology, along with other paradigms of African American theology. See also the more recent offering of Anthony B. Bradley, *Liberating Black Theology: The Bible and the Black Experience in America*, Wheaton, IL: Crossway, 2010.

43 This term reflects a growing consciousness of theologians and critical scholars whose work has emerged from nations and contexts that have been marginalized by the twin threats of colonialism and neo-colonialism and the economic rapacity of free-market economic globalization. See Marcella Althaus-Reid, Ivan Petrella and Luiz Carlos Susin (eds), *Another Possible World*, London: SCM, 2007; R. S. Sugirtharajah (ed.), *Voices from the Margin: Interpreting the Bible in the Third World*, London and Maryknoll, New York: SPCK/Orbis, 1995; John Parratt (ed.), *An Introduction to Third World Theologies*, Cambridge: Cambridge University Press, 2004; Virginia Fabella and R. S. Sugirtharajah (eds), *Dictionary of Third World Theologies*, Maryknoll, NY: Orbis, 2000.

44 EATWOT stands for the Ecumenical Association of Third World Theologians, which was founded in 1976. A helpful summary of the formation, identity and character of the organization can be found in Fabella and Sugirtharajah (eds), *Dictionary of Third World Theologies*, pp. 70–2.

45 See Alistair Kee, *The Rise and Demise of Black Theology*, London: SCM, 2008, pp. vii–x.

Black Theology makes no pretence to be fair. As we have seen in previous chapters, the oppression and marginalization of ordinary Black people is built on the basis of a profound disregard for them as sentient human subjects. Their needs and wishes are often disregarded. There is nothing fair about exploitation. Yet, as the critics of Black Theology would charge it for the unfairness of its critical response to the structural injustice that is imposed on the poorest in the world, they themselves are often silent when it comes to speaking up for the poor.[46]

I want to highlight the approach of some Black and Womanist scholars in this area, as key examples for how Black Theology has addressed the issue of world poverty of Black and other peoples from non-European cultures. These scholars will demonstrate the deliberately structured frameworks that seek to limit and position predominantly Black people as *Person 1* in the exercise.

Beginning with James Cone: the problem is racism!

James Cone would not describe himself as a Marxist, nor could his work be seen as an expression of Marxist ideology. There is no doubt, however, that his early work saw in Marxism a helpful tool for constructing his Black Theology of liberation. Cone argued that Black Theology, as a theology of liberation, was committed to challenging and overturning the vicious White power structure that had long imprisoned Black people – both literally and figuratively.[47] As we have seen previously, Cone's approach to Black Theology is informed by his continued commitment to the biblical revelation of God. He is arguing for a clear difference between the Kingdom of God and that of the world economic system.[48] While Cone's early work used aspects of Marxist frameworks as a way of critiquing the socio-economic system of America, his preferred approach to undertaking Black Theology, and its resultant attack on White power, has come from the Bible.

Cone's biblical theology provides a robust theological rationale for outlining the essential difference between the characteristics of the Kingdom of God and that of the world economic system. His Jesus-centred approach to liberation for Black people is one that seeks to use Black history and experience, and to link these to biblical models of justice. His aim is to create a theological model that critiques the structures of the present world order, one based on White privilege.[49] Cone does not engage in the analysis of class and how class distinctions between wealthy people who own capital

---

46 See Cone, 'Theology's Great Sin', pp. 139–52.
47 Cone, *God of the Oppressed*, p. 156.
48 Cone, *God of the Oppressed*, pp. 39–114.
49 See Cone, 'Theology's Great Sin', pp. 139–52.

and the poor at the bottom of society constitute the basis for how most societies are run. This latter perspective is one that is more commonly found in Latin American liberation theology.[50]

For Cone, it is no coincidence that the people most likely to be poor in a world of global capitalism run by White people with power are poor Black people and other non Euro-Americans.[51] For Cone, poverty has a colour. It is his contextualized and particular reading of oppression that separates him from the more generic, class-based approaches to the subject that one often finds in Latin American liberation theologians, for example.[52] Cone's analysis of people most likely to be in *Person 1* will be that they are Black. As we will see, one weakness of Cone's analysis is that, in failing to engage with issues of gender in his early work, his default position regarding the identity of those in *Person 1* is one that assumes a male subject. In actual fact, any serious analysis of global poverty will show that gender is a major contributory factor in the workings of world economic systems. In such systems, the more likely identity of an individual in *Person 1* is that of a Black woman and not a Black male. As we will see, when looking at the work of Womanist theologians, if poverty has a colour, then it also has a gender.

Cone notes that the 'free market' proponents of the world economic system will assert the goodness, generosity and the efficiency of choice that is gained for all people across the globe from this mode of economic activity. Cone, however, is clear that this is a smokescreen, not unlike the kinds of 'diversionary tactics' I have illustrated previously in this chapter.[53] The proponents of 'free trade' would like it to be believed that this system is for the benefit of ordinary people in the world, but the evidence from the peoples themselves tells another story.[54] Cone's approach to analysing why people are poor is one that is very much drawn from his commitment to anti-racism. While he has focused attention on the ways in which American capitalism has impoverished the poor, across the globe,[55] the

---

50 Cone's work does include some aspects of class analysis, where he looks at economic structures and shows how they impact on poor Black people. See Cone, *God of the Oppressed*, pp. 108–37. For a better understanding of Latin American liberation theology, see Christopher Rowland (ed.), *The Cambridge Companion to Liberation Theology*, Cambridge: Cambridge University Press, 1999.

51 See Cone, 'Theology's Great Sin', pp. 142–5.

52 See James H. Cone, *My Soul Looks Back*, Maryknoll, NY: Orbis, 1986, pp. 114–38.

53 See James H. Cone 'Looking Back, Going Forward: Black Theology as Public Theology', in Dwight N. Hopkins (ed.) *Black Faith and Public Talk: Critical Essays on James H. Cone's Black Theology and Black Power*, Maryknoll, NY: Orbis, 1999, pp. 246–59.

54 See the excellent Christian Aid video *Life and Debt*, New Yorker Films, 2001, for the differing accounts on the impact of free trade on poor neo-colonial countries like Jamaica. Black Theology sides with the first-hand accounts of the poor themselves and not with the free-market apologists like the officers from the International Monetary Fund (IMF).

55 See Cone, *My Soul Looks Back*, pp. 93–113.

bulk of his work has been directed at the historical experiences of African Americans.

While some Black theologians have critiqued Cone and other African American Black theologians for their short-sightedness in looking only at their own experiences,[56] I would argue that, on the contrary, Cone and his ilk are simply being true to the basic tenets of 'contextual theology'. In a previous chapter, I highlighted the contextual nature of Black Theology by looking, particularly, at two key examples of the movement in Britain. In highlighting examples drawn from Black Theology in Britain, it does not mean I am not concerned with, or have no interest in, the plight of Black people in other parts of the globe. In seeking to draw from experience, however, as a source for undertaking theological reflection, I do not think it is unreasonable that Black theologians commence their work from the narratives that are of primary importance for them.

As a contextual theologian, the immediacy of Cone's view is the United States. For him, the individual in *Person 1* would be an African American. This would be the case, not because other peoples do not suffer, but because the impact on his own experience and consciousness has been shaped by being born and socialized within the United States of America. Cone's racialized, theological reflections illustrate the gap between the world economic system of White privilege and the gospel of Jesus Christ. The latter is one of equity, justice and liberation for all marginalized and economically dispossessed people, most of whom have non-European backgrounds.[57]

As the dominant voice in Black Theology, since its inception as an academic discipline, James Cone has set the tempo for the movement, in which the analysis of 'race'-based oppression has largely been the norm. The strength of this approach to understanding the nature of world poverty is that it has 'put a face' to the individual crouched in *Person 1*. That person is most likely to be a Black person. The inequities of racism and the notion and practice of White supremacy have impacted on Black people. This has occurred within many White-majority societies (and Black-majority ones in Africa also). In such contexts, little account has been taken of the dignity and rights of Black people. Black Theology under the aegis of James Cone has attacked the privileging of White concerns, particularly as it arises from White people with power. He has shown that a Black retelling of the story, and the accompanying reinterpretation of the gospel, is critical for the development of a Black Theology of liberation.[58]

---

56 See Delroy A. Reid-Salmon, 'A Sin of Black Theology: The Omission of the Caribbean Diasporan Experience from Black Theological Discourse', *Black Theology* 6:2 (2008), pp. 139–52.

57 Hopkins and Lewis, *Another World Is Possible*.

58 See James H. Cone, *Speaking the Truth: Ecumenism, Liberation and Black Theology*, Grand Rapids, MI: Eerdmans, 1986.

While Cone's engagement with the class-based analysis of Marxist thought has been relatively peripheral to his overall work, the same cannot be said of the work of Cornel West. West analyses the nexus between Black Theology and Marxism, seeking to outline how a comprehensive critique of capitalism can expose the power-hungry tendencies of the market.[59] This market system is one that has given rise to interlocking systems of poverty and oppression for poor and underclass people across the world.

The Black Theology perspective outlined by West has prophetically denounced laissez-faire, liberal capitalism. In using this term, West is speaking to the 'hands-off' approach of governments and regulatory systems, who, coupled with the freedom of such large corporations, invariably act for their own benefit and not for the needs of the poor. West sees this model of socio-economic activity as being an aberration and contrary to the 'theology for hope' that has been a central plank of European political theology, for example, since the Second World War.[60] The most substantive articulation of this prophetic revolutionary vision for Black Christianity and its accompanying Black Theology can be found in one of Cornel West's classic later works.[61] I have limited my look at West to these relatively brief comments because I recognize the central challenge of trying to decide whether West is primarily a theologian or a philosopher. Given this question, I have decided to devote greater space to those who would identify themselves as theologians in the first instance.

Poverty not only has a colour – it has a gender also!

In looking at Cone's perspectives on wrestling with the issue of world poverty we saw that his approach was one that focused on issues of White supremacy and racism. Central to his critique was the failure of White Christian theology to even acknowledge these concerns, let alone challenge them. If we liken his stance to the metaphorical exercise I described earlier in this chapter we will see that the individual in *Person 1* is most likely to be a Black person. In Cone's contextual work, this person most probably (but not exclusively, I might add) will be an African American. What was lacking in Cone's early work was any substantial acknowledgement that poverty, marginalization and oppression not only have a colour or ethnicity (some-

59 See Cornel West, 'Black Theology and Marxist Thought', in Wilmore and Cone (eds), *Black Theology 1966–1979*, pp. 552–67.

60 See Cornel West, 'Black Theology of Liberation as Critique of Capitalist Civilisation', in James H. Cone and Gayraud S. Wilmore (eds), *Black Theology: A Documentary History, Volume Two, 1980–1990*, Maryknoll, NY: Orbis, 1993, pp. 410–25.

61 Cornel West, *Prophecy Deliverance! An Afro-American Revolutionary Christianity*, Louisville, KY: Westminster John Knox, 2003.

thing Latin American liberation theology has largely ignored)[62] but also a gender.

The question of world poverty and its relationship to the identity of the individual in *Person 1* is a concern that has been addressed by Womanist theologians. African American Womanist ethicists such as Katie Cannon and Emilie Townes have reflected theologically on the socio-cultural structures and the impact these have made upon Black women and other poor people of colour in the USA and across the world.[63]

Unlike Cone, Cannon and Townes have added an important gender critique to the politically charged, gendered perspectives on the ills that have imposed themselves upon *Person 1*. As we will see, Womanist theologians have added more specificity to the challenge of identifying not only the causes of *Person 1*'s situation but also, of equal importance, *her* identity too.

Liberation theologians will identify the *Person 1* as someone from the so-called 'Third World' or the 'Global South'. Cone and most first- and second-generation Black theologians will identity *Person 1* as a Black person who is poor. Womanists, however, will see that person as a poor Black woman. Namely, that while poverty and economic hardship can befall all peoples, statistically we can see that in our present world order it is predominantly Black women who are the holders of the unwanted title of 'the least of the least'.[64]

While a number of Womanist theologians have written eloquently about the underlying poverty facing predominantly Black women in the world, the work of Keri Day, a newer, emerging Womanist ethicist, has contributed

---

62 Ivan Petrella charts the history of, and outlines a new future for, liberation theology and chides Black Theology for being overly concerned with issues of Blackness and mining their own resources. He fails, however, to acknowledge the epistemological (or knowledge-based) privilege he confers on White western ideas, without any attempt to draw from the intellectual ideas generated by Africa or people of African descent or, indeed, from indigenous people in Latin America. This is a minor argument, in all truth, because, in the final analysis, Black and liberation theologies have much more in common than the comparatively smaller number of issues that divide them. See Ivan Petrella, *The Future of Liberation Theology: An Argument and Manifesto*, London: SCM, 2006. See Cone, *My Soul Looks Back*, pp. 93–113, for an account of the relationship between Black Theology, liberation theology and Third World theologies.

63 With regard to this work, see Katie Cannon, *Katie's Canon: Womanism and the Soul of the Black Community*, New York: Continuum Publishing, 1995, pp. 144–61, and Emilie Townes, *Womanist Ethics and the Cultural Production of Evil*, New York: Palgrave Macmillan, 2006, pp. 111–38.

64 See Elaine E. Thomas, 'Macroeconomy, Apartheid and the Rituals of Healing in an African Indigenous Church', in Dwight N. Hopkins, Lois Ann Lorentzen, Eduardo Mendieta and David Batstone (eds), *Religions/Globalizations: Theories and Cases*, London and Durham: Duke University Press, 2001, pp. 135–60, where the author identifies the subjectivity of the likely victims of the global economy and the means by which African Christians are seeking to survive against this neo-imperialistic backdrop.

greatly to this debate.[65] What makes Day's work most compelling, particularly for the purposes of this chapter, is the greater precision she brings to the debate in terms of the identity of *Person 1*. Day looks in great detail at the existing approaches of Black and Womanist theologians in regards to the challenges posed by global poverty and shows how the excellence of this work has, nevertheless, been limited by some important omissions.

Day argues that previous Black theologians who have addressed the area of world poverty have not offered a practical economic framework for exploring the struggle for truth that confronts ordinary Black people. This struggle is one between the need for a wholesale change of the world structure that condemns so many Black women to poverty and the need to identify what might constitute 'full life' and dignity for these people. In other words, as these analyses attempt to make sense of asking the 'back story' of why ordinary Black people are poor, they must not become some soulless and dry exercise. Such analysis must also be about people and how they are enabled to live, and to do so abundantly.

Day's work explores how Black and Womanist liberation theologies can respond to the chronic poverty experienced by communities of colour around the world. Day argues that Black liberation theologies have performed the theological task of rethinking the world system, often doing so by rereading the Gospels from the margins of society. What they have not accomplished to the same degree of success, however, is to link this interpretive theological work with the practical task of guiding these communities in what an alternative, non-exploitative, non-capitalistic world or society looks like.

Day's work commences with an acknowledgement that she is not the first person to try and write in solidarity with Black women who live at the bottom of the economic ladder, often occupying the identity of *Person 1* in the exercise. Day acknowledges the debt she owes to the two major Womanist ethicists of their generation, Katie Cannon and Emilie Townes. She acknowledges the distinctive patterns of racism and how this underlying economic structure makes possible the exploitation of Black people.[66] Alternatively, she identifies the manner in which public policies reinforce the socio-economic deprivation of the poor in America.[67]

A central thesis of Day's argument is that Black and Womanist theologies need to provide a theoretical paradigm for imaging an 'economy of hope'. Day writes:

> Black liberation and Womanist theologies need a social critique that not
> only spells out the roots of advanced capitalist crisis but also provides

---

65 See Day, 'Global Economics', pp. 9–33.
66 See Cannon, *Katie's Canon*, p. 160.
67 See Townes, *Womanist Ethics*, p. 126.

BLACK THEOLOGY AND SOCIAL ANALYSIS

possibilities within this mode of economic activity. This social critique, which provides the roots and possibilities of capitalist crisis, might enable Black liberation and Womanist discourses to offer more insightful theological reflection on what liberation for the global poor might look like within such arrangements.[68]

As a means of theorizing around what an economy of hope might look like for the global poor people of colour, Day argues for the construction of a set of contextual indicators that might embody the lived realities of human rights and social justice.[69] The concepts that Day puts forward are not abstract 'pie-in the-sky' visions for what we might describe as the 'ideal world'. Rather, her model for the 'economy of hope' is one that draws on the specific stories, experiences and cultures of the many differing contexts in which poor Black women live; she is not pushing for one specific model by which Black women might be understood as achieving a measure of freedom from economic and material poverty.

Day puts forward a worked example for what constitutes the improved life and living for Black women. This concept is based on a specific hermeneutical or interpretative framework that can be applied in a flexible manner to the many differing contexts across the globe. The model she has in mind is that of the *imago Dei* or the 'image of God' as understood in terms of the Christian tradition. When adopting this term, Day is pushing Black and Womanist theologies to begin to articulate a broader range of concepts that might assist the global poor (predominantly Black women) to envision what shape or form communal thriving might take for them. The theological articulation of the *imago Dei* is placed in dialogue with Martha Nussbaum's call for 'universal values'.[70] The latter concept from Nussbaum is one that calls for a platform for illustrating the concrete, material realities of communal living for the poor, in terms of the present world economic structure.

Day's commitment is to creating a clearer theo-ethical model for what constitutes liberation and full life for Black women across the globe. She is arguing for a more precise engagement of Black and Womanist theologies as they seek to critique the present world economic system. She is careful, however, not to suggest one specific or particular framework, underpinning this commitment to liberation for Black women and other peoples from non-European cultures. She recognizes that using the *imago Dei* presents certain limitations, in terms of its usefulness to poor people across the world, particularly those who do not adhere to the Christian faith.

---

68 Day, 'Global Economics', p. 24.

69 Day, 'Global Economics', pp. 24–9.

70 See Martha Nussbaum, *Women and Human Development: The Capabilities Approach*, Cambridge: Cambridge University Press, 2000.

This presents a challenge for the largely Christian character of Black Theology. Hence, there is a need for the notion and practice of liberation for poor Black women across the world that is worked out contextually, in each particular setting, by the protagonists themselves.[71] The challenge of writing from a powerful central position, as an African American woman, does present some major difficulties for Day. Is it possible to outline a model of radical solidarity with the poor across the world and not end up, even by accident, imposing American models, frameworks and standards on other cultures and contexts? How do poor Black women in Africa resist the urge to mimic North American frameworks when there is a huge disparity in power, influence and visibility between the contexts of the former and the vast machinery of theological power that is constructed in the latter? In fairness to Day, she is mindful of the power she holds as an African American woman. She does not seek to map out a universal model for what constitutes liberation and an 'economy of hope' for people who are fixed in the identity of *Person 1*. The challenge that has faced Day and other Black and Womanist theologians before her is that of seeking to effect models of transformative change (as outlined in the previous chapter) for people trapped in the guise of *Person 1*. It is at this point that the hitherto unmentioned *Person 2* comes into play.

When this exercise has been performed with many ordinary Black people, they have often ignored *Person 2*, until the question of what constitutes progress is discussed. Clearly, *Person 2* is in transition, growing from the image of one who is trapped, in *Person 1,* towards becoming the triumphant and defiant one in *Person 3*.[72] The structural and systemic factors that impinge on and condemn *Person 1* to 'her' lowly position have been discussed in this chapter. These range from pernicious forms of free-market capitalism, White supremacist racism, through to the impact of colonialism, media manipulation and spiritualized, theological conservatism. All the aforementioned, and many other factors, can be blamed for limited and constricting the perspectives and opportunities for those in *Person 1*.

The rise of neo-Pentecostalism: the challenge to Black Theology

When discussing the strategies by which those who identified as *Person 1* can rise into that of *Person 2*, the Black people with whom I have shared this exercise have alighted on a specific response. To my mind, this response,

---

71 Day, 'Global Economics', pp. 27–9.

72 This image served as the basic metaphor for my initial doctoral work that sought to provide an education-focused approach to Black Theology for the purposes of the conscientization of ordinary Black people. It has served as an important conceptual framework for some of my previous work. See Anthony G. Reddie, *Growing into Hope: Vol. 1, Believing and Expecting*, and Vol. 2, *Liberation and Change*, Peterborough: Methodist Publishing House, 1998. See also Anthony G. Reddie, *Nobodies to Somebodies: A Practical Theology for Education and Liberation*, Peterborough: Epworth, 2003.

unlike what has been detailed before, is not consistent with Black Theology. I believe this response, as often identified by ordinary Black people, runs counter to what Black Theology has asserted. In the first instance I want to look at the rise of Black 'neo-Pentecostalism' as an important framework for transforming the life experiences of Black poor people in *Person 1*.

The latter part of the last century witnessed the exponential growth of a new type of Christianity. Pentecostalism has been the huge success of the twentieth century, accounting for the accelerated growth of Christianity across the globe. Pentecostalism, with its pronounced emphasis on the manifestation of the Spirit in general, and speaking in tongues (glossolalia) in particular, has witnessed a tremendous growth, especially among the poor across the world. There can be no doubting of the effective power of a tradition that gives hope to the poor, in the belief that in God, through the power of the Holy Spirit, all things are possible, including startling material, economic change.

In using the term 'neo-Pentecostalism' I am distinguishing it from the traditional models that first emerged in the 1920s and 30s with their roots in Black cultural experiences.[73] The rise of this newer form of Pentecostalism is one that does not have an explicit identification with, and a commitment to, the sociopolitical concerns of Black communities, as was the case with the traditional Black church. One can witness this phenomenon in the rhetoric of many of these newer Pentecostal churches, in that they do not use an explicit language that identifies with what might be described as 'Black issues'. Indeed the 'colour blind' theology to which I have drawn attention in a previous piece of work is very consistent with the specific 'Universal' and 'International' identity many neo-Pentecostal churches have asserted in their publicity.[74]

In the context of this discussion around Black Theology and social analysis, especially in terms of understanding the root cause of Black poverty and oppression, neo-Pentecostalism offers a significant and important challenge. This new mode of thinking has emerged particularly in terms of what is perceived to be God's activity or agency. This is especially the case vis-à-vis wealth creation and the empowerment of the individual. It can be argued that this development is giving rise to what many are terming a new model or pattern for the Black Church in America.[75]

Constraints of space prevent a more detailed exploration of the genesis and the finer characteristics of what many are now terming 'mega-churches'[76]

---

73 See Aldred, *Respect*; Mark Sturge, *Look What the Lord Has Done! An Exploration Black Christian Faith in Britain*, Milton Keynes: Scripture Union, 2005.

74 See Reddie, *Working against the Grain*, pp. 25–9.

75 See Dwight N. Hopkins, *Heart and Head: Black Theology Past, Present and Future*, New York: Palgrave Macmillan, 2002, pp. 19–20.

76 Important work has been undertaken on the phenomenon of mega-churches. See Stephanie Mitchem, *Name It and Claim It: Prosperity Teaching in the Black Church*, Cleveland, OH: Pilgrim Press, 2007. See also Jonathan L. Walton, *Watch This: The Ethics and Aesthetics of Black Televangelism*, New York and London: New York University Press, 2009.

(which are the archetypal expression of this new phenomenon). It is important, however, that we realize that this new phenomenon reflects a seismic shift in the theological engagement with the global poor. In the context of seeking the uplift of *Person 1* and the development into *Person 2*, these new mega-churches represent a clear divergence from the central tenets of Black Theology. Black and Womanist theologies have offered leftist critiques of, and have opposed the present world system of, liberal economics and global capitalism. Mega-churches, however, offer a largely uncritical endorsement of the merits of wealth creation and God's providence from within the existing world order. The theology that has arisen from these largely neo-Pentecostal churches is one that has been characterized by African American Womanist theologian Stephanie Mitchem as offering a 'name it and claim it' ethic towards prosperity and social development.[77]

This model of empowering the poor is one that is very different from the model provided by Black Theology. Central to the 'name it and claim it' philosophy is that the work of the Holy Spirit, allied to faithful giving to the church, can give rise to Spirit-led forms of transformative change. These forms of change are different to those identified in the previous chapter in terms of 'liberative praxis'. They do not require concerted communitarian or collective action, nor do they require radical or revolutionary struggle to change, or even dismantle, the present system. This form of spiritually engendered change is identified by Robert Beckford as 'selfish faith', as its chief outcome is the personal enrichment of the individual, with no accompanying commitment to the transformation of the whole community. In addition to the aforementioned, there is also a lesser commitment to challenging systemic injustice, to the ultimate overthrow of a sinful and oppressive system.[78]

Clearly, one needs to be mindful of Walton's charge regarding a flat and seemingly simplistic reading of these churches (particularly as they relate to global economic matters).[79] I believe it is fair, however, to assert that there are specific characteristics in the theological stance adopted and endorsed within this specific model of the Black church that differs from the past. Vincent Wimbush has identified non-contextualized, fundamentalist readings of the Bible as one of the core characteristics of this fast-evolving movement.[80] Such readings of the Bible are ones that often lead to a theological assessment of the world that has moved beyond the racialized suspicions of the Black Theology approach, as detailed by Cone (see above)

---

77 Mitchem, *Name It and Claim It*, pp. 45–51.

78 See Robert Beckford, 'Theology in the Age of Crack: Crack Age, Prosperity Doctrine and "Being There"', *Black Theology in Britain* 4:1 (2001), pp. 9–24.

79 Walton, *Watch This*, pp. 11–17.

80 Vincent L. Wimbush, *The Bible and African Americans: A Brief History*, Minneapolis: Fortress, 2003, pp. 63–75.

The theology of mega-churches is one that argues for a more individualistic understanding of personal blessing and material progress than that found in any of the approaches I have identified in this chapter. The power of God to bless the believer in return for one's personal devotion to Jesus is not based on an overturn of the present world economic system.

I think it is fair to say that the dominant articulation of Black Theology in terms of social analysis is one that has placed greater emphasis on Spirit-filled approaches to systemic change than one of personal blessing for specific individuals. One can detect very little that might be understood as a 'hermeneutic of suspicion', in terms of the merits or otherwise of concrete material change coming in the form of specific material blessings for some, and not for all people.

Both the Black Theology and the neo-Pentecostal approach use the Christian framework for their accompanying theological positions, in terms of seeking solutions to the impoverishment of Black people. For example, the latter would see the benefits of Spirit-filled notions of change as being reserved solely for those who espouse the 'correct' mandatory relationship with Jesus Christ.[81] The providential gifts and opportunities provided by a gracious God include the technological breakthrough of mass communications that has been the generosity of this new global capitalist economy.[82]

For those who have encouraged the use of 'prosperity teaching' as a means of enabling ordinary poor Black people to move from *Person 1* to *Person 2*, greater emphasis is placed upon Spirit-filled tithing and seeking material blessing from God. This is accomplished via the church, in exchange for a faithful commitment to God alone. In and of itself, this is not necessarily a bad thing. It is a position, however, that does not encourage radical collectivist action, in which all people, irrespective of specific commitment to Jesus or not, can be included. In a previous chapter, I outlined a model of Black Christology that encouraged Black people to move beyond a limited perspective that saw 'Jesus as the only way' and the sole portal through which the Black liberation struggle could be envisaged. The model of liberation that is envisaged via neo-Pentecostal perspectives places less emphasis upon human activity as understood as the Spirit of Liberation in and for us that is articulated by Dwight Hopkins.[83]

The neo-Pentecostal movement within North America has embraced the potentiality of global communications for its mission and evangelism. It has

---

81 This doctrinal point regarding the exclusivity of Jesus Christ represents the critical difference between what might be understood as 'traditional' Christianity and the prophetic tradition in African American theology. The latter, however, has consistently argued for full life and liberation for all poor people of colour, irrespective of faith adherence or none.

82 T. D. Jakes, *The Great Investment: Faith, Family and Finance*, New York: G. P. Putnam's Sons, 2000, pp. 13–14.

83 See Hopkins, *Heart and Head*, pp. 77–90.

seized on these possibilities as a means of disseminating their message.[84] Indeed, one can point to the desirability of using the media as their alternative model of effecting solidarity with the poor of the world.[85] The global success of this approach to evangelism and mission arises from an enticing message that is wrapped within a Spirit-filled, inspired, self-improvement ethic. This model of evangelism is one that shifts the emphasis from a collective struggle for systemic change to a more personalized transformative mode of material change.[86]

One could note a form of endorsement for the present workings of the world economic system in the theological outworking of this movement. The working practices of the mega-churches resemble the secular, multi-media corporations that previous models of Black Theology have denounced.[87]

The new perspective and tradition in Black Christianity, particularly as it applies to social analysis and concerns the empowerment of the poor, is very different from that advocated by Black Theology. The work of Hopkins, for example, is very clear that there are no quick 'spiritual fixes' for Black

---

84 See the mission statement of 'God TV', the most successful satellite networking of neo-Pentecostal ministries and teaching in the world, which includes a significant African American presence in the shape of well-known figures like T. D. Jakes and Creflo Dollar. See http://www.god.tv/node/1 for further information.

85 Walton, *Watch This*, pp. 199–227.

86 This model of ecclesiology and its resultant theological stance, vis-à-vis the world economy, has given rise to a number of parallel developments in other contexts. In the UK, the largest church (of any denominational stance or ethnicity) is the Kingsway Christian Centre, which is pastored by Nigerian-born Matthew Ashimolowo. This church operates as a multi-million pound, global enterprise in the mould of its African American progenitors and endorses a prosperity-inspired form of ministry that attracts thousands of people. For further details on this church and the developing movement in the UK, see Israel Olofinjana, *Reverse in Ministry and Mission: Africans in the Dark Continent of Europe – a Historical Study of African Churches in Europe*, Milton Keynes: Authorhouse, 2010, pp. 58–72.

87 The most articulate voice in Black Theology that offered a biting critique against the doubtful practices of global capitalism is that of Dwight N. Hopkins. One of Hopkins's key insights is his theological critique of 'Monopoly capitalism'. In using this term, which is a key insight in his social analysis, Hopkins is speaking to the accumulation of capital and the private possession and ownership of the means of production, within the elite group of people who would be defined as the super rich. Hopkins has also argued that 'globalization' is itself a form of religion for the 'political right' and stands in sharp distinction to the freedom, generosity and openness of the Kingdom of God. His key texts in this regard are: Dwight N. Hopkins, 'Theologies in the USA', in Althaus-Reid, Petrella and Susin (eds), *Another Possible Wolrld*, pp. 98–100, and 'The Religion of Globalization', in Hopkins, Lorentzen, Mendieta and Batstone (eds), *Religions/Globalizations*, pp. 7–32. See Hopkins, *Heart and Head*, pp. 109–25 and 127–9; 'New Orleans Is America', in Kirk-Duggan (ed.), *The Sky Is Crying*, pp. 59–68; 'Black Christian Worship: Theological and Biblical Foundations', in Hopkins and Lewis (eds), *Another World Is Possible*, pp. 338–40.

people to move from *Person 1 to Person 3*. Indeed, the need to turn the whole system on its head is one that leads Black Theology to question the very working of the model itself, which has (most likely) a crouching Black woman at the bottom and an erect, triumphalistic White male at the top.[88]

The movement of the Spirit in transforming individuals *within* the existing structures and systems (as opposed to demolishing the existing framework itself) is often seen within neo-Pentecostalism as being consistent with the scope of God's activity. This is not that dissimilar from perspectives put forward by White, neo-conservative evangelicals in America and across the world. So questions of Black people being cursed or needing to be 'delivered' from demons and evil spirits (as opposed to fighting the material evils of capitalism and racism) become the alternative approach to social analysis.

Black Theology, to my mind, should oppose this particular brand and means of assessing 'who are the poor in the world and why?' It should do so because this form of social analysis mirrors, too closely, the racialized intent of many conservative White evangelicals who are prone to engage in the same kinds of rhetoric.

An antidote to neo-Pentecostalism

The important antidote to Black neo-Pentecostalism is one that seeks to utilize the tools and perspectives that I have outlined previously in this chapter. In the first instance, as I have asserted, it begins with the belief that the Kingdom of God is incompatible with the present world system as millions of poor people experience it on a daily basis.

An alternative approach, one rooted in the leftist politics of Black Theology, begins with the radical, counter-cultural nature of the Kingdom of God. The Kingdom of God speaks against all notions of exploitation of the poor and the vested self-interests of the rich and powerful. Black Theology has used the social-political criticism of Black biblical scholars such as Randall Bailey, Itumeleng Mosala and Oral Thomas.[89] These individuals have offered an alternative understanding of God's justice to that found in

---

88 See David Isiorho, 'Buying the Poor for Silver and the Needy for a Pair of Sandals (Amos 8:6): The Fit between Capitalism and Slavery as Seen through the Hermeneutic of the Eighth-Century Prophet Amos', in Anthony G. Reddie (ed.), *Black Theology, Slavery and Contemporary Christianity*, Aldershot: Ashgate, 2010, pp. 59–68.

89 See Randall C. Bailey, *Yet with a Steady Beat: Contemporary U.S. Afrocentric Biblical Interpretation*, Atlanta, GA: Society for Biblical Literature, 2003; Randall C. Bailey, Tat-siong Benny Liew and Fernando F. Segovia (eds), *They Were All Together in One Place? Toward Minority Biblical Criticism*, Atlanta, GA: Society for Biblical Literature, 2009; Mosala, *Biblical Hermeneutics*; Oral A. W. Thomas, *Biblical Resistance Hermeneutics within a Caribbean Context*, London: Equinox, 2010.

prosperity-led, neo-Pentecostal forms of social analysis. They have been useful to Black Theology's analysis of social structures because they start from the belief that all knowledge and truth is a struggle for power. This struggle is one between those who can assert their own perspectives (as seen in Chapter 1) and those who are denied power. This work demonstrates that such forms of contestation can be seen in the biblical text itself; that is, the Bible does not necessarily provide us with a neutral or an entirely trustworthy picture of what constitutes the 'will of God'.

So, for example, let us start by looking at a specific text that holds some significance for the purposes of this discussion. Many ordinary Black people in the earlier exercise highlighted Luke 21.1–4 – 'the widow's mite' – as an example of the importance of paying tithes and supporting the church in order to receive a material blessing from God. This text was highlighted with regard to my previous comments on neo-Pentecostalism and the 'quick-fix' approach to seeking change as opposed to that of costly liberative praxis.

A critical, social-political reading of the text will begin not by spiritualizing the text, but rather it takes into account the contested power relationships in its very construction, in addition to the imbalances in the relationship of those who read it. So, such a reading will not suggest that it offers an example for modern-day Christians to follow. Rather, one starts by acknowledging the social and political context in which the author is writing. So, for example, it has been asserted by a number of scholars that Luke's Gospel was written as a challenge to the rich, Gentile followers of Jesus.[90]

One of the social-political and economic tools for interpreting the Bible that has been used by biblical scholars and Black theologians is that of 'postcolonial theory'.[91] Postcolonial theory is a critical, scholarly approach to challenging and critiquing representations of truth that have been shaped by the seemingly all-powerful frameworks of colonialism and empire. The importance of this theory arises when one is reminded that there are a great many similarities between the context in which the Bible was written and the experience of many Diasporan African people over the past century and a half. What links the two is the issue of colonialism and postcolonialism. Postcolonialism does not necessarily mean 'the end of colonialism'. Rather, it refers to the continuation of it within the cultural imagination and practices of the people who were formerly colonized. So, although independence might have arrived for a colonized people, the influence of the process of colonization might still exist.

---

90 See Mosala, *Biblical Hermeneutics*, pp. 154–89.

91 See R. S. Sugirtharajah, *The Bible and the Third World: Precolonial, Colonial and Postcolonial Encounters*, Cambridge: Cambridge University Press, 2001, and *Postcolonial Criticism and Biblical Interpretation*, Oxford: Oxford University Press, 2002; Fernando F. Segovia and R. S. Sugirtharajah (eds), *A Postcolonial Commentary on the New Testament Writings*, London: T & T Clark, 2007.

First-century Judaea, where Jesus' ministry was largely located, was an occupied colony of the Roman Empire. In such contexts, exploitation of the poor, in which a few people are benefiting from the system and the majority are condemned to poverty, rings many bells in our present age. Given the context in which the writer of the Gospel of Luke was writing, it cannot be a stretch to think that these issues would have concerned and indeed influenced the writing of this account of Jesus' life. What happens to our socially informed, political reading if we imagine the widow as *Person 1*? If there is, then, a clear colonial context that may well have shaped the writing of this Gospel,[92] it is perfectly possible for Jesus' telling of the story of the widow's mite to be one that is influenced by the socio-political and economic context in which he is located.

In this passage, a postcolonial reading sees Jesus condemning the exploitation of the poor (seen in the widow's mite). In so doing, he is challenging the whole system of Temple worship. Jesus can be seen to be issuing a critical attack upon the very structure and system in which this poor widow is located.

As Jesus shares this narrative, it cannot have gone unnoticed that he is condemning the whole structure and system of the religious–social–cultural–economic setting, in which the Temple is a key institution in regulating and stipulating the norms of society. In challenging and perhaps even denouncing the Temple system, which asks a poor widow to give all that she has, Jesus can be read as undermining the status quo, not championing it.

Consider the differences between a Black Theology approach to social analysis, which ultimately calls for a radical reversal of the three figures in the exercise, and one that seeks to operate within it. The latter perspective often assumes the system to be acceptable, if not actually representing God's own interests.

This text reminds us of the way in which even religious institutions are often guilty of exploiting the poor. How do we respond to the challenges presented by this text? Have Black mega-churches, and indeed churches of all shapes, traditions and theologies, been guilty of colluding with the exploitation of the poor in our present world order? How many have offered a seductive message of 'come and join in with our system (of monopoly capitalism) and you will be OK'? At the present time, a number of prominent Black Christian churches and their leaders are experiencing significant exponential growth. Many of them often do so on the back of attracting largely poor Black people (often economic migrants in many countries in western Europe, for example). What does this text have to say to and against these particular practitioners of the Christian faith?

---

92 See Virginia Burrus, 'The Gospel of Luke and the Acts of the Apostles', in Segovia and Sugirtharajah (eds), *A Postcolonial Commentary on the New Testament Writings*, pp. 133–55.

Was this widow persuaded to put in all she had as an offering on the basis that she might receive great financial blessings as a result? Is this not the case with many of the successful practitioners of 'prosperity gospel'-led approaches to Christian mission and ministry? The Black Theology message, informed by postcolonial theory, is a critique of the existing social–cultural–economic system. Jesus seems to be offering to the first hearers of his story an 'upside-down' Kingdom. This message is one that still applies in our current era. Namely, why should the poor and the socially marginalized give all they have to sustain rich organizations that should be supporting them financially, and not the other way around?

The challenge of the gospel is to be counter-cultural. In a world dominated by monopoly capitalism and the wholesale exploitation of the poor, the Church has to undertake a root-and-branch exercise in soul searching in order to examine its own complicity with regard to its historic relationship with the poor. An ideological, Black Theology, postcolonial-influenced approach to the interpretation of Scripture reminds us that the Kingdom of God is not merely a promise of everlasting life in heaven. It is also a promise of full life (John 10.10) in the flesh and blood realities of this world, prior to death.

The salient question remains, how can the Church be a counter-cultural force that challenges the seemingly all-pervasive power of rich western economic frameworks that take from the poor in order to enrich themselves? Why should the promise of full life and progress for the poor be predicated on the basis of upholding and sustaining the rich? Even if the rich are the Church and the pastors who live well at the poor's expense?

This final brief rereading of the biblical text has been effected in order to show how a social-political interpretation of the Bible, allied to the reflections undertaken previously, can provide a much-needed means of social analysis. This form of analysis is one that reminds us why certain people are poor. Black Theology is unashamedly biased in its approach to critically analysing societies and their structures and systems. It does so in order to uncover the reasons why predominantly Black people, particularly women, are located in the crouched position as *Person 1*. The question has often been posed – why are certain people in this position? As a follow-up, one can ask how they can rise up through the position of *Person 2*, in order to be represented in *Person 3*. Black Theology wishes to (and indeed should) be asking a more fundamental question: do these figures represent God's intention for all humanity, within the parameters of what we describe as the 'Kingdom of God'? Black Theology argues 'no'. This stance has always been an unpopular one, increasingly so, as we consider the rise of neo-Pentecostalism among Black people across the world. But the challenges of the cross, as detailed by James Cone, remind us that there is no liberation or transformative change without struggle! There is no other way!

Questions

1. Is it so bad that ordinary Black people seek individual, spiritual solutions to their problems as opposed to more material ones, in terms of social and political forms of collective action? If yes, then why, and if not, then why not?
2. Do you feel Black Theology's relationship with leftist perspectives on social issues is problematic and does that limit its engagement with ordinary Black people? If yes, then why, and if not, then why not?
3. Black Theology appears to have a major problem with neo-Pentecostalism – is this fair? Are there advantages to the neo-Pentecostal approach to personal empowerment when compared to the models advocated by Black Theology?

7

Putting All This Together

This chapter marks a slight departure from the previous ones. It does not seek to outline any specific aspect or theme within Black Theology. Instead, the aim is to draw together all the insights from the previous chapters and to link these to a specific, practical issue confronting ordinary Black people.

May I remind you once again of the dual nature of this book? This text is based upon the twin hopes of assisting the reader to *understand* Black Theology. The first hope is to explain the basic ideas and themes of Black Theology by showing how Black Theology functions as an academic discipline. The second hope is to assist the reader in understanding the basic intent of Black Theology by illustrating how Black Theology operates as a practical movement committed to liberating ordinary, predominantly poor Black people from the oppressive structures and systems that impinge on their lived realities in the world.

In terms of the second hope, I believe that one of the failings of Black Theology is that it has given the impression of only being concerned with its first identity as an academic discipline. I have used participative, experiential exercises drawn from Transformative Popular Education in order to show how the academic concerns of Black Theology can speak to and engage with the life experiences of ordinary Black people and vice versa.

This form of interaction, linking academic theory to attempts to develop practical action is what is known as 'praxis'. This book is an attempt to illustrate the praxis basis of Black Theology by means of its engagement with Black Theology theory and with ordinary Black people. This coming together of theory and practice-based experiences of ordinary Black people is intended to alert us to the practical challenges that face Black Theology in the twenty-first century.

This chapter seeks to synthesize all that has gone before. Rather than commence with an exercise this chapter will look at a practical, contentious issue and will show how, by means of Black Theology, one can seek to better understand and transform it. I want to show how Black Theology can be used as an interpretive tool for analysing contemporary issues in addition to being an academic discipline in its own right.

Identifying a contemporary issue

The summer of 2011 saw Britain engulfed by a serious of urban riots across the country. The catalyst for these urban riots was the death of Mark Duggan in Tottenham, North London, shot dead by the Metropolitan Police. The police claimed that Duggan had been armed and that they had killed him fearing there was an imminent threat from this armed individual.[1]

The community's anguish at the death of Duggan, a popular figure in the area, was exacerbated by the poor communication between the police in Tottenham and the wider Black community. What started out as a peaceful demonstration and vigil outside the police station in Tottenham subsequently turned into a riot. In the days following this initial event in Tottenham, there was a series of riots across London and in many other cities and towns across Britain.[2]

Countless column inches and government-sponsored academic research has been undertaken seeking to explain the reasons for these major events. At the time of writing, the latest explanation for the riots has come from the Black local Member of Parliament for the Opposition Labour Party, David Lammy. Lammy has claimed that the government prohibition on parents smacking their children (as part of the armoury for instilling discipline and creating a moral framework) is one of the underlying causes for the riots.[3] Lammy is putting forward the view that parents should be permitted to smack their children in order to discipline them. This form of discipline, so it is asserted, will prevent them from joining gangs and participating in the kinds of destructive, anti-social and criminal forms of behaviour, seen in the rioting in Tottenham and other parts of the country.

What is of interest for the purposes of this work is the identity of Lammy and the constituency that he represents in North London. David Lammy is a Black man of African Caribbean origin. He was born in London. His parents are from the Caribbean/South American country of Guyana, which was a former British colony, prior to its independence in 1966. The parliamentary constituency that Lammy represents (Tottenham) has a high concentration of Black people (of African and Caribbean origin) living within it. Tottenham is an area with many socio-economic problems, including high unemployment, crime (burglary and muggings) and drug dealing and misuse. The area was also the scene of major riots in October 1985 on a large estate named Broadwater Farm.[4]

The relationship of Lammy with his largely Black constituents is what interests me in the continuing debates surrounding the desirability or otherwise

---

1   See the following link for the genesis of this story, http://www.bbc.co.uk/news/ukengland-london-14459516 (accessed 29 February 2012).

2   For brief details on the riots see http://en.wikipedia.org/wiki/2011_England_riots (accessed 29 February 2012).

3   For the basic outline of this story, see http://www.huffingtonpost.co.uk/2012/01/29/lammy-smacking-laws-riots_n_1239759.html (accessed 29 February 2012).

4   See the following link for brief details on the Broadwater Farm riots in 1985, http://en.wikipedia.org/wiki/Broadwater_Farm_riot (accessed 29 February 2012).

of parents smacking their children in order to instil discipline. Conversations with a number of prominent Black Christians in Britain have revealed the high level of support David Lammy has received for his comments. Many Black Christian parents have argued that smacking children is an indispensable part of the formation and nurturing process for Black children. Many will point to Black cultural traditions and the Bible for evidence of the desirability of this practice. Others will argue that the imposition of the government in the domestic affairs of Black parents represents the heavy-handed imposition of the 'nanny state' on ordinary people. This imposition is a contributory factor in the levels of Black crime and violence committed by many Black young people in a number of urban contexts in Britain.

The fact that so many Black Christians agree with Lammy is not simply anecdotal reporting on my part. Rather, it is linked to a number of long-standing issues and concerns in some Diasporan Black communities on how to raise Black children, in the hope that they will be safe and will prosper.

So, in this chapter, I want to deploy many of the themes and ideas that have been discussed in previous chapters in order to demonstrate how Black Theology is not just an abstract intellectual discipline. I want to show how it is also a praxis-based movement, committed to social transformation, justice and equity for all people. In the light of the comments made by David Lammy, which have been supported by a number of ordinary Black people, I am going to reflect upon the relationship between the religious convictions of 'some' Black Christians and how these belief systems then get played out in some of the practical aspects of their faith. I am particularly interested in how Black Theology can offer a critical perspective on the relationship between what people say they believe, which then shapes their practice, especially when they feel there is a faith or moral perspective, and their actions.

For the purposes of this chapter, I want to look at some of the debates about how, as a society, we engage with children, particularly in terms of their nurture and overall socialization. So although I will be looking at how Black Christians attempt to construct their notions of what constitutes the 'Godly approach' to bringing up children, this work should not be seen as distinct material on 'children's ministry' per se. Rather, it is as an example of how 'Christian' thinking can be challenged by the methods and themes that emanate from Black Theology.

In this final chapter, I hope to show how Black Theology provides some important, critical tools for enabling ordinary Black people of faith to engage with the broader debates pertaining to the 'rights of children' and the associated questions around issues of discipline and corporal punishment. So this chapter is really a 'case-study' for the broader questions pertaining to how Black Christian faith in the UK (and in other contexts) engages with activities and forms of behaviour that have public policy issues and concerns imbued within them. This question is becoming increasingly important as the work of the Equalities and Human Rights Commission (EHRC)[5] in the UK has been contested by a number of Christians (of all ethnic and cultural groups) who regard the seeming imposition of the Equalities Bill as an example of so-called 'political correctness'. The provisions of the EHRC are seen by many conservative Black Christians as being contrary to the very essence of Christianity.

Part of my approach in this chapter is to engage Black Theology in dialogue with some of the resources utilized by practical theologians in order to better understand the ways in which human societies construe values and establish truth. This can assist in explaining how and why particular faith groups seek to use specific biblical narratives as a means of establishing their cultural norms for the contemporary practices in nurturing children. This is particularly germane in terms of the insistence of some on their rights to smack their children. In effect, I want to assess how we can open our eyes to the often covert ways in which our self-constructed assumptions of truth create frameworks for determining how the Bible is read. Then, as a corollary, what can be learnt from its many narratives, particularly as these texts affect our understanding of and the relationship with children.

It is worth remembering that these reflections are made in the light of the theory and practice of Black Theology! The central premise of Black Theology is that the term 'Black' comes to represent God's symbolic and actual solidarity with oppressed people. The majority of ordinary Black people have been consigned to the marginal spaces of the world solely on the grounds of their very Blackness.[6] I am using a Black theological method as a means of posing a number of ideological and socio-political points about the use and abuse of Holy Scripture and Christian tradition as it collides with contemporary Black experience and human life. Black Theology is committed to challenging the systemic frameworks that serve the interests of the powerful, often using the dictates of 'orthodoxy' as a means of attacking the perspectives of the marginalized. The perspectives of the latter are often labelled as 'unorthodox' at best and completely 'unacceptable' at worst.[7]

Finally, by way of an explanatory overview of this work, I should say that this chapter makes reference to working practices of Black communities, whether continental Africa, the UK, the Caribbean or North America. It should not be assumed that my reference to these communities or contexts denotes a specific or particular problem for these groups alone. There is a sense that all communities have their failings and examples of poor practice, aided and abetted by even poorer theology (more of which in a short while)

---

5 See the following link for further information, http://www.equalityhumanrights. com/ (accessed 29 February 2012).

6 See James H. Cone, *A Black Theology of Liberation*, Maryknoll, NY: Orbis, 1986.

7 See Kwok Pui-Lan, *Postcolonial Imagination and Feminist Theology*, Louisville, KY: Westminster John Knox, 2005.

in terms of their relationship to children. In highlighting these particular arenas, I am simply seeking to be honest about my own specific methodology and vocation as a Black theologian and informal, popular educator! I cannot, nor do I, write for everyone. Instead, I begin from a place that is familiar to me and address my thoughts to the spaces, places and people with whom I share some immediate sense of identity. My work proceeds from the shared narratives and historic resonances around what it means to be a Black human being.[8]

Determining the historical and contextual background

As we have seen in the early chapters, the starting point for Black Theology is the experience and realities of being a Black person in the world. Although Black Theology is undoubtedly a theological discipline, its starting points are not intellectual reflections on the nature, presence or, indeed, even the very existence of God. Rather, the starting point is the concrete reality of human existence. Previously I have argued that an important phrase in African Caribbean culture is that of 'who feels it, knows it'. The question that arises from this phrase is 'what have we felt and how do we know it is true, and what are the consequences if these experiences are actually true?' So, in order to construct a Black Theology-inspired approach to looking at this issue of how and why particular ideas or practices are invoked in the treatment of Black children, we need to explore the historical context that has shaped Black people in this respect. These historical reflections (like other Black Theology work that has explored 'slave narratives')[9] are intended to show the development of ideas and practices over an extended period of time.

So, for example, in order to understand the role played by Christianity in the nurture of Black children, one needs to know something of the development of Black Christianity in the African Diaspora, over the period of the last 500 years. Black Christianity in the Americas and the Caribbean (the site of my own recent ancestry) developed within the ongoing struggles of Black peoples to affirm their identity and very humanity in the face of seemingly insuperable odds.[10]

---

8 For an imaginative and incisive exploration of the shared and complex nature of what it means to be a human being, see Dwight N. Hopkins, *Being Human: Race, Culture and Religion*, Minneapolis: Fortress, 2005.

9 See Dwight N. Hopkins, *Down, Up and Over: Slave Religion and Black Theology*, Minneapolis: Fortress, 2000; Dwight N. Hopkins and George C. L. Cummings (eds), *Cut Loose Your Stammering Tongue: Black Theology in the Slave Narratives*, 2nd edn, Louisville, KY: Westminster John Knox, 2003; Carol Troupe, 'Re-Reading Slave Writing through the Lens of Black Theology', in Anthony G. Reddie (ed.), *Black Theology, Slavery and Contemporary Christianity*, Aldershot: Ashgate, 2010, pp. 165–84.

10 See Hopkins, *Down, Up and Over*, pp. 11–36.

As has been stated in other places, the 'invention' of Blackness, as opposed to being 'African' is a construction of the Enlightenment.[11] There already existed ways of seeing and understanding Black people and others of darker skin within the cultural thinking and imaginary gaze of Europeans. Nevertheless, the overall development of theories that saw Black people as 'less than' arose during the epoch of slavery.[12] In short, at some point in the long gestation period of the era of slavery, African people became Negroes, and went from being subjects to becoming objects of the racialized gaze of others.[13]

Black people in the African Diaspora became Christians in mass numbers during the 'Great Awakening' in the middle of the eighteenth century.[14] The Christianity into which they were socialized was an exploitative framework that stated that Black people were inherently and divinely sanctioned as being inferior to White people.[15] Black people were not passive imbibers, however, of this biased and self-serving brand of Christian education. Rather, Black slaves began to 'steal away' from beneath the close confines of their slave masters to worship God in their own self-constructed spaces.[16]

Black Christianity was born of the essential need to create safe frameworks in which the Black self could rehearse the basic rules of what it meant to be a human being.[17] These brief reflections on Diasporan Black African Christian history are very much a brief reminder of what has gone before in this text. They have been restated in order to emphasize the point that one has to reflect on the historical frameworks and analyse them in order to assess how and why particular ideas, concepts and practices develop. These, in turn, have shaped the lived experiences of ordinary Black people.

Wrestling with the Bible: the challenge for Black Christianity in Britain and across the world

In a previous chapter I have spoken about the need to 'tell a new story'. This work is very much centred on the Bible, as this resource remains a key component of Black Christian experience, and is a part of the arsenal

---

11 See Emmanuel C. Eze, *Race and the Enlightenment*, New Malden, MA, and Oxford: Blackwell, 1997.

12 See Dwight N. Hopkins, *Being Human*, pp. 113–60.

13 See Anthony B. Pinn, *Terror and Triumph: The Nature of Black Religion*, Minneapolis: Fortress, 2003, pp. 1–25.

14 See Anne H. Pinn and Anthony B. Pinn, *Fortress Introduction to Black Church History*, Minneapolis: Fortress, 2002, pp. 6–8.

15 See Sylvester A. Johnson, *The Myth of Ham in Nineteenth-Century American Christianity: Race, Heathens and the People of God*, New York: Palgrave Macmillan, 2004.

16 Henry H. Mitchell, *Black Church Beginnings: The Long-Hidden Realities of the First Years*, Grand Rapids, MI and Cambridge, UK: Eerdmans, 2004, pp. 24–45.

17 Mitchell, *Black Church Beginnings*, pp. 8–45.

of Black Theology's method of thinking about God in the light of Black experiences of struggle and marginalization. In terms of the former, Black religious scholarship, whether it is committed to Black Theology, or simply reflects on the Black experience in the light of religious themes, has undertaken work looking at the relationship of Black people to the Bible.[18] In terms of Black Theology, more specifically, Dwight Hopkins states:

> The second building block in the development of a black theology of liberation is a rereading of the bible from the perspective of the majority of society, those who are poor and working people. Black theology of liberation believes in a relationship between God's freeing activity in the African American community and that same liberating activity documented in the Hebrew and Christian Scriptures. In contrast to dominant ideas about theology, which claim to offer impartial thinking or talking about God, black theology sees and experiences the spirit of freedom clearly on the side of the African American poor.[19]

As we have seen, the exercise of rereading the Bible in the light of one's own lived experiences and reality is central to the attempt to 'tell a new story' about the Black self to the world and, indeed, to one's very self. It is a process of moving from being 'nobodies to somebodies'.[20] It should be noted, however, that the Bible is not an innocent text. What I mean by this is that it has the power invested in it by human beings who believe that it can transform and energize human experience. Therefore, given its importance, this makes it incumbent on us not to take it lightly. As we have seen, the Bible has been used to justify slavery, colonization, rape and homophobic violence. It has been used as a weapon against Black people. That is why Black biblical scholars like Randall Bailey and Oral Thomas talk about the need to read against the text.[21]

---

18 See Vincent L. Wimbush (ed.), *African Americans and the Bible: Sacred Texts and Social Textures*, New York and London: Continuum, 2000; Vincent L. Wimbush, *The Bible and African Americans: A Brief History*, Minneapolis: Fortress, 2003; Michael Joseph Brown, *The Blackening of the Bible: The Aims of African American Biblical Scholarship*, Harrisburg, PA: Trinity Press International, 2004; Patricia Sheerattan-Bisnauth (ed.), *Righting Her-Story: Caribbean Women Encounter the Bible Story*, Geneva: World Communion of Reformed Churches, 2011.

19 See Dwight N. Hopkins, *Introducing Black Theology of Liberation*, Maryknoll, NY: Orbis, 1999, p. 23.

20 See Anthony G. Reddie, *Nobodies to Somebodies: A Practical Theology for Education and Liberation*, Peterborough: Epworth, 2003.

21 See Randall C. Bailey, 'The Danger of Ignoring One's Own Cultural Bias in Interpreting the Text', in R. S. Sugirtharajah (ed.), *The Postcolonial Bible*, Sheffield: Sheffield Academic Press, 1998, pp. 66–90, and 'But It's in the Text: Slavery, the Bible, and the African Diaspora', in Reddie (ed.), *Black Theology, Slavery and Contemporary Christi-*

Reading against the text is the realization that biblical texts represent the active involvement of human beings in context, often writing in the light of their material interests when trying to talk about God's revelation. Inspired by the scholarship of Bailey, and more recently Thomas,[22] it is my belief that biblical texts are better understood as a sacred 'Word *about* God' rather than 'the Word *of* God'. They are not nuggets of God-dictated prose that fell from the heavens in an unadulterated form.

With this in mind, it is important, then, that Black Theology enables ordinary Black people to become increasingly aware of the ideological power of the Bible. It is incumbent that all of us are reminded of the need to engage with it faithfully, but critically, as I have indicated in a previous chapter.

Telling a new story requires a strategic engagement with the Bible, but not only in terms of it being the 'Word of God', as understood by so many ordinary Black people. I believe there is also a pragmatic role in this process as well that is important for our consideration. One of the important characteristics of Black Christianity is the centrality of the Bible. This is not to suggest that the Bible is not central to the formulations of other Christian groups or persons. It is a generalized truth, however, that every branch of Black Christianity across the world holds Scripture to be the supreme rule of faith and the only means by which one can understand God's revelation in Christ.

Despite its radical roots in countering racism and Black dehumanization, many Black churches and the Christians who have emerged from them, whether in the USA or in the Caribbean or Britain, have remained wedded to a form of nineteenth-century White evangelicalism. What I mean by this is that the frameworks through which many Black Christians were converted (the evangelical revival of the eighteenth century) were provided by White-European Christianity. While Black people clearly invested the various classical doctrines and beliefs with aspects of their own sensibilities, courtesy of their West African roots,[23] there is no doubting that a good deal of European thinking remained locked within their religious experiences.

Sadly, however, the vestiges of this influence have largely remained and are often manifested in anti-African/anti-Black sentiments. Black scholars have demonstrated the extent to which the theological development of Christianity as a global religion has been impacted by Eurocentric philosophical thought forms, often ignoring or down-playing the African

---

anity, pp. 31–46. See also Oral A. W. Thomas, *Biblical Resistance Hermeneutics within a Caribbean Context*, London: Equinox, 2010.

22 See Oral A. W. Thomas, 'A Resistant Biblical Hermeneutic within the Caribbean', *Black Theology* 6:3 (2008), pp. 330–42.

23 See Robert E. Hood, *Must God Remain Greek? Afro-Cultures and God-Talk*, Minneapolis: Fortress, 1990; Dianne M. Stewart, *Three Eyes for the Journey: African Dimensions of the Jamaican Religious Experience*, New York and London: Oxford University Press, 2005.

influence.[24] Black Christianity has imbibed these overarching Eurocentric, Greek-influenced thought forms, often at the expense of their own identity and African-based forms of knowledge and their resultant truth claims. One of the elements that Black Christianity has internalized is the idea that they are 'people of the book'. This adherence to the Bible as the sole basis for any legitimate talk about God is one that continues to exist in many branches of Black Christianity across the world.

For many Black Christians, while not necessarily describing themselves as 'evangelical', nevertheless, construct their faith in terms that owe very little to the more progressive developments in biblical studies and Christian theology. As I have outlined previously, historical-critical biblical studies will mean very little to them.[25] It is interesting to observe the ways in which many Black Christians seek to construct their world-view in terms of the Bible. This often takes the shape of seeking biblical bases for any form of action, as opposed to drawing on other forms of knowledge to supplement what the Bible might be saying.

Prior to undertaking this work, I found myself involved in a vigorous conversation with a leading Black Pentecostal church leader at a major lecture I had given on the subject of 'Black spiritualities'. The substance of the talk concerned the need for Black people to learn to incorporate more of their African cultural ancestry in their working practices of the Christian faith. I felt that this was important because it was a means of giving praxis to the totality of their existence. Namely, that Eurocentric, western-dominated schemes of religious knowledge, theory and practice were not serving the totality of Black Christianity well in twenty-first-century Britain. The initial reaction of this church leader was to reject any notion of 'Black spiritualities'. Not only was the idea an abhorrent one but also there was no such thing. My response to this retort was to 'play it safe'; I did not go on the offensive and argue for the radical, subversive nature of Black spiritualities. Rather, I settled for a more emollient line of argument. I simply made the point that all peoples, living in their particular contexts, had developed specific ways of connecting with the non-material that was within and beyond them. I emphasized that African peoples were no different in this regard. Then I asked the 64-million-dollar question. How did they account for the different types of spiritualities that existed in the world, if such contextual differences, like Black spiritualities, did not exist?

---

24 See Hood, *Must God Remain Greek?* See also Gay L. Byron, *Symbolic Blackness and Ethnic Difference in Early Christian Literature*, New York: Routledge, 2002.

25 I think it is important to realize that this facet is not unique to African and African Caribbean people. I would imagine that the majority of churchgoers in the UK have not found any engagement with the developments in 'liberal theology' or critical approaches to the Bible in their ongoing daily faith formations and Christian discipleship. But in this work I am concerned with Black Christians, particularly those of Caribbean descent.

My respondent countered, first by rejecting wholesale all notions of African schemes of knowledge and ways of knowing. It was reiterated that there was simply no such thing as Black spiritualities and, if such a thing existed, then it was clearly contrary to God's will. When I pressed the question about how did they account for different types of spiritualities in the world, they pointed first to the 'fall' and, second, to the tower of Babel (as depicted in Gen. 11.1–9) for their explanation.

In short, there was no legitimacy for drawing upon ideas from outside the biblical source for seeking to explain material cultures and their accompanying practices. Their reaction against anything that might be perceived as African was also made on the assumption that there was nothing from this source in the underlying themes and theological ideas of the Bible. To engage in such reflections was to indulge in aberrant forms of spirituality that had no basis in a 'proper' version of the Christian faith.

Rethinking how we see the Bible

At this point, the question of syncretism becomes a major area of controversy. When I asked why she was so resistant to the possibility of her faith and spirituality being influenced by African traditions, the words 'contamination' and 'pollution of the pure source' were used to validate the abhorrence. As I have asserted in a previous chapter, there is a need for a more expansive notion of Black religiosity, one which goes beyond just 'creedal Christianity'. It is imperative that we recognize that (a) not all Black people are Christians and (b) that the roots of our religious identities in many Black families is not solely Christian. The Diasporan journey of Black religio-cultural traditions, throughout the centuries, is one that has assimilated myriad influences and perspectives along the way. In fact, this is true of all communities, cultures and ethnic groups. There is nothing pure about any community of people, no matter how far back they can trace their lineage. It is imperative that ordinary Black people are enabled to be less doctrinaire over what is considered orthodox or acceptable. Assisting ordinary Black people to rethink how they read the Bible is essential to the process of 'telling a new story'. As we will see at a later point in this final chapter, reading the Bible in ways that ignore the religio-cultural history of a people can have damaging and even dangerous results.

In the many workshops I have led over the years as a participative Black Theologian, many Black Christians have argued against the inclusion of 'African cultural practices' within the orbit of their Christian faith. This tendency is perhaps amplified when such people have recently come to the UK from the African continent. The more recent work of Gayraud Wilmore in the USA[26] has not persuaded many Black Christians to rethink the extent to which they

---

26 See Gayraud S. Wilmore, *Pragmatic Spirituality: The Christian Faith through an Africentric Lens*, New York and London: New York University Press, 2004, pp. 87–152.

might be persuaded to see their Christian faith as more than the mere adherence to biblical texts and narratives. Oftentimes, this adherence to the Bible is secured on the grounds of biblical literalism and even fundamentalism.

The question of how we read the Bible in the context of the plural, and oftentimes increasingly complex, religious landscape is very much a vexed question. The challenge to the Church and Christians from other religious philosophical positions, such as 'Humanism' or post-Enlightenment secular notions of civic life, are very real. For many Black Christians, the response to this challenge is to delve even further into the Bible and to seek to use it as a rule book as opposed to a guide. So, when such individuals and communities cite biblical sanction for and against particular ideas or examples of social policy, they often do so on the basis of not acknowledging the complexity and ambiguity of the Bible itself as a source for their religious praxis.

Some ordinary Black people will miss the fact that parts of the Bible incorporate alternative religious and philosophical ideas. The consequence of this is that it can be a means of encouraging Christians to interpret the actions of God within other thought forms. Sadly, this facet of reading has eluded some Black Christians (and other people of course, I should add). A good example of this can be seen in the Prelude to John's Gospel. This is constructed in terms of Greek philosophical thought and not strictly a form of 'traditional' Jewish-Hebrew tradition. The depiction of the Cosmic Christ as the 'Logos' is in fact a Greek import by the writer of the Fourth Gospel. It was used as a means of showing the universalizing basis of the Christ of faith for the whole of humankind.

I am sure that for some early readers of the Fourth Gospel, particularly those from Jewish religio-cultural backgrounds, this kind of 'syncretism' must have seemed outrageous and distinctly dangerous. This move, however, is now viewed with equanimity by most Christians throughout the world. I can safely report that I have never seen or heard of any Black Christian in Britain voice any doubt about the efficacy or legitimacy of the opening sections of the Fourth Gospel. The use of Greek ideas to talk about a Jewish rabbi from Galilee does not concern them.[27]

Many people will counter this point by making recourse to the unfolding role of authority within Christendom on matters pertaining to Christian doctrine and biblical interpretation. It would seem that syncretism is acceptable when the controlling powers of church authority deem it to be so. This brings me back to my central contention of the anti-African/

---

27 As Hood reminds us, it would appear that so long as 'White' European cultures and thought forms are being intertwined with so-called 'pure' Christianity, then any notion of syncretism (often rarely admitted as such, however) can be tolerated. But when Black African traditions are being utilized, like Vodun in Haiti or Santeria in Cuba, then the dictates of White Euro-American hegemony are brought to bear, often at the expense of the latter. See Hood, *Must God Remain Greek?*, pp. 43–102.

anti-Black perspectives that have been imbibed by some ordinary Black Christians. So long as largely White western religious authorities can dictate what is orthodox and who can be saved and who is allowed within or is excluded from the Church then most Black Christians are content to acquiesce. When moves are made to incorporate African-centred perspectives into our notions of Black religiosity, suddenly all bets are off! One can witness aspects of this disdain in terms of the reception afforded Michelle Gonzalez's work in Cuba. Michelle Gonzalez has sought to align Roman Catholicism with Santeria,[28] within the Cuban context. When I have explained the merits of Gonzalez's work to ordinary Black Christians, many of them have cried foul, asserting that this kind of move is dangerous.

If we look at the development of 'Imperial Mission Christianity'[29] over the past 400 years, for example, one could well argue that the countless deaths at the hand of the Christian orthodoxy of John 14.6 would make the alleged dangers of Santeria seem like 'child's play'. So why is it that one kind of importation is permissible and even seen as desirable (for a number of people, the Fourth Gospel remains their favourite within the New Testament canon) and another is not? Some will argue for the inspiration of the Holy Spirit (the same Spirit who championed Greek texts in the New Testament canon and not African/Coptic ones?). Others will point to the legitimizing and authenticating process of church tradition. I want to assert, however, the 'hermeneutic

---

28 Santeria is a religious tradition that has its origins in West Africa and is an amalgam of inherited African religious themes and European Roman Catholicism. See Michelle A. Gonzalez, *Afro-Cuban Theology: Religion, Race, Culture and Identity*, Gainesville: University of Florida Press, 2006.

29 In using this term I am speaking of a historical phenomenon in which there existed (and continues to this day) an interpenetrating relationship between European expansionism, notions of White superiority and the material artefact of the apparatus of empire. In terms of the last, one must note the relationship between external and internal forms of socio-political and cultural imposition upon client states, who exhibit limited agency within these forms of geo-political arrangements. When speaking of external imposition, I am referring to externalized control of territory from European metropolitan centres (London, Paris, Brussels, Madrid, Berlin, Lisbon etc.) usually via colonial apparatchiks, such as viceroys, governors and more faceless bureaucrats in the civil service. In terms of internal imposition, I am referring to the axiomatic epistemological (knowledge-based) superiority of Eurocentric socio-cultural norms, manners, aesthetics and morality, which affected the social arrangements between the colonized and the colonizer. All this took place within the body politic of those nations ruled under the aegis of empire. There is a vast literature pertaining to the development, facets and characteristics of colonialism and empire, particularly, within the purview of the Christian Church. For a selective reading of this phenomenon, particularly from a liberationist perspective, see John Parratt (ed.), *An Introduction to Third World Theologies*, Cambridge: Cambridge University Press, 2004; R. S. Sugirtharajah (ed.), *Voices from the Margin: Interpreting the Bible in the Third World*, Maryknoll, NY, and London: Orbis/SPCK, 1995; Virginia Fabella and R. S. Sugirtharajah (eds), *Dictionary of Third World Theologies*, Maryknoll, NY: Orbis, 2000.

of suspicion' at this point. As we have seen in a previous chapter, this term refers to a mode of scepticism and suspicion at the claims that are made for accepted truth and orthodoxy. What is often constituted as truth and ortho-doxy is often dictated by people with power and authority. This, in turn, is linked to those who have much to benefit from the assumptions that par-ticular ideas cannot be challenged. I want to ask the critical question of who benefits from the parameters we set concerning orthodoxy and heterodoxy? I pose the question because such matters are as often concerned with issues of power as they are with religious or theological matters. Why are some Black Christians happier to champion White, western orthodoxy at the expense of Black attempts to refashion a version of Christianity that is fit for purpose for the complex, postmodern world of the twenty-first century?

The construction of Jesus as the 'Logos', for example, is the kind of rethink-ing of religious ideas that so many ordinary Black Christians find eminently acceptable. Yet, this is a radical philosophical and theological innovation. In this new development, Jesus is understood in a new form for the purposes of Christian mission in a predominantly Greek-influenced world. As the Church moved away from its purely Jewish moorings (for good or ill), so it found new thought forms in which to reflect the truths of Jesus the Christ as an agent for righteousness and liberation.

In the British context, it is disappointing that Robert Beckford's coura-geous attempts to do something similar with Jesus at the end of the twentieth century, in casting him as 'dread', within the frameworks provided by Rasta and reggae culture, never took off.[30] The ingenious skill of Beckford was to locate within the 'Jesus of faith' a means of encapsulating a saving Christ for Black people in postcolonial Britain. This saving Christ was Black, Ca-ribbean, contemporary, edgy and anti-establishment. This Black Christ was not limited by the dictates of Christian orthodoxy (after all, what has dread and Rasta to do with first-century Galilee or Christian tradition?). Rather, this Jesus was an anti-imperial sacred figure, committed to the overturning of White privilege and its resultant supremacy.

The kind of theological intuition advocated by Beckford and other Black theologians, in terms of how one engages with alternative thought forms and frameworks for assessing truth, remains a threat for many ordinary Black people. For the most part, Black Christianity in Britain is often locked into literalistic readings of the Bible, in which many adherents claim to be-lieve the whole of the canon as being divinely inspired and the supreme authority in all matters.[31] This adherence to Scripture is selective like *all*

---

30 See Robert Beckford, *Jesus Is Dread*, London: Darton, Longman and Todd, 1998, and *Dread and Pentecostal: A Political Theology for the Black Church in Britain*, Lon-don: SPCK, 2000.

31 See 'The Statement of Faith' of the Influential *Council for Black-Led Churches*. http://www.cblcuk.com/membership/index.php?pageID=429 (Accessed 22 March 2010.)

approaches to reading the Bible. I emphasize *all* because I think it is of crucial import in the context of this discussion. All of us are selective, idiosyncratic and contradictory in the way in which we handle the Bible.

The last statement can be witnessed when one reflects on the salient truth
of our inconsistent approaches to biblical authority, as recounted by Miguel
de la Torre.[32] As de la Torre suggests, in the context of how Christian parents should remonstrate with and discipline their children, the Bible calls for
disobedient children to be executed (Lev. 20.9). He continues by reminding
us that the Bible is not the fullest revelation of God because Jesus is 'the
Word'; Jesus is the norm by which all the other elements of the Bible are to
be interpreted. But the fact is that many Christian communities do not treat
'the Word' as being Jesus, but rather sanction the whole of Scripture as
being literally dictated by God and therefore understood as the sole means
of salvation.

The issue of the inconsistency in our reading strategies can be found in
the manner in which certain passages of the Bible are taken as literally true
(and are to be followed accordingly) while others are not. As I have stated,
all people read the Bible in idiosyncratic and contradictory ways, even those
who claim to read it literally, as if it were the *actual words* of God. As
Miguel de la Torre reminds us, if the Bible were the literal word of God
then God would be guilty of genocide, infanticide, patricide and regicide.
When de la Torre points to the fact that the Bible calls for disobedient children to be executed he does so in an ironic mode, knowing full well that
no right-minded society supposedly adhering to Christian values will casu-
ally sanction the execution of disobedient children. Many may well believe
the Bible to be the literal word of God, but some form of interpretative
framework is at work to ensure that, for the most part, catastrophic events
like murdering children do not become a regular occurrence. While most
Christian communities have ways of regulating their literal understanding
of violent and bloodthirsty texts,[33] I would argue that the underlying frameworks people hold about the Bible and the nature of God still inform the
overarching values for how we treat and engage with children.

It is comparatively rare that violence is committed against children as normative practice, which is then justified on biblical grounds. It is my belief,
however, that the underlying notions of God and the Bible held by many
people provide the substantive framework that makes such religious and
cultural horrors possible. There are dangers when we attempt to engage
with the Bible as if this material artefact provides the normative framework
for our ethics, without being influenced by or even attempting to interpret

---

32 Miguel A. de la Torre, 'Scripture', in Miguel A. de la Torre (ed.), *Handbook of
U. S. Theologies of Liberation*, St Louis: Chalice Press, 2004, pp. 85–6.

33 See Renita J. Weems, *Battered Love: Marriage, Sex, and Violence in the Hebrew
Prophets*, Minneapolis: Fortress, 1995.

it in the light of new theories or knowledge of human life. In such cases, we run the risk of being able to sanction the worst kind of religious atrocities, because 'God told us to do it'.

I argue in this work that it is imperative that ordinary Black Christians are encouraged to engage with alternative and differing philosophical frameworks when reflecting on how they construct their faith-based ways of living. It is important that we consider new ways of seeing and interpreting what it means to be human. Alternative theories, at their best, can pour additional light onto the nature of Christian discourse and practice, rather than obscuring or polluting it. Just as Greek philosophical thought offered a new focus on 'Jesus as the Christ' for the early Church, so then engaging with differing religio-cultural frameworks can assist Black Christians in their engagement with social policy-related issues in twenty-first-century Britain. For the purposes of this chapter I am interested in the public policy issue of how Black Christian parents nurture and socialize their children in this present era.

In a previous piece of work, I showed that many Black Christians possess a form of dialectical spirituality, which provides the frameworks for how they read and interpret the Bible.[34] In that work, I argued that within many Black religious communities there exists a religious-cultural framework, whereby people can read in support of what the biblical text has said and against it, depending upon the ways in which their traditional norms were either being supported or challenged by the Bible.[35] In effect, we can take the Bible literally or find some means of 'squaring it' with our existing prejudices and cultural norms, depending upon whether biblical texts collude with or challenge our existing cultural norms.

Back to the children

One of the most important tasks for any society is that of nurturing the next generation. The British state, for example, will spend billions of pounds in providing free public education in order that children are educated and socialized for their future life as citizens within the nation. Alongside the provision of education in all its various manifestations, the state also provides statutory social services in order to ensure the safe welfare and care of children. Children are of immense importance to the body politic of any nation.

Alongside the provision of the state, Christian communities are also charged with the care and nurture of children. This can be seen in a plethora of reports, or in the amount of electronic and printed curriculum

---

34 See Anthony G. Reddie, *Working against the Grain: Re-Imaging Black Theology in the 21st Century*, London: Equinox, 2008, pp. 49–74.

35 Reddie, *Working against the Grain*, pp. 68–74.

and learning materials for promoting child nurture and instruction into the Christian faith. In short, considerable amounts of resources are spent by the churches in Britain on work with children.

Why this is important

In the summer of 2007, as Britain commemorated the bicentenary of the passing of the abolition of the slave trade act, I and a number of colleagues organized a major Black Theology conference seeking to address the legacies of slavery. At the conclusion of the second night, a group of participants, all of us second-generation African Caribbean people, born in the UK and socialized within Black Christian families, began to share our experiences of growing up in our various households. This was a spontaneous outpouring of emotions and memories. Amid much laughter and good-natured banter, the ten of us all remembered the wonderfully idiosyncratic child-rearing practices of our Caribbean parents, all of whom had come to the UK as part of the *Windrush* generation, between 1948 and 1965.

What was common to the experience of all ten was the casual way in which discipline was administered within the home. While none of the group exhibited any sense of animosity or anger at the kinds of punishment that were levied out to us in our formative years, it was nevertheless some-what disconcerting to see the extent to which these practices were so commonplace. One of the members of that group intimated that there should be some form of research undertaken into this phenomenon. It was clear that this jocular and amusing discussion had, nonetheless, resonated with us all. Perhaps it had struck a raw nerve?

Earlier, I spoke of the ways in which cultural frameworks are often conflated with biblical texts in order to provide the ethical and moral basis for particular forms of action. In the context of the child-rearing practices of some African Caribbean parents one can cite two seemingly inviolate 'proof texts' from the Bible. In the first instance there are the pithy remarks to be found in Proverbs 13.24, which states, 'Those who spare the rod hate their children, but those who love them are diligent to discipline them.' These remarks are followed by Proverbs 23.13–14, which say, 'Do not withhold discipline from your children; if you beat them with a rod, they will not die. If you beat them with the rod, you will save their lives from Sheol.'

In both cases, these texts, particularly the latter, are quite explicit in the relationship between using the rod and sparing a child from going to hell. Clearly, what loving and responsible parent would not want to spare their child the excesses of everlasting damnation for the sake of some correctly administered discipline using the rod? Such injunctions will, of course, run contrary to the explicit dictates of the state, which has taken a negative view on the notion of corporal punishment, while stopping short of outlawing it completely.[36] For many Black Christian parents, the state's belief that parents should not strike their children is seen as a direct challenge to what many will see as clear biblical teaching. It is in this context that David Lammy's remarks are seen to have struck a chord with the 'common-sense wisdom' of ordinary Black Christian parents in the UK and perhaps in other parts of the world also.

The importance of the Bible in shaping historic and perhaps more contemporary child-rearing practices can perhaps be more clearly discerned in an in-depth look at another 'proof text', of sorts, in terms of how one should treat one's children. I have chosen to look at Abraham's aborted sacrifice of his son in Genesis 22, because it has been quoted by some ordinary Black Christian parents as an exemplar for the kind of dutiful, faith-based, parental observance insisted upon by a righteous and stern God.

Reflecting upon Genesis 22.1–14

I have chosen to reflect upon this text because it is one of those difficult passages that is (for very good reason) often overlooked by many people who work with children. It has been deemed as an 'unfriendly text' for children. There is no doubt that once one digs beneath the spiritualized veneer of this text one cannot help but be appalled at the actions of the main protagonist in the narrative. What are we to make of Abraham's seemingly reckless actions, in being prepared to sacrifice his son at the behest of a disembodied voice, claiming to be God? How this text is read tells us much about the underlying frameworks some Black Christians hold in terms of their assessment of the theological value of young children.

'Some years later God decided to test Abraham, so he spoke to him' (Gen. 22.1, CEB). Thus begins this infamous text. The voice of God speaks to Abraham and he, responding, agrees to take his son Isaac to the land of Moriah. Abraham gets up early in the morning and begins to chop wood in order to raise a sacrifice to God on an altar.

It is interesting to note that nowhere in the text does it say that Abraham sought the opinion of his wife Sarah on this matter. As I have stated in a previous piece of work, there is always an inherent danger in the sole, individual voice, responding to what they notionally believe to be the 'voice of God', and acting in potentially destructive ways, later claiming that 'God told them to do it'.[37] The collective and corporate ethic in Christian theology and practice as a means of discerning God's revealed presence and

---

36 This issue was reported in more popularist terms by the BBC, back in 2005. See http://news.bbc.co.uk/1/hi/uk/4175905.stm (accessed 23 February 2012).

37 See Anthony G. Reddie, *Acting in Solidarity: Reflections in Critical Christianity*, London: Darton, Longman and Todd, 2005, p. 19.

activity is hugely important. It remains an important theological method within Methodism (and other churches, of course), for example, for such dangerous and unrepresentative of occasions as this one![38]

If we applied a 'hermeneutic of suspicion' at this point, we would be able to look more critically at the lone patriarch who is the sole recipient of revelatory experience. Black Theology should emphasize the collective and not notions of hierarchical and top-down models of revelatory, inspired practices of authority and leadership.[39] I believe that Black and Womanist theologies offer us alternative, collective, communitarian ways of discerning God's presence and what might be construed as God's will. These models would force ordinary Black people reading this text to note that the male patriarch did not consult his wife in order to check on the veracity of the message. Perhaps a dispassionate voice from the one who gave birth to the child in the first instance would have forced the male protagonist to 'think again' about the desirability of the action he was considering undertaking? This kind of critical reading has important implications for how many Black churches are run. How would church life be different if sole patriarchal men consulted disenfranchised Black women more often?

When Isaac asks his father about the seeming absence of a ram that will be used for the sacrifice, Abraham responds by stating, 'My Son . . . God will provide the ram' (v. 6). The unmistaken and uncomfortable echoes of christological atonement can be read into this verse. 'God will provide the ram' can be seen as an early portent of the 'lamb whose death takes away the sin of the world'. Womanist theologians such as Terrell and Williams[40] have critiqued normative atonement theories for their valourizing of the mechanics of suffering, mutilation and death, seemingly as an act of will from a bloodthirsty, patriarchal God.

Delores Williams, in particular, has offered a trenchant riposte to the notion that sacrificial action can be understood as redemptive. Williams is particularly concerned with the cross and Christ's atonement serving as a kind of model or example for Black women to emulate. In other words, Christ's suffering was redemptive, therefore the same can be true for you! The idea of sacrificing oneself for the sake of others undoubtedly has noble connotations and is the kind of heroic example often told in mythic tales of heroism. It is problematic, argues Williams, when it becomes the expected and sole mode of engagement open to Black women. This, as corollary, then

---

38 See Angela Shier-Jones, 'Conferring as Theological Method', in Clive Marsh, Brian Beck, Angela Shier-Jones and Helen Wareing (eds), *Unmasking Methodist Theology*, London: Continuum, 2004, pp. 82–94.

39 Michael N. Jagessar and Anthony G. Reddie (eds), *Black Theology in Britain: A Reader*, Oakwood and London: Equinox, 2007, pp. 305–6.

40 See JoAnne Marie Terrell, *Power in the Blood? The Cross in the African American Experience*, Maryknoll, NY: Orbis, 1998, pp. 17–34; Delores Williams, *Sisters in the Wilderness: The Challenge of Womanist God-Talk*, Maryknoll, NY: Orbis, 1993, pp. 161–7.

denies them other forms of resistance and activity, save that of heroic, silent suffering for others.[41] It is worth quoting Williams at length here because I feel her biting critique of notions of redemptive suffering has an important role to play in how we think about the issue of the physical disciplining or smacking of children. Williams says:

> Women must question (Deotis) Roberts's way of seeing such positive value in oppressed black women identifying with Christ through their common suffering wrought by cross-bearing. Black women should never be encouraged to believe that they can be united with God through this kind of suffering. There are quite enough black women bearing the cross by rearing children alone, struggling on welfare, suffering through poverty, experiencing inadequate health care, domestic violence and various forms of sexism and racism.[42]

While Williams's comments do not pertain to the issue of child-rearing, they do nevertheless call into question the efficacy of sacrifice as a means of pleasing God. They also challenge the belief that one might witness or experience desirable and spiritually fulfilling outcomes in submitting oneself to such sacrificial acts.

What is important to note about this text is the seeming patriarchal collusion between a bloodthirsty male God and a complicit male patriarch. That God should seek to test Abraham using a seemingly 'dispensable' child should invite serious comment. This, however, is then compounded by the fact that Abraham does not seem to challenge or question the veracity of the voice and its outlandish command.

Many from a more conservative evangelical tradition will cry foul at my 'hermeneutic of suspicion' that is clearly in evidence as I read this text. Some will cry out at my irreverent and unholy readings of Scripture. I would remind them that if challenging or questioning the voice of God is a wholly illegitimate exercise, then what are we to make of Job, who does that very thing and is not reprimanded by God?[43] In actual fact, a close reading of the book of Job shows that it is his so-called friends who give him erroneous advice who are chastised, not Job himself.

If we can allow ourselves the honesty of not sacralizing the text, one cannot but help consider the alacrity with which Abraham appears willing to offer up his son as a sacrifice to God. The frightening aspect of this text is the way in which it is used in much *adult* Christian education work as a prime exemplar of human obedience. In effect, this becomes a kind of theological and spiritual test case for the kind of sacrificial denying of self that

---

41 Williams, *Sisters in the Wilderness*, pp. 161–7.

42 Williams, *Sisters in the Wilderness*, p. 169.

43 See Reddie, *Acting in Solidarity*, pp. 22–30.

is replete within Christian theology. It is strange that more questioning of this text does not take place. Surely it is not unreasonable to speculate on whether Abraham had taken leave of his senses? After all, are not such actions potentially the stuff of headlines on the late-night news, when persons are seen to have 'gone off the rails'? Instead, for many, this story is a great example to follow. If we see this narrative as a great example and not as a cautionary tale, we find ourselves in treacherously deep waters. Clearly, it must be the case that what we are meant to follow is the *spirit* of the narrative and not the specific example itself. For to do so would surely mean a lengthy prison sentence. However, as we know, there are *some* people who are prone to read the Bible in literalistic ways. One of the consequences of such literalistic readings is that spiritual exemplars such as this one (which are still problematic, as I have shown) have an unfortunate habit of sometimes becoming *actual* events and practices. The dangers of such texts are exacerbated when we are also dealing with people who have not seen the concealed, ironic 'nod and a wink', denoting that they were not meant to take it *too seriously*.

This text is clearly one of the most non-child-friendly narratives in the Bible. The fact that it is rarely used in the formal contexts of Christian formation, when working with children, is testament to the dangerous precedents it seems to set around the apparent disposability of children, at the whim of God. It is perhaps the nature of these 'texts of terror',[44] coupled with the post-Second World War developments in cognitive psychology that led to the growing awareness of the needs of learners, particularly young children. These developments led to an increased appreciation of the role of psychology in the Christian education of children.[45] Namely, that the messages we send out through smacking children are potentially harmful. If striking an adult can be deemed to be assault, then how might a child potentially interpret such actions? This must be a point of some concern given the greater vulnerability of children to exploitation when compared to adults. One rarely hears such concerns from the advocates of this form of action.

The vulnerability of Black children in terms of exploitation, and the need to support and empower the most vulnerable, is a central tenet of all theologies of liberation, including Black Theology. The realities of pain and suffering have to be more important than the seemingly simple, doctrinaire application of biblical proof texts. They have to be more important than the belief in certain theological ideas relating to suffering and pain being redemptive. I am reminded that central to any Black Theology analysis is the belief that the sole criteria for the desirability of any theological doctrine or

---

44 See Phyllis Trible, *Texts of Terror: Literary-Feminist Readings of Biblical Narratives*, London: SCM, 1992.

45 John Sutcliffe (ed.), *Tuesday's Child: A Reader for Christian Educators*, Birmingham: Christian Education, 2001, pp. 46–71.

theme are whether they promote emancipation and liberation. At this point it is worth quoting James Cone who amplifies this point when he states that 'Black Theology is not prepared to discuss the doctrine of God, man, Christ, Church, Holy Spirit – the whole spectrum of Christian theology – without making each doctrine an analysis of the emancipation of black people.'[46]

Incorporating alternative forms of knowledge to help us understand the truth

Earlier in this book, I demonstrated how Black Theology has been adept at using alternative theories and concepts as ways of looking critically at any issue or concern. One of the tools that can be used by Black Theology are the insights of developmental psychology. These can enable us to understand the critical issues at play in our reflections on the Christian formation of children.

In the context of this discussion, it is interesting to note the clear disparity between many of the formal processes adopted by many churches in the UK to the question of the socialization of children, and those utilized by some Black Christian parents. In terms of the former, one can still deduce the influence of the impact of developmental psychology of the 1960s on how the state and many churches engage with children. Developmental psychology, sometimes known as 'human development', is the study of the psychological processes that emerge throughout the course of human life. There is a particular concern on how these factors impact on and affect human personality and behaviour.[47] The role of developmental psychology, particularly its application to the nurture of children, has been one of the ground-breaking movements of the twentieth century. This movement gave greater clarity and insight into the developmental nature of human life. It offered an important riposte to the competing notions regarding human growth and consciousness. On the one hand, there was the belief that human development was chiefly a product of environmental forces, including notions of child nurture. On the other hand, the counter view asserted that human beings were shaped entirely by God's grace. In terms of the former, the work of James Fowler on faith development has been immensely instructive.[48] Fowler has shown that human beings are active in the construction of their faith as a means of making sense of and interpreting the world. In other words, Christian faith is not solely a gift of grace, but is also a product of experience.

---

46 James H. Cone, *Black Theology and Black Power*, Maryknoll, NY: Orbis 1989 [1969], p. 121.

47 See, for example, Erik H. Erikson, *The Life Cycle Completed*, New York: Norton, 1997; Urie Bronfenbrenner, *The Ecology of Human Development: Experiments by Nature and Design*, Cambridge, MA: Harvard University Press, 1979.

48 See James W. Fowler, *Stages of Faith: The Psychology of Human Development and the Quest for Meaning*, San Francisco: HarperCollins, 1985.

With specific reference to the nurture and development of children raised within a Christian context or within the orbit of the Church, the research of Ronald Goldman has been of immense importance. Goldman's work led to a wholesale reassessment of the role of the Bible in the formation and nurture of children.[49] Goldman contended that the Bible was an adult book and wholly unsuited to the nurture and developmental needs of children.[50] He writes: 'I suggest that it is impossible to teach the Bible as such to children much before adolescence, and that we must look for another approach which offers a more realistic alternative to our present ills.'[51]

Goldman's ideas are less popular these days, as the progressive insights of the 1960s are being increasingly rejected. Despite this, however, it should be noted that an important legacy of developmental psychology has been the notion that children are not 'miniature adults' or mere 'dependants', lacking in agency or autonomy of their own. This has demonstrated the importance of children's rights, among them the right to be recognized as 'spiritual beings' endowed with the capacity to know God for themselves and to be able to articulate their innate sense of spirituality.

The broader developments in child nurture and socialization, both within the Church and by the state, has adopted a broadly 'liberal' perspective. Conversely, the practices often adopted by some Black Christian parents remain rooted in a seemingly fixed model of strict biblical literalism and an accompanying adherence to the 'Word of God'. Whether it is a literal reading of selected texts from the book of Proverbs or a literalist reading of the Abraham narrative from Genesis 22, it is not uncommon to find some Black Christian parents extolling the 'Good Book'. Many will ignore the claims of the broader insights in child development and socialization, often dismissing these as 'secular' and 'political correctness'.

It is not my intention to attack every aspect of the child-rearing practices of all Black Christian parents. I was born into and socialized in such an environment, and I am thankful for my parents. For many ordinary Black people, especially those who are Christian parents, the underlying frameworks that govern the nurture and socialization of their children have developed over a long period of time. Often, such parental models have been informed by the historic context of religious faith responding to real material hardship. One should not forget that the historic background and development of Black Christianity in Britain and across the other parts of the African Diaspora, as I have stated previously, was one that emerged as a response to the reality of oppression.[52]

---

49 See Ronald Goldman, *Readiness for Religion*, London: Routledge and Kegan Paul, 1965.

50 Goldman, *Readiness for Religion*, pp. 3–39.

51 Goldman, *Readiness for Religion*, p. 8.

52 See Pinn, *Terror and Triumph*, pp. 81–156.

A number of critical perspectives have arisen from the Diasporan African experience of slavery, colonialism, reconstruction and postcolonialism. One of the key insights has been the sense that many Black people learnt very quickly that the world was not a place to be trusted. The world of White people was one in which Black communities lived in terms of fear, trepidation and the constant threat of death. Consequently, many Black communities became cautiously conservative in their socialization patterns and child-rearing practices. Grant Shockley, looking at the Christian education of African American children, for example, reflects upon the conservative and didactic models of teaching used in the nurture and Christian formation within many historic Black churches.[53]

The nature of the threat to Black life was such that no concessions were made in terms of socializing and nurturing children. Such patterns of child-rearing had to respond to the contextual struggles of simply trying to stay alive in a hostile environment. They also needed to inculcate Black children into the necessary survival skills for navigating themselves through such dangerous environments. It is in such contexts that Christian faith often became the means of overcoming these very real environmental threats. Janice Hale amplifies this point when commenting on the importance of African-derived stories of experience:

> These stories transmit the message to Black children that there is a great deal of quicksand and many land mines on the road to becoming a Black achiever . . . They also transmit the message that it is possible to overcome these obstacles. These stories help Black children de-personalise oppression when they encounter it and enable them to place their personal difficulties into the context of the overall Black liberation struggle.[54]

African Diasporan practices of nurture and formation, which emerged from the fiery furnace of slavery and racism, have alighted on the central importance of Christian faith. They have done so, often seeing faith as the primary means (some might even assert as the only means) by which Black people can survive in a discriminatory and hostile environment.[55]

While the extremities of the past are no longer the reality for many Black children, the inherited frameworks of biblical literalism and

---

53   See Grant Shockley, 'Historical Perspectives', in Charles R. Foster and Grant S. Shockley (eds), *Working with Black Youth: Opportunities for Christian Ministry*, Nashville, TN: Abingdon, 1989, pp. 9–29.

54   Janice Hale, 'The Transmission of Faith to Young African American Children', in Randall C. Bailey and Jacquelyn Grant (eds), *The Recovery of Black Presence*, Nashville, TN: Abingdon, 1995, pp. 193–207 (207).

55   Colleen Birchett, 'A History of Religious Education in the Black Church', in Donald B. Rogers (ed.), *Urban Church Education*, Birmingham, AL: Religious Education Press, 1989, pp. 69–76 (76).

neo-conservatism remain. This facet is visible in how children are often perceived in terms of their individual agency.

One can see aspects of this biblical-religio-cultural framework in the work of Joe Aldred, one of the leading Black Christian figures in Britain. He is the secretary for Minority Ethnic Christian Affairs for Churches Together in England (CTE). In an interview for the *Birmingham Post*, Aldred is reported to have stated that 'Black Children fail for the want of discipline'. Aldred continues by stating:

> It started a long time ago with all the politically correct stuff about the degree to which parents should control children. In a Caribbean home a good slap on the backside for a child that is misbehaving is seen as nothing wrong. If you do it now, you get reported to the police.[56]

In fairness to Aldred, I must stress that in citing his words I am in no way inferring that Aldred in any sense condones violence against Black children. Indeed, one can cite his work in challenging the unrepresentative practices of some Black churches, predominantly in London, in terms of their anti-Christian behaviour to children who are alleged to be demon-possessed.[57]

To be clear, I do not believe that Aldred accepts any notion of the acceptability of abusing children in the name of exorcism. I am bound to remark, however, that his easy assumption that the lack of corporal punishment can lead to deteriorating social behaviour conforms to the religious framework I have described thus far. This brings me back to the comments of David Lammy. For Lammy, the inability of predominantly Black parents to smack their children can be seen as a contributory cause of riots in London and across the country in August 2011.

Even the most cursory or basic adherence to notions of critical social analysis (such as that adopted in the previous chapter) would alert us to the fact that Lammy's contentions are risible. It is a struggle to find any research evidence to suggest that there is *any* relationship between children being smacked and resultant better social behaviour.

Of greater concern, however, for the purposes of this work on Black Theology are the underlying theological models or images of God that seem to fuel these particular notions on child-rearing. The necessity of disciplining children using physical force remains acceptable if one possesses conservative or even biblically literalist frameworks for assessing the theological virtue of physical punishment and suffering. These theological frameworks are then 'aided and abetted' by historically conservative religious values that

---

56 *Birmingham Post*, 31 March 2004. From http://www.corpun.com/uks00403.htm.

57 See http://www.wwrn.org/article.php?idd=17775&sec=39&cont=5 for an example of Aldred's leadership on this issue in his capacity as the Chair of the Council of Black-Led Churches.

essentially believe 'any kind of action is necessary to safeguard children from hell, sin and the outside world'.

Aldred and Lammy assume that the potentially confused messages we send out to children when we use physical forms of restraint and correction are justifiable if they lead to regulated behaviour and any resultant learning. This view, of course, is predicated on the non-existent evidence that there is any causal link between corporal punishment and resultant behaviour.

I should stress once again that I am not seeking to attack all Black Christian parents. Rather, I am trying to engage with Black parents as a means of questioning the wider challenges posed by constricted and literalist readings of the Bible. I am also concerned at the use of traditional atonement theories that seek to validate suffering and physical pain as being redemptive. In this chapter, I have attempted to explore the relationship between religious convictions and one's subsequent actions. I believe that one can see elements of this in the models of socialization and nurture adopted by some Black Christian parents.

The problem with such interpretative strategies for raising one's children is that they operate on the basis of the Bible providing 'closed' forms of knowledge. These forms of knowledge are rarely impacted upon by other sources or bases for how we come to know what is true. It is at this juncture that the importance of Black Theology comes into its own. As I have demonstrated in a previous chapter, my work has sought to use sources of knowledge that lie outside the official canon of the Bible. I have used these additional resources for assisting us in discerning 'what is the word of God', 'what is a word about God'[58] or, alternatively, 'what word is simply limited to its own context'. In fact one can go even further and suggest 'what is not of God at all', but is simply a form of projection used by people in order to bolster their particular perspective. Using the ideas and frameworks of Transformative Popular Education can be a means of helping ordinary Black people to read the Bible more critically. It can assist them to undertake theology in a more contextual fashion.

For example, in my own previous work, I have incorporated notions of 'critical openness' as a means of enabling ordinary Black people to reflect theologically in a more critical manner.[59] Critical openness is a process of formation and reflection in which the learner is enabled to grow in faith, in a context of freedom and openness. It is a form of theological reflection that enables the learner to engage with forms of knowledge and truth that emerge from a variety of perspectives. It does not believe in a closed-world

---

58 I make this distinction when assessing how Black Theology seeks to interpret the Bible in ways that are consistent with the thrust for full life and liberation for all people. See Reddie, *Working against the Grain*, pp. 108–10.

59 See Anthony G. Reddie, *Dramatizing Theologies: A Participative Approach to Black God-Talk*, Oakville, CT, and London: Equinox, 2006, pp. 105–6.

'biblical Truth'. Rather, God can speak from within a variety of perspectives and vantage points. The mode of reflection and learning is one that is open to plural influences and ideas from other religious traditions and secular philosophies. It is a form that does not limit the bounds of religious and theological knowledge.[60]

Critical openness can be used as a helpful tool for enabling African Caribbean Christian parents to adopt a more nuanced and amplified approach to their biblically inspired, religio-cultural frameworks. For example, critical openness can assist them in the judgements they make when engaging with their children. When allied to the historic experiences of being Black in a White-dominated world, critical openness can enable some of these individuals to perceive the world in a very different manner from the more constricted perspectives that existed in former eras.

In a previous piece of work I wrote about the importance of the oral tradition within African Caribbean life.[61] In this work, I argue that long before people began to depend upon the written text as the primary medium for the development and dissemination of knowledge, many Black people used wise sayings and narratives as ways of 'passing on' truth.

One of my inspirations for this work was my maternal grandmother who lived all her life in the eastern parish of Portland, Jamaica. She probably travelled no more than 40 or so miles from the place in which she was born and yet she was an exceedingly wise and knowledgeable person.[62] Her oral-based wisdom, told through the medium of countless anecdotes, family stories and reminiscences, had been informed by a close, communitarian world of the village in which she grew up and was nurtured. It was also informed by the immediate prevalence of colonialism and endemic rural poverty. In such contexts, the realities of life might well necessitate a literalist reading of the Bible. Such contexts might necessitate the careful selection of verses from the book of Proverbs or seeing the Abraham narrative in Genesis 22 as a paradigm for the ideal, God-fearing Christian parent. I doubt, however, that either of my siblings would agree with such readings as the basis for their contemporary practices of raising my niece and nephew.

In the present context, critical openness is acknowledged as their children engage with plural influences in school and in the broader society. These influences are then juxtaposed with the African Caribbean, religio-cultural traditions of their Baptist great-grandmother. A Black Theology 'hermeneutic of suspicion' will critically assess the helpfulness of such biblical texts,

---

60 See John Hull, 'Critical Openness in Christian Nurture', in Jeff Astley and Leslie Francis (eds), *Critical Perspectives on Christian Education*, Leominster: Grace-wing, 1994, pp. 251–75.

61 See Anthony G. Reddie, *Is God Colour Blind? Insights from Black Theology for Christian Ministry*, London: SPCK, 2009, pp. 23–36.

62 Reddie, *Is God Colour Blind?*, pp. 23–4.

such as Genesis 22. It will critically assess the desirability of a sole patriarch hearing a disembodied voice, but failing to consult others before taking action. Such an approach will discuss his potentially ruinous behaviour for the community as a whole. There will be recognition of the dangers of sole voices interpreting 'God's will'. If my previous comments appear somewhat fanciful, 'over- the- top', or even fantastical, then consider the actions of David Koresh in Waco, Texas, in April 1993 or, prior to that, Jim Jones in Jonestown in Guyana, in November 1978. In both cases, we witnessed mass tragedies under the leadership of a sole male patriarch who professed to hear the voice of God!

Perhaps the greater contextual challenges are not reserved for such outlandish occasions as the ones just described. Rather, I believe we have to assess the working practices of many Black churches in the contemporary era. How many are presently operating with patriarchal models of leadership? Ones in which a sole male patriarch interprets God's will without being encumbered to seek the advice of others? How often are Black women included in these discernment processes and decision-making practices? How often are Black women and children expected to suffer, physically, psychologically and spiritually, for the betterment of the whole church community? How often is physical punishment and suffering invoked as a 'badge of honour'?

I hope that this case-study has suggested ways in which the armoury of tools employed by Black Theology can offer critical perspectives for how ordinary Black people can exhibit greater levels of liberative praxis in their daily operations of life. Black Theology is far too important to be left to the experts!

Questions

1. Do you think Black Theology can be accused of 'pandering to political correctness' by challenging the parental right to smack or strike children in the name of disciplining them? If yes, then why, and if not, then why not?
2. What are the gains and losses of rereading and critiquing the Bible in the way it is undertaken in this chapter?
3. This issue may be seen as part of the larger 'culture wars' that are taking place in many western societies between the state and the Church. What are some of the other 'cultural' issues to which Black Theology should attend?
4. Can the Black Theology method adopted in this chapter offer any insight to these other challenges, and if so, then how?

Conclusion

Black Theology remains a vital resource for enabling Black people to live in a liberative fashion. It can assist in finding complementary sources of knowledge and the relevant tools for creating liberative, transformative and healthy modes of action.

By adopting Black Theology as the underlying framework for 'interpreting the world', I believe that ordinary Black people can be encouraged to think more critically about how they attempt to live out their faith in the world. Black Theology can support and encourage more critical responses to inherited religious dogma and ask the question, 'Is this truly of God? Is it liberative for *all people*?'

The biggest challenge that faces Black Theology in the twenty-first century is that of relevance. In its earliest incarnation as an academic discipline, the biggest challenge that faced Black Theology was that of legitimacy. Noel Erskine has shown the ways in which early Black Theologians were eager to engage in dialogue with prominent White Euro-American theologians, but exhibited a kind of myopia when it came to dialoguing with Black women.[1]

In the present era, Black Theology's problem is not one of legitimacy but, instead, is a challenge of relevance. Is Black Theology still relevant? Has a movement supposedly committed to liberative praxis exchanged the dangerous, prophetic commitment to systemic change and personal conscientization for bland, polite academic rhetoric?[2]

This work has attempted to explain the central ideas of Black Theology. It has also attempted to do something other than this. It has tried to incorporate Transformative Popular Education as a means of showing how Black Theology can attend to the issues that impact on ordinary Black people. This work is not about trying to save Black Theology. Black Theology is not

---

1 Noel Leo Erskine, *Black Theology and Pedagogy*, New York: Palgrave Macmillan, 2008, pp. 45–7.

2 See Elonda Clay's brave and challenging article that seeks to investigate the reasons for Black Theology's present struggle. See Elonda Clay, 'A Black Theology of Liberation of Legitimation? A Postcolonial Response to Cone's *Black Theology and Black Power* at Forty', *Black Theology* 8:3 (2010), pp. 307–26.

dying, and I make no claims to possess any salvific qualities. I do believe, however, Black Theology needs to regain its verve. It needs to discover the images and visions that can inspire ordinary Black people to live out a radical faith that is committed to transformative change.

Black Theology's ultimate commitment must be to serving God, via the practical concerns and needs of ordinary Black people. Theory in and of itself has its place, but I do not believe this can account for the central intent of Black Theology. Black Theology, with its roots in the life experiences of ordinary Black people, and being fired into life by Black clergy and other activists, needs to be more than 'just another academic discipline'. It must retain its commitment to rigorous theological analysis *and* liberative praxis, born out of an intense engagement with ordinary Black people. I trust that this text has offered some modest examples of how this can be done!

Bibliography

Abernathy, Ralph D., *And the Walls Came Tumbling Down*, New York: Harper and Row, 1989.

Ackah, William, 'Back to Black or Diversity in the Diaspora: Re-Imagining Pan-African Christian Identity in the Twenty-First Century', *Black Theology* 8:3 (2010), pp. 341–56.

Adi, Hakim, and Marika Sherwood (eds), *Pan-African History: Political Figures from Africa and Diaspora since 1787*, London: Routledge, 2003.

Alread, J. D., *Respect: Understanding Caribbean British Christianity*, Peterborough: Epworth, 2005.

Aldred, Joe, 'The Holy Spirit and the Black Church', in Aldred and Ogbo (eds), *Black Church in the 21st Century*, pp. 45–62.

Aldred, Joe, and Keno Ogbo (eds), *The Black Church in the 21st Century*, London: Darton, Longman and Todd, 2010.

Alexander, Valentina, 'Passive and Active Radicalism in Black-Led Churches', in Jagessar and Reddie (eds), *Black Theology in Britain*, pp. 52–69.

Ali, Carroll A. Watkins, *Survival and Liberation: Pastoral Theology in African American Context*, St Louis: Chalice Press, 1999.

Althaus-Reid, Marcella, Ivan Patrella and Luis Carlos Susin (eds), *Another Possible World*, London: SCM, 2007.

Amoah, Elizabeth, '"Poverty is madness": Some Insights from Traditional African Spirituality and Mental Health', in Dwight N. Hopkins and Marjorie Lewis (eds), *Another World Is Possible: Spiritualities and Religions of Global Darker Peoples*, Oakwood and London: Equinox, 2009, pp. 207–18.

Anderson, Victor, *Beyond Ontological Blackness: An Essay on African American Religious and Cultural Criticism*, New York: Continuum, 1995.

Anderson, Victor, *Creative Exchange: A Constructive Theology of African American Religious Experience*, Minneapolis: Fortress, 2008.

Andrews, Dale P., *Practical Theology for Black Churches: Bridging Black Theology and African American Folk Religion*, Louisville, KY: Westminster John Knox, 2002.

Anyabwile, Thabita M., *The Decline of African American Theology: From Biblical Faith to Cultural Captivity*, Downers Grove, IL: IVP Academic, 2007.

Asante, Molefi Kete, *Afrocentricity*, Trenton, NJ: Africa World Press, 1980.

Asante, Molefi Kete, 'Afrocentricity and Culture', in Molefi Kete Asante and Kariamu Welsh Asante (eds), *African Culture: The Rhythms of Unity*, Trenton, NJ: First Africa World Press, 1990, pp. 3–12.

Ashby Jr, Homer U., *Our Home Is over Jordan: A Black Pastoral Theology*, St Louis: Chalice Press, 2003.

Austin, Algernon, *Achieving Blackness: Race, Black Nationalism and Afrocentrism in the Twentieth Century*, New York and London: New York University Press, 2006.

Baer, Hans A., *The Black Spiritual Movement: A Religious Response to Racism*, Knoxville: University of Tennessee Press, 1984.

Bailey, Randall C., 'But It's in the Text! Slavery, the Bible and African Diaspora', in Anthony G. Reddie (ed.), *Black Theology, Slavery and Contemporary Christianity*, Farnham: Ashgate, 2010, pp. 31–46.

Bailey, Randall C., 'The Danger of Ignoring One's Own Cultural Bias in Interpreting the Text', in R. S. Sugirtharajah (ed.), *The Postcolonial Bible,* Sheffield: Sheffield Academic Press, 1998, pp. 66–90.

Bailey, Randall C., Cheryl Kirk-Duggan, Madipoane Masenya (ngwan'a Mphahlele) and Rodney S. Sadler Jr, 'African and African Diasporan Hermeneutics', in Page Jr (Gen. Ed.), *Africana Bible*, pp. 19–24.

Bailey, Randall C., Tat-siong Benny Liew and Fernando F. Segovia (eds), *They Were All Together in One Place? Toward Minority Biblical Criticism*, Atlanta, GA: Society for Biblical Literature, 2009.

Bailey, Randall C., (ed.), *Yet with a Steady Beat: Contemporary U.S. Afrocentric Biblical Interpretation*, Atlanta: Society for the Study of Biblical Literature, 2003.

Bailey, Randall C., and Jacqueline Grant (eds), *The Recovery of Black Presence: An Interdisciplinary Exploration*, Nashville, TN: Abingdon, 1995.

Balasuriya, Tissa, 'Liberation of the Affluent', *Black Theology* 1:1 (2002), pp. 83–113.

Baldwin, Lewis V., *Towards the Beloved Community: Martin Luther King Jr and South Africa*, Cleveland, OH: Pilgrim Press, 1995.

Banks, James A. (ed.), *Multicultural Education, Transformative Knowledge and Action: Historical and Contemporary Perspectives*, New York: Teachers College Press, 1996.

Banks, James A., *Race, Culture and Education: The Selected Works of James A. Banks*, London and New York: Routledge, 2006.

Baker-Fletcher, Karen, *Dancing with God: The Trinity from a Womanist Perspective*, St Louis: Chalice Press, 2007.

Baker-Fletcher, Karen, *Sisters of Dust, Sisters of Spirit: Womanist Wordings on God and Creation*, Minneapolis: Fortress, 1998.

Baker-Fletcher, Karen, and Garth Kasimu, *Bible Witness in Black Churches*, New York: Palgrave Macmillan, 2009.

Baker-Fletcher, Karen, and Garth Kasimu, *My Sister, My Brother: Womanist and Xodus God-Talk*, Maryknoll, NY: Orbis, 1997.

Barton, Mukti, *Rejection, Resistance and Resurrection: Speaking Out on Racism in the Church*, London: Darton, Longman and Todd, 2005.

Battle, Michael, *The Black Church in America*, Oxford: Blackwell, 2006.

Battle, Michael (ed.), *The Quest for Liberation and Reconciliation: Essays in Honour of J. Deotis Roberts*, Louisville, KY: Westminster John Knox, 2005.

Beckford, Robert, *Dread and Pentecostal: a Political Theology for the Black Church in Britain*, London: SPCK, 2000.

Beckford, Robert, 'Dread and Rahtid: Robert Beckford's Canon', in Michael N. Jagessar and Anthony G. Reddie (eds), *Black Theology in Britain: A Reader*, Oakwood and London: Equinox, 2007, pp. 81–108.

Beckford, Robert, *God and the Gangs*, London: Darton, Longman and Todd, 2004.

Beckford, Robert, *God of the Rahtid: Redeeming Rage*, London: Darton, Longman and Todd, 2001.

Beckford, Robert, *Jesus Dub*, London: Routledge, 2006.

Beckford, Robert, *Jesus Is Dread*, London: Darton, Longman and Todd, 1998.

Beckford, Robert, 'Theology in the Age of Crack: Crack Age, Prosperity Doctrine and "Being There"', *Black Theology in Britain* 4:1 (2001), pp. 9–24.

Bevans, Stephen B., *Models of Contextual Theology*, Maryknoll, NY: Orbis, 2004.

Bhogal, Inderjit, *A Table for All*, Sheffield: Penistone, 2000.

Bikos, Steve, *I Write What I Like: A Selection of His Writings*, ed. Aelved Stubbs, London: Heinemann Educational, 1979.

Birchett, Colleen, 'A History of Religious Education in the Black Church', in Donald B. Rogers (ed.), *Urban Church Education*, Birmingham, AL: Religious Education Press, 1989, pp. 69–76.

'Black Power: Statement by the National Committee of Negro Churchmen, July 31, 1966', in Gayraud S. Wilmore and James H. Cone (eds), *Black Theology: A Documentary History, 1966–1979*, Maryknoll, NY: Orbis, 1979, pp. 23–30.

Blount, Brian K. (ed.), *True to Our Native Land: An African American New Testament Commentary*, Minneapolis: Fortress, 2007.

Blyden, Edward, 'Africa's Service to the World: Discourse Delivered before the American Colonization Society, May 1880. The Scope and Meaning of "Ethiopia"', in Cain Hope Felder (ed.), *The Original African Heritage Study Bible*, Nashville, TN: James C. Winston Publishing Company, 1993, pp. 109–21.

Boesak, Allan A., *Farewell to Innocence: A Socio-Ethical Study on Black Theology and Black Power*, Maryknoll, NY: Orbis, 1977.

Boesak, Allan A. *The Fire Within: Sermons from the Edge of Exile*, Glasgow: Wild Goose, 2007.

Boesak, Allan A, and Charles Villa-Vicencio, *When Prayer Makes the News*, Philadelphia: Westminster, 1986.

Bradley, Anthony B., *Liberating Black Theology: The Bible and the Black Experience in America*, Wheaton, IL: Crossway, 2010.

Bronfenbrenner, Urie, *The Ecology of Human Development: Experiments by Nature and Design*, Cambridge, MA: Harvard University Press, 1979.

Brooten, Bernadette (ed.), *Beyond Slavery: Overcoming Religious and Sexual Legacies*, Basingstoke: Palgrave Macmillan, 2010.

Brown, Michael J., *The Blackening of the Bible: The Aims of African American Biblical Scholarship*, Harrisburg, PA: Trinity Press International, 2004.

Brown, Michael J., *The Lord's Prayer through North African Eyes*, London: T & T Clark, 2004.

Burrus, Virginia, 'The Gospel of Luke and the Acts of the Apostles', in Segovia and Sugirtharajah (eds), *A Postcolonial Commentary on the New Testament Writings*, pp. 133–55.

Byron, Gay L., *Symbolic Blackness and Ethnic Difference in Early Christian Literature*, New York: Routledge, 2002.

Callahan, Allen D., *The Talking Book: African Americans and the Bible*, New Haven: Yale University Press, 2006.

Callender, Christine, *Education for Empowerment: The Practice and Philosophies of Black Teachers*, Stoke-On-Trent: Trentham, 1997.

Cannon, Katie G., *Black Womanist Ethics*, Atlanta, GA: Scholars Press, 1988.

Cannon, Katie G., *Katie's Cannon: Womanism and the Soul of the Black Community*, New York: Continuum, 1995.

Carruthers, Iva E., Frederick D. Haynes III and Jeremiah A. Wright Jr (eds), *Blow the Trumpet in Zion: Global Vision and Action for the 21st Century Black Church*, Minneapolis: Fortress, 2005.

Carter, J. Kameron, *Race: A Theological Account*, New York: Oxford University Press, 2008.

Cassidy, Laurie M., and Alex Mikilich (eds), *Interrupting White Privilege: Catholic-Theologians Break the Silence*, Maryknoll, NY: Orbis, 2007.

Charles, Ronald, 'Interpreting the Book of Revelation in the Haitian Context', *Black Theology* 9:2 (2011), pp. 177–98.

Chinula, Donald M., *Building King's Beloved Community: Foundations for Pastoral Care and Counselling with the Oppressed*, Cleveland, OH: United Church Press, 1997.

Clark, Jawanza Eric, 'Reconceiving the Doctrine of Jesus as Savior in Terms of the African Understanding of an Ancestor: A Model for the Black Church', *Black Theology* 8:2 (2010), pp. 140–59.

Clay, Elonda, 'A Black Theology of Liberation of Legitimation? A Postcolonial Response to Cone's *Black Theology and Black Power* at Forty', *Black Theology* 8:3 (2010), pp. 307–26.

Coleman, Monica A., *Making a Way Out of No Way: A Womanist Theology*, Minneapolis: Fortress, 2008.

Coleman, Will, *Tribal Talk: Black Theology, Hermeneutics, and African/American Ways of 'Telling the Story'*, University Park, PA: University of Pennsylvania Press, 2000.

Cone, James H., *Black Theology and Black Power*, New York: HarperSanFrancisco, 1989.

Cone, James H., *A Black Theology of Liberation*, Maryknoll, NY: Orbis, [1970].

Cone, James H., *The Cross and the Lynching Tree*, Maryknoll, NY: Orbis, 2011.

Cone, James H., *For My People: Black Theology and the Black Church*, New York: Orbis, 1984.

Cone, James H., *God of the Oppressed*, New York: Seabury, 1975.

Cone, James H., *Martin, Malcolm and America*, Maryknoll, NY: Orbis, 1992.

Cone, James H., *My Soul Looks Back*, New York: Orbis, 1986.

Cone, James H., *The Spirituals and the Blues*, New York: Seabury, 1972.

Cone, James H., 'Theology's Great Sin: Silence in the Face of White Supremacy', *Black Theology* 2:2 (2004), pp. 139–52.

Cone, James H., and Gayraud S. Wilmore, *Black Theology: A Documentary History, Vol. 1, 1966–1979*, Maryknoll, NY: Orbis, 1992.

Cone, James H., and Gayraud S. Wilmore, *Black Theology: A Documentary History, Vol. 2, 1980–1992*, Maryknoll, NY: Orbis, 1993.

Copeland, M. Shawn, *Enfleshing Freedom: Body, Race and Being*, Minneapolis: Fortress, 2009.

Crawford, H. Elaine, *Hope in the Holler: A Womanist Theology*, Louisville, KY: Westminster John Knox, 2002.

Crawley, Ashon T., '"Let's Get It On": Performance Theory and Black Pentecostalism', *Black Theology* 6:3 (2008), pp. 308–29

Davis, Kortright, *Emancipation Still Comin'*, Maryknoll, NY: Orbis, 1990.

Day, Keri, 'Global Economics and U. S. Public Policy: Human Liberation for the Global Poor, *Black Theology* 9:1 (2011), pp. 9–33.

De la Torre, Miguel A., 'Scripture', in Miguel A. de la Torre (ed.), *Handbook of U. S. Theologies of Liberation*, St Louis: Chalice Press, 2004, pp. 85–6.

Dick, Devon, *Rebellion to Riot: The Jamaican Church in Nation Building*, Kingston, Jamaica: Ian Randle, 2003.

Douglas, Kelly Brown, *The Black Christ*, Maryknoll, NY: Orbis, 1994.

Douglas, Kelly Brown, *Sexuality and the Black Church: A Womanist Perspective*, Maryknoll, NY: Orbis, 1999.

Douglas, Kelly Brown, *What's Faith Got to Do with It? Black Bodies/Christian Souls*, Maryknoll, NY: Orbis, 2005.

Du Bois, W. E. B., *The Education of Black People: Ten Critiques, 1906–1960*, New York: The Monthly Review Press, 1973.

Du Bois, W. E. B., *The Souls of Black Folk*, New York: Bantam Books, 1989.

Dube, Musa W., *Postcolonial Feminist Interpretation of the Bible*, St Louis: Chalice Press, 2000.

Duncan, Carol B., *This Spot of Ground: Spiritual Baptists in Toronto*, Waterloo, Ontario: Wilfred Laurier Press, 2008.

Dyson, Michael Eric, *Holler If You Hear Me: Searching for Tupac Shakur*, Pittsburgh: University of Pennsylvania Press, 2002.

Dyson, Michael Eric, *I May Not Get There With You: The True Martin Luther King, Jr*, New York: Simon and Schuster, 1999.

Dyson, Michael Eric, *Reflecting Black: African American Cultural Criticism*, Minneapolis: University of Minnesota Press, 1993.

Earl Jr, Riggins R., *Dark Salutations: Ritual, God, and Greetings in the African American Community*, Harrisburg, PA: Trinity Press International, 2001.

Earl Jr, Riggins R., *Dark Symbols, Obscure Signs: God, Self, and Community in the Slave Mind*, Knoxville, TN: University of Tennessee Press, 2003.

Echols, James (ed.), *I Have a Dream: Martin Luther King Jr. and the Future of Multicultural America*, Minneapolis: Fortress, 2004.

Edmonds, Ennis B., and Michelle A. Gonzalez, *Caribbean Religious History: An Introduction*, New York and London: New York University Press, 2010.

Edmonds, Ennis B., and Michelle A. Gonzalez, *Religious History: An Introduction* New York and London: New York University Press, 2010.

Eppehimer, Trevor, 'Victor Anderson's Beyond Ontological Blackness and James Cone's Black Theology: A Discussion', *Black Theology* 4:1 (2006), pp. 87–106.

Erikson, Erik H., *The Life Cycle Completed*, New York: Norton, 1997.

Erskine, Noel L., *Black Theology and Pedagogy*, New York: Palgrave Macmillan, 2008.

Erskine, Noel L., *Decolonizing Theology: A Caribbean Perspective*, Maryknoll, NY: Orbis, 1981.

Erskine, Noel L., *From Garvey to Marley*, Gainesville: University of Florida Press, 2007.

Erskine, Noel L., *King among the Theologians*, Cleveland, OH: Pilgrim Press, 1994.

Evans, Curtis J., *The Burden of Black Religion*, New York and London: Oxford University Press, 2008.

Evans Jr, James H., *We Have Been Believers: An African American Systematic Theology*, Minneapolis: Fortress, 1992.

Eze, Emmanuel C. (ed.), *Race and the Enlightenment*, New Malden, MA, and Oxford: Blackwell, 1997.

Fabella, Virginia, and R. S. Sugirtharajah (eds), *Dictionary of Third World Theologies*, Maryknoll, NY: Orbis, 2000.

Fanon, Frantz, *Black Skin, White Masks*, New York: Grove, 1967; London: MacGibbon & Kee, 1968.

Fanon, Franz, *The Wretched of the Earth*, London: Penguin, 1967.

Felder, Cain Hope, 'Exodus', in Felder (ed.), *Original African Heritage Study Bible*, pp. 85–94.

Felder, Cain Hope (ed.), *Troubling Biblical Waters: Race, Class, and Family*, Maryknoll, NY: Orbis, 1989.

Felder, Cain Hope (ed.), *Stony the Road We Trod: African American Biblical Interpretation*, Minneapolis: Fortress, 1991.

Felder, Cain Hope (ed.), *The Original African Heritage Study Bible*, Nashville, TN: The James C. Winston Publishing Company, 1993.

Floyd-Thomas, Stacey M. (ed.), *Deeper Shades of Purple*, New York: New York University Press, 2006.

Floyd-Thomas, Stacey M., *Mining the Motherlode*, Cleveland, OH: Pilgrim Press, 2006.

Fowler, James W., *Stages of Faith: The Psychology of Human Development and the Quest for Meaning*, San Francisco: HarperCollins, 1985.

Frazier, E. Franklin, *The Negro Church in America*, New York: Schocken Books, 1963.

Freire, Paulo, *Education for Critical Consciousness*, New York: Continuum, 1990 [1973].

Gafney, Wil, 'Reading the Hebrew Bible Responsibly', in Page Jr (Gen. Ed.), *Africana Bible*, pp. 45–53.

Garvey Amy Jacques (ed.), *The Philosophy and Opinions of Marcus Garvey*, vol. 3, *More Philosophy and Opinions of Marcus Garvey*, selected and edited from previously unpublished material by E. U. Essien-Udom and Amy Jacques Garvey, London: Cassell, 1977.

Genovese, Eugene, *Roll Jordan Roll*, New York: Vintage Books, 1980.

Gichaara, Jonathan, 'Issues in African Liberation Theology', *Black Theology* 3:1 (2005), pp. 75–85.

Gilkes, Cheryl Townsend, *If It Wasn't for the Women: Black Women's Experience and Womanist Culture in Church and Community*, Maryknoll, NY: Orbis, 2001.

Goatley, David Emmanuel, *Black Religion, Black Theology: The Collected Essays of J. Deotis Roberts*, Harrisburg, PA: Trinity Press International, 2003.

Goldman, Ronald, *Readiness for Religion*, London: Routledge and Kegan Paul, 1965.

Gonzalez, Michelle A., *Afro-Cuban Theology: Religion, Race, Culture, and Identity*, Gainesville: University of Florida Press, 2006.

Gorringe, Timothy J., *Furthering Humanity: A Theology of Culture*, Aldershot: Ashgate, 2004.

Gossai, Hemchand, and Nathaniel Samuel Murrell (eds), *Religion, Culture and Tradition in the Caribbean*, Basingstoke and London: Macmillan, 2000.

Graham, Elaine, Heather Walton and Francis Ward, *Theological Reflection: Methods*, London: SCM, 2005.

Graham, Elaine, Heather Walton and Francis Ward, *Theological Reflection: Sources*, London: SCM, 2007.

Grant, Colin, *Negro with a Hat: The Rise and Fall of Marcus Garvey*, New York and London: Oxford University Press, 2008.

Grant, Jacquelyn, 'A Theological Framework', in Charles R. Foster and Grant S. Shockley (eds), *Working with Black Youth: Opportunities for Christian Ministry*, Nashville, TN: Abingdon, 1989, pp. 55–76.

Grant, Jacquelyn, *White Women's Christ and Black Women's Jesus: Feminist Christology and Womanist Response*, Atlanta, GA: Scholar's Press, 1989.

Grant, Paul, and Raj Patel (eds), *A Time to Act: Kairos 1992*, Birmingham: A joint publication of Racial Justice and the Black Theology Working Group, 1992.

Grant, Paul, and Raj Patel (eds), *A Time to Speak: Perspectives of Black Christians in Britain*, Birmingham: A joint publication of Racial Justice and the Black Theology Working Group, 1990.

Griffin, Horace L., *Their Own Receive Them Not: African American Lesbians and Gays in Black Churches*, Cleveland, OH: Pilgrim Press, 2006.

Groome, Thomas H., *Christian Religious Education: Sharing Our Story and Vision*, San Francisco: Jossey-Bass, 1980.

Groome, Thomas H., *Sharing Faith: A Comprehensive Approach to Religious Education and Pastoral Ministry*, San Francisco: HarperSanFrancisco, 1991.

Gruchy, Steve de, 'Jesus the Christ', in John de Gruchy and C. Villa-Vicencio (eds), *Doing Theology in Context: South African Perspectives*, Cape Town and Johannesburg: David Philip Publishers, 1994, pp. 55–67.

Habermas, Jürgen, *Knowledge and Human Interests*, Boston: Beacon, 1971.

Hale, Janice, 'The Transmission of Faith to Young African American Children', in Randall C. Bailey and Jacquelyn Grant (eds), *The Recovery of Black Presence*, Nashville, TN: Abingdon, 1995, pp. 193–207.

Harding, Vincent, 'Black Power and the American Christ', in Gayraud S. Wilmore and James H. Cone (eds), *Black Theology: A Documentary History, 1966–1979*, Maryknoll, NY: Orbis, 1979, pp. 35–42.

Harding, Vincent, *Martin Luther King: The Inconvenient Hero*, Maryknoll, NY: Orbis, 2008 [1996].

Harris, James H., 'Black Church and Black Theology: Theory and Practice', in James H. Cone and Gayraud S. Wilmore (eds), *Black Theology: A Documentary History, Vol. 2, 1980–1992*, Maryknoll, NY: Orbis, 1993, pp. 85–98.

Hardy III, Clarence E., *James Baldwin's God: Sex, Hope, and Crisis in Black Holiness Culture*, Knoxville, TN: University of Tennessee Press, 2003.

Harris, James H., *Pastoral Theology: A Black-Church Perspective*, Minneapolis: Fortress, 1991.

Hart, William David, *Black Religion: Malcolm X, Julius Lester and Jan Willis*, New York: Palgrave Macmillan, 2008.

Harvey, Marcus Louis, 'Engaging the Orisa: An Exploration of the Yoruba Concepts of *Ibeji* and *Olokun* as Theoretical Principles in Black Theology', *Black Theology* 6:1 (2008), pp. 61–82.

Haslam, David, *The Churches and 'Race': A Pastoral Approach*, Cambridge: Grove, 2001.

Haslam, David, *Race for the Millennium: A Challenge to Church and Society*, London: Church House for the Churches' Commission on Racial Justice (CCRJ), 1996.

Hayes, Diana L., *Standing in the Shoes My Mother Made: A Womanist Theology*, Minneapolis: Fortress, 2010.

Hayes, Diana L., 'We, Too, Are America: Black Women's Burden of Race and Class', in Kirk-Duggan (ed.), *The Sky Is Crying*, pp. 69–79.

Haynes, Stephen R., *The Curse of Ham: Race and Slavery in Early Judaism, Christianity and Islam*, Princeton, NJ: Princeton University Press, 2005.

Haynes, Stephen R., *Noah's Curse: The Biblical Justification of American Slavery*, Oxford and New York: Oxford University Press, 2002; David M. Goldenberg.

Hendricks Jr, Obery M., *The Universe Bends Towards Justice: Radical Reflections on the Bible, Church and the Body Politic*, Maryknoll, NY: Orbis, 2011.

Hertzog II, William R., *Parables as Subversive Speech: Jesus as Pedagogue of the Oppressed*, Louisville, KY: Westminster John Knox, 1994.

Hill, Johnny Bernard, *The Theology of Martin Luther King, Jr. and Desmond Mpilo Tutu*, New York: Palgrave Macmillan, 2007.

Hood, Robert E., *Begrimed and Black: Christian Traditions on Blacks and Blackness*, Minneapolis: Fortress, 1994.

Hood, Robert E., *Must God Remain Greek? Afro-Cultures and God-Talk*, Minneapolis: Fortress, 1990.

Hooks, bell, *Teaching to Transgress: Education as the Practice of Freedom*, New York: Routledge, 1994, pp. 93–128.

Hopkins, Dwight N., 'Black Christian Worship: Theological and Biblical Foundations', in Hopkins and Lewis (eds), *Another World Is Possible*, pp. 338–40.

Hopkins, Dwight N., *Being Human: Race, Culture and Religion*, Minneapolis: Fortress, 2005.

Hopkins, Dwight N. (ed.), *Black Faith and Public Talk: Critical Essays on James H. Cone's Black Theology and Black Power*, Maryknoll, NY: Orbis, 1999.

Hopkins, Dwight N., *Black Theology USA and South Africa: Politics, Culture and Liberation*, Maryknoll, NY: Orbis, 1989.

Hopkins, Dwight N., *Down, Up and Over: Slave Religion and Black Theology*, Minneapolis: Fortress, 2000.

Hopkins, Dwight N., *Heart and Head: Black Theology – Past, Present and Future*, New York and London: Palgrave, 2002.

Hopkins, Dwight N., *Introducing Black Theology of Liberation*, Maryknoll, NY: Orbis, 1999.

Hopkins, Dwight N., 'New Orleans Is America', in Kirk-Duggan (ed.), *The Sky Is Crying*, pp. 59–68.

Hopkins, Dwight N., 'The Religion of Globalization', in Hopkins, Lorentzen, Mendieta and Batstone (eds), *Religions/Globalizations*, pp. 7–32.

Hopkins, Dwight N., 'Theologies in the USA', in Althaus-Reid, Patrella and Susin (eds), *Another Possible World*, pp. 94–101.

Hopkins, Dwight N., and George Cummings, *Cut Loose Your Stammering Tongue: Black Theology and the Slave Narratives*, Maryknoll, NY: Orbis, 1991.

Hopkins, Dwight N., and George C. L. Cummings (eds), *Cut Loose Your Stammering Tongue: Black Theology in the Slave Narratives*, 2nd edn, Louisville, KY: Westminster John Knox, 2003.

Hopkins, Dwight N., and Marjorie Lewis (eds), *Another World Is Possible: Spiritualities and Religions of Global Darker Peoples*, London: Equinox, 2009.

Hopkins, Dwight N., Lois Anne Lorentzen, Eduardo Mendieta and David Batstone (eds), *Religions/Globalizations: Theories and Cases*, Durham, NC, and London: Duke University Press, 2001.

Hopkins, Dwight N., and Linda E. Thomas (eds), *Walk Together Children: Black and Womanist Theologies, Church and Theological Education*, Eugene, OR: Cascade Books, 2010.

Howard, Charles Lattimore, 'Black Stars and Black Poverty: Critical Reflections upon Black Theology from a Garveyite Perspective', *Black Theology* 9:3 (2011), pp. 312–33.

Hull, John M., 'Critical Openness in Christian Nurture', in Jeff Astley and Leslie J. Francis (eds), *Critical Perspectives on Christian Education*, Leominster: Gracewing, 1994, pp. 251–75.

Isiorho, David, 'Black Identities and Faith Adherence: Social Policy and Penal Substitution in the Epoch of the SS *Empire Windrush*', *Black Theology* 7:3 (2009), pp. 282–99.

Isiorho, David, 'Buying the Poor for Silver and the Needy for a Pair of Sandals (Amos 8:6): The Fit between Capitalism and Slavery as Seen through the Hermeneutic of the Eighth-Century Prophet Amos', in Anthony G. Reddie (ed.), *Black Theology, Slavery and Contemporary Christianity*, Aldershot: Ashgate, 2010, pp. 59–68.

Jackson, Anita, *Catching Both Sides of the Wind: Conversations with Five Black Pastors*, London: British Council of Churches, 1985.

Jagessar, Michael N., 'A Brief Con-version: A Caribbean and Black British Postcolonial Scrutiny of Christian Conversion', *Black Theology* 7:3 (2009), pp. 300–24.

Jagessar, Michael N., 'Early Methodism in the Caribbean: Through the Imaginary Optics of Gilbert's Slave Women – Another Reading', *Black Theology* 5:2 (2007), pp. 153–70.

Jagessar, Michael N., *Full Life for All: The Work and Theology of Philip A. Potter – a Historical Survey and Systematic Analysis of Major Themes*, Zoetermeer: Boekencentrum, 1997.

Jagessar, Michael N., 'Is Jesus the Only Way? Doing Black Christian God-Talk in a Multi-Religious City (Birmingham, UK)', *Black Theology* 7:2 (2009), pp. 200–25.

Jagessar, Michael N., 'Liberating Cricket: Through the Optic of Ashutosh Gowariker's Lagaan', *Black Theology* 2:2 (2004), pp. 239–49.

Jagessar, Michael N., 'Review Article: Critical Reflections on John Wesley, Thoughts Upon Slavery', *Black Theology* 5:2 (2007), pp. 250–5.

Jagessar, Michael N., and Stephen Burns, *Christian Worship: Postcolonial Perspectives*, London: Equinox, 2011.

Jagessar, Michael N., and Stephen Burns, 'Liturgical Studies and Christian Worship: The Postcolonial Challenge', *Black Theology* 5:1 (2007), pp. 39–62.

Jagessar, Michael N., and Anthony G. Reddie (eds), *Black Theology in Britain: A Reader*, London: Equinox, 2007.

Jagessar, Michael N., and Anthony G. Reddie (eds), *Postcolonial Black British Theology*, Peterborough: Epworth, 2007.

Jakes, T. D., *The Great Investment: Faith, Family and Finance*, New York: G. P. Putnam's Sons, 2000.

Jennings, Willie James, *The Christian Imagination: Theology and the Origins of Race*, New Haven and London: Yale University Press, 2010.

Johnson, Matthew V., *The Tragic Vision of African American Religion*, Basingstoke: Palgrave Macmillan, 2010.

Johnson, Sylvester A., *The Myth of Ham in Nineteenth-Century American Christianity: Race, Heathens, and the People of God*, New York: Palgrave Macmillan, 2005.

Jones, William R., *Is God a White Racist? A Preamble to Black Theology*, Boston: Beacon, MA, 1998.

Joy, David C. I., *Mark and Its Subalterns: A Hermeneutical Paradigm for a Postcolonial Context*, London: Equinox, 2008.

Julien, Isaac, 'Black Is, Black Ain't: Notes on De-Essentializing Black Identities', in Gina Dent (ed.), *Black Popular Culture*, Seattle: Bay Press, 1992, pp. 255–63.

Karran, Kampta, 'Changing Kali: From India to Guyana to Britain', *Black Theology in Britain* 4:1 (2001), pp. 90–102.

Kee, Alistair, *The Rise and Demise of Black Theology*, London: SCM, 2008.

Keller, Catherine, Michael Nausner and Mayra Rivera (eds), *Postcolonial Theologies: Divinity and Empire*, St Louis: Chalice Press, 2004.

Kelly Miller Smith Institute Incorporated, 'What Does It Mean to be Black and Christian', in Cone and Wilmore (eds), *Black Theology*, pp. 164–74.

Kirk-Duggan, Cheryl, *Exorcizing Evil: A Womanist Perspective on the Spirituals*, Maryknoll, NY: Orbis, 1997.

Kirk-Duggan, Cheryl (ed.), *The Sky Is Crying: Race, Class and Natural Disaster*, Nashville, TN: Abingdon, 2006.

Kretzschmar, Louise, *The Voice of Black Theology in South Africa*, Johannesburg: Raven Press, 1986.

Kunnie, Julian, *Models of Black Theology: Issues in Class, Culture and Gender*, Valley Forge, PA: Trinity Press International, 1994.

Lartey, Emmanuel Y., *In Living Colour: Intercultural Approaches to Pastoral Care and Counselling*, London and Philadelphia: Jessica Kingsley, 2003.
Lartey, Emmanuel Y., 'Practical Theology as a Theological Form', in James Woodward and Stephen Pattison (eds), *The Blackwell Reader in Pastoral and Practical Theology*, Oxford: Blackwell, 2000, pp. 128–34.
Lartey, Emmanuel Y., 'Theology and Liberation: The African Agenda', in Althaus-Reid, Patrella and Susin (eds), *Another Possible World*, pp. 80–93.
Leech, Kenneth, *Race: Changing Society and the Churches*, London: SPCK, 2005.
Leech, Kenneth, *Struggle in Babylon*, London: Sheldon Press, 1988.
Lewis, Berrisford, 'Forging an Understanding of Black Humanity through Relationship: An Ubuntu Perspective', *Black Theology* 8:1 (2010), pp. 69–85.
Lewis, Marjorie, 'Diaspora Dialogue: Womanist Theology in Engagement with Aspects of the Black British and Jamaican Experience', *Black Theology* 2:1 (2004), pp. 85–109.
Lewis-Cooper, Marjorie, 'Some Jamaican Rites of Passages: Reflections for the Twenty-First Century', *Black Theology in Britain* 6 (2001), pp. 53–71.
Lincoln, C. Eric, and Lawrence Mamiya, *The Black Church in the African American Experience*, Durham, NC: Duke University Press, 1990.
Long, Michael G., *Martin Luther King Jr. on Creative Living*, St Louis: Chalice Press, 2004.

Martin, Tony (ed.), *Message to the People: The Course of African Philosophy*, Dover, MA: Majority Press, 1986.
McCalla, Doreen W., *Unsung Sheroes in the Church: Singing the Praises of Black Women Now!*, Bloomington, IN: Authorhouse, 2007.
McCrary, P. K., *The Black Bible Chronicles: From Genesis to the Promise Land*, New York: African American Family Press, 1993.
McCrary, P. K., *The Black Bible Chronicles: Rappin' with Jesus*, New York: African American Family Press, 1994.
Mercer, Kobena, *Welcome to the Jungle: New Positions in Black Cultural Studies*, London: Routledge, 1994.
Miller, Michael St Aubin, 'He said I was Out of Pocket: On Being a Caribbean Contextual Theologian in a Non-Caribbean Context', *Black Theology* 9:2 (2011), pp. 223–45.
Milwood, Robinson A., *Liberation and Mission: A Black Experience*, London: African Caribbean Education Resource Centre (ACER), 1997.
Mitchell, Henry H., *Black Church Beginnings: The Long-Hidden Realities of the First Years*, Grand Rapids, MI: Eerdmans, 2004.
Mitchell, Henry H., and Nicola Copper-Lewter, *Soul Theology: The Heart of American Black Culture*, San Francisco: Harper and Row, 1986.
Mitchem, Stephanie Y., *Introducing Womanist Theology*, Maryknoll, NY: Orbis, 2002.
Mitchem, Stephanie Y., *Name It and Claim It: Prosperity Teaching in the Black Church*, Cleveland OH: Pilgrim Press, 2007.
Mosala, Itumeleng J., *Biblical Hermeneutics and Black Theology in South Africa*, Grand Rapids, MI: Eerdmans, 1989.

Mosala, Itumeleng J., and Butio Tlhagale (eds), *The Unquestionable Right to Be Free: Black Theology from South Africa*, Maryknoll, NY: Orbis, 1986.

Moses, Wilson Jeremiah (ed.), *Classical Black Nationalism: From the American Revolution to Marcus Garvey*, New York and London: New York University Press, 1996.

Mothlabi, Mokgethi, *African Theology/Black Theology in South Africa: Looking Back, Moving On*, Pretoria: University of South Africa Press, 2008.

Mothlabi, Mokgethi, *The Theory and Practice of Black Resistance to Apartheid: A Socio-Ethical Analysis*, Johannesburg: Scotaville Publishers, 1984.

Mullings, Lynnette, 'Teaching Black Biblical Studies in the UK: Special Issues for Consideration and Suggested Hermeneutical Approaches', *Discourse* 8:2 (2009), pp. 81–126.

Mulrain, George, 'The Caribbean', in John Parratt (ed.), *An Introduction to Third World Theologies*, Cambridge: Cambridge University Press, 2004, pp. 163–81.

Murove, Munyaradzi Feliz, 'Perceptions of Greed in Western Economic and Religious Traditions: An African Communitarian Response', *Black Theology* 5:2 (2007), pp. 220–43.

Murphy, Larry, 'Piety and Liberation: A Historical Exploration of African American Religion and Social Justice', in Iva E. Carruthers, Frederick D. Haynes III and Jeremiah A. Wright Jr (eds), *Blow the Trumpet in Zion: Global Vision and Action for the 21st Century Black Church*, Minneapolis: Fortress, 2005, pp. 35–58.

Murrell, Nathaniel Samuel, William David Spencer and Adrian Anthony McFarlane (eds), *Chanting Down Babylon: The Rastafari Reader*, Philadelphia: Temple University Press, 1998.

Nelson, Clarice Tracey, 'The Churches, Racism and the Inner-Cities', in Raj Patel and Paul Grant (eds), *A Time to Speak: Perspectives of Black Christians in Britain*, Birmingham: A joint publication of Racial Justice and the Black Theology Working Group, CCRU/ECRJ, 1990, pp. 3–10.

Noel, James A., and Matthew V. Johnson (eds), *The Passion of the Lord: African American Reflections*, Minneapolis: Fortress, 2005.

Nussbaum, Martha, *Women and Human Development: The Capabilities Approach*, Cambridge: Cambridge University Press, 2000.

Oduyoye, Mercy Amba, *Beads and Strands: Reflections of an African Woman on Christianity*, Maryknoll, NY: Orbis, 2004.

Oduyoye, Mercy Amba, *Introducing African Women's Theology*, Sheffield and Cleveland, OH: Sheffield Academic Press and Pilgrim Press, 2001.

Oduyoye, Mercy Amba, and Musimbi R.A. Kanyoro (eds), *The Will to Arise: Women, Tradition and the Church in Africa*, Maryknoll, NY: Orbis, 1997.

Olofinjana, Israel, *Reverse in Ministry and Mission: Africans in the Dark Continent of Europe – a Historical Study of African Churches in Europe*, Milton Keynes: Authorhouse, 2010.

Page Jr, Hugh R. (Gen. Ed.), *The Africana Bible: Reading Israel's Scriptures from Africa and the African Diaspora*, Minneapolis: Fortress, 2010.

Paris, Peter J., *The Social Teachings of the Black Churches*, Minneapolis: Fortress, 1985.

Paris, Peter J., *The Spirituality of African Peoples: The Search for a Common Moral-Discourse*, Minneapolis: Fortress, 1995.

Parratt, John (ed.), *An Introduction to Third World Theologies*, Cambridge: Cambridge University Press, 2004.

Perkinson, James W., *Shamanism, Racism and Hip-Hop Culture: Essays on White-Supremacy and Black Subversion*, New York: Palgrave Macmillan, 2005.

Perkinson, James W., *White Theology*, New York: Palgrave Macmillan, 2004.

Petrella, Ivan, *The Future of Liberation Theology: An Argument and Manifesto*, London: SCM, 2006.

Phiri, Isabel Apawo, and Sarojini Nadar (eds), *African Women, Religion and Health: Essays in Honor of Mercy Amba Ewudziwa Oduyoye*, Maryknoll, NY: Orbis, 2006.

Pinn, Anne, and Anthony B. Pinn, *Fortress Introduction to Black Church History*, Minneapolis: Fortress, 2002.

Pinn, Anthony B., *African American Humanist Principles: Living and Thinking like the Children of Nimrod*, New York: Palgrave Macmillan, 2005.

Pinn, Anthony B. (ed.), *Black Religion and Aesthetics: Religious Thought and Life in Africa and the African Diaspora*, New York: Palgrave Macmillan, 2009.

Pinn, Anthony B., *Embodiment and the New Shape of Black Theological Thought*, New York and London: New York University Press, 2010.

Pinn, Anthony B. (ed.), *Noise and Spirit: The Religious and Spiritual Sensibilities of Rap Music*, New York and London: New York University Press, 2003.

Pinn, Anthony B., 'Sweaty Bodies in a Circle: Thoughts on the Subtle Dimensions of Black Religion as Protest', *Black Theology* 4:1 (2006), pp. 11–26.

Pinn, Anthony B., *Terror and Triumph: The Nature of Black Religion*, Minneapolis: Fortress, 2003.

Pinn, Anthony B., *Varieties of African American Religious Experience*, Minneapolis: Fortress, 1998.

Pinn, Anthony B., *Why Lord? Suffering and Evil in Black Theology*, New York: Continuum, 1995.

Pinn, Anthony B., and Dwight N. Hopkins, *Loving the Body: Black Religious Studies and the Erotic*, New York: Palgrave, 2004.

Pollard III, Alton B., and Love Henry Whelchel Jr (eds), *How Long This Road: Race, Religion and the Legacy of C. Eric Lincoln*, New York: Palgrave Macmillan, 2004.

Pui-Lan, Kwok, *Postcolonial Imagination and Feminist Theology*, Louisville, KY: Westminster John Knox, 2005.

Raboteau, Albert, *A Fire in the Bone*, Boston: Beacon, 1995.

Rabateau, Albert, *Slave Religion: The 'Invisible Institution' in the Antebellum South*, New York: Oxford University Press, 1978.

Ray Jr, Stephen G., 'Contending for the Cross: Black Theology and the Ghosts of Modernity', *Black Theology* 8:1 (2010), pp. 53–68.

Reddie, Anthony G., *Acting in Solidarity: Reflections in Critical Christianity*, London: Darton, Longman and Todd, 2005.

Reddie, Anthony G., *Black Theology in Transatlantic Dialogue*, New York: Palgrave Macmillan, 2006.

Reddie, Anthony G., *Black Theology, Slavery and Contemporary Christianity*, Farnham: Ashgate, 2010.

Reddie, Anthony G., *Dramatizing Theologies : A Participative Approach to Black God-Talk*, Oakville, CT, and London: Equinox, 2006.

Reddie, Anthony G., 'Editorial', *Black Theology: An International Journal* 45:2 (2006), pp. 134–5.

Reddie, Anthony G., *Faith, Stories and the Experience of Black Elders: Singing the Lord's Song in a Strange Lane*, London: Jessica Kingsley, 2001.

Reddie, Anthony G., *Growing into Hope, Vol. 1, Believing and Expecting*, Peterborough: Methodist Publishing House, 1998.

Reddie, Anthony G., *Growing into Hope, Vol. 2, Liberation and Change*, Peterborough: Methodist Publishing House, 1998.

Reddie, Anthony G., *Is God Colour Blind? Insights from Black Theology for Christian Ministry*, London: SPCK, 2009.

Reddie, Anthony G., *Nobodies to Somebodies: Practical Theology for Education and Liberation*, Peterborough: Epworth, 2003.

Reddie, Anthony G., 'Pentecost – Dreams and Visions (A Black Theological Reading of Pentecost)', in Maureen Edwards (ed.), *Discovering Christ: Ascension and Pentecost*, Birmingham: IRBA, 2001, pp. 27–42.

Reddie, Anthony G., *Re-Imaging Black Theology in the 21st Century*, London: Equinox, 2008.

Reddie, Anthony G., *Working against the Grain: Re-Imaging Black Theology in the 21st Century*, London, Equinox, 2008.

Reddie, Richard S., *Abolition*, Oxford: Lion/Hudson, 2007.

Reddie, Richard S., *Black Muslims in Britain*, Oxford: Lion/Hudson, 2009.

Reddie, Richard S., *Martin Luther King Jr: History Maker*, Oxford: Lion, 2011.

Reid-Salmon, Delroy A., 'Faith and the Gallows: The Cost of Liberation', in Anthony G. Reddie (ed.), *Black Theology, Slavery and Contemporary Christianity*, Aldershot: Ashgate, 2010, pp. 151–64.

Reid-Salmon, Delroy A., *Home away from Home: The Caribbean Diasporan Church in the Black Atlantic Tradition*, London: Equinox, 2008.

Reid-Salmon, Delroy A., 'A Sin of Black Theology: The Omission of the Caribbean Diasporan Experience from Black Theological Discourse', *Black Theology* 6:2 (2008), pp. 139–52.

Roberts, J. Deotis, *Africentric Christianity*, Valley Forge, PA: Judson Press, 2000.

Roberts, J. Deotis, *Bonhoeffer and King: Speaking Truth to Power*, Louisville, KY: Westminster John Knox, 2005.

Rodney, Walter, *The Groundings with My Brothers*, London: Bogle-L'Ouverture Publications, 1990 [1969].

Ross, Rosetta E., *Witnessing and Testifying: Black Women, Religion and Civil Rights*, Minneapolis: Fortress, 2003.

Rowland, Christopher (ed.), *The Cambridge Companion to Liberation Theology*, Cambridge: Cambridge University Press, 1999.

Sanders, Cheryl, *Living the Intersection*, Minneapolis: Fortress, 1995.

Sant'Ana, Antonio (National Ecumenical Commission to Combat Racism, Brazil), 'Black Spirituality: The Anchor of Black Lives', in Dwight N. Hopkins and Marjorie

Lewis (eds), *Another World Is Possible: Spiritualities and Religions of Global Darker Peoples*, London: Equinox, 2009.

Santos, Diana Fernandes dos (Youth of the Methodist Church, Brazil), 'Black Heritage in Brazil', in Dwight N. Hopkins and Marjorie Lewis (eds), *Another World Is Possible: Spiritualities and Religions of Global Darker Peoples*, London: Equinox, 2009.

Segovia, Fernando S., and R. S. Sugirtharajah (eds), *A Postcolonial Commentary on the New Testament Writings*, London: T & T Clark, 2007.

Sheerattan-Bisnauth, Patricia (ed.), *Righting Her-Story: Caribbean Women Encounter the Bible Story*, Geneva: World Communion of Reformed Churches, 2011.

Shockley, Grant, 'Historical Perspectives', in Charles R. Foster and Grant S. Shockley (eds), *Working with Black Youth: Opportunities for Christian Ministry*, Nashville, TN: Abingdon, 1989, pp. 9–29.

Sims, Angela D., *Ethical Complications of Lynching: Ida B Wells's Interrogation of African American Terror*, New York: Palgrave Macmillan, 2010.

Singleton III, Harry H., *Black Theology and Ideology: Deideological Dimensions in the Theology of James H. Cone*, Collegeville, MN: The Liturgical Press, 2002.

Sivanandan, A., *Communities of Resistance: Writings on Black Struggles for Socialism*, London: Verso, 1990.

Smith Jr, Archie, *Navigating the Deep River: Spirituality in African American Families*, Cleveland, OH: United Church Press, 1997.

Smith Jr, Robert L., *From Strength to Strength: Shaping a Black Practical Theology for the 21st Century*, New York: Peter Lang, 2007.

Smith, Theophus, *Conjuring Cultures: Biblical Formations in Black America*, New York: Oxford University. Press, 1994.

Smith, Yolanda Y., *Reclaiming the Spirituals: New Possibilities for African American Christian Education*, Cleveland, OH: Pilgrim Press, 2004.

Sneed, Roger A., *Representations of Homosexuality: Black Liberation Theology and Cultural Criticism*, New York: Palgrave Macmillan, 2010.

Sobrino, Jon, *Jesus the Liberator: A Historical-Theological View*, Maryknoll, NY: Orbis, 1993.

Society for Biblical Literature, *Reading the Bible in the Global Village: Cape Town*, (no. 3) Atlanta, GA: Society for Biblical Literature, 2002.

Spencer, William David, *Dread Jesus*, London: SPCK, 1999.

Stewart, Dianne M., *Three Eyes for the Journey: African Dimensions of the Jamaican Religious Experience*, New York and Oxford: Oxford University Press, 2005.

Stewart III, Carlyle Fielding, *Black Spirituality and Black Consciousness*, Trenton, NJ: Africa World Press, 1999.

Stinehelfer, Jeffrey N., 'Dig This: The Revealing of Jesus Christ', *Religious Education* 64:6 (1969), pp. 467–70.

Sturge, Mark, *Look What the Lord Has Done! An Exploration of Black Christian Faith in Britain*, Milton Keynes: Scripture Union, 2005.

Sugirtharajah, R. S., *The Bible and Empire: Postcolonial Considerations*, Cambridge and New York: Cambridge University Press, 2005.

Sugirtharah, R. S., *The Bible and the Third World: Precolonial, Colonial and Postcolonial Encounters*, Cambridge: Cambridge University Press, 2001.

Sugirtharah, R. S., *The Post Colonial Bible*, Sheffield: Sheffield Academic Press, 1998.

Sugirtharajah, R. S., *Postcolonial Criticism and Biblical Interpretation*, Oxford: Oxford University Press, 2002.

Sugirtharajah, R. S., *Postcolonial Reconfigurations: An Alternative Way of Reading the Bible and Doing Theology*, London: SCM, 2003.

Sugirtharah, R. S., *Voices from the Margins*, Maryknoll, NY, and London: Orbis and SPCK, 1991.

Sugirtharajah, R. S. (ed.), *Voices from the Margin: Interpreting the Bible in the Third World*, London and Maryknoll, New York: SPCK/Orbis, 1995.

Sutcliffe, John (ed.), *Tuesday's Child: A Reader for Christian Educators*, Birmingham: Christian Education, 2001.

Terrell, JoAnne Marie, *Power in the Blood? The Cross in the African American Experience*, Maryknoll, NY: Orbis, 1998.

Thomas, Elaine E., 'Macroeconomy, Apartheid and the Rituals of Healing in an African Indigenous Church', in Dwight N. Hopkins, Lois Ann Lorentzen, Eduardo Mendieta and David Batstone (eds), *Religions/Globalizations: Theories and Cases*, London and Durham: Duke University Press, 2001, pp. 135–60.

Thomas, Linda E. (ed.), *Living Stones in the Household of God: The Legacy and Future of Black Theology*, Minneapolis: Fortress, 2004.

Thomas, Linda E., *Under the Canopy: Ritual Process and Spiritual Resilience in South Africa*, Columbia, SC: University of South Carolina Press, 1999.

Thomas, Oral A. W., *Biblical Resistance Hermeneutics within a Caribbean Context*, London: Equinox, 2010.

Thomas, Oral A. W., 'A Resistant Biblical Hermeneutic within the Caribbean', *Black Theology* 6:3 (2008), pp. 330–42.

Tillich, Paul, *Systematic Theology*, vol. 1, Chicago: University of Chicago Press, 1967.

Tomlin, Carol, *Black Language Style in Sacred and Secular Contexts*, New York: Caribbean Diaspora Press, 1999.

Townes, Emilie M., *Womanist Ethics and the Cultural Production of Evil*, New York: Palgrave Macmillan, 2006.

Townes, Emilie M., *Womanist Justice, Womanist Hope*, Atlanta, GA: Scholars Press, 1993.

Tracy, David *The Analogical Imagination: Christian Theology and the Culture of Pluralism*, London: SCM, 1981.

Tribble, Jeffrey L., *Transformative Pastoral Leadership in the Black Church*, New York: Palgrave Macmillan, 2005.

Trible, Phyllis, *Texts of Terror: Literary-Feminist Readings of Biblical Narratives*, London: SCM, 1992.

Troupe, Carol, 'Re-Reading Slave Writing through the Lens of Black Theology', in Anthony G. Reddie (ed.), *Black Theology, Slavery and Contemporary Christianity*, Aldershot: Ashgate, 2010, pp. 165–84.

Valentina Alexander, 'Passive and Active Radicalism in Black-Led Churches', in Michael N. Jagessar and Anthony G. Reddie (eds), *Black Theology in Britain: A Reader*, London: Equinox, 2007, pp. 52–69.

Vincent, Theodore G., *Black Power and the Garvey Movement*, San Francisco: Rampart Press, 1972.

Walker, Robin, *When We Ruled*, London: Every Generation Media, 2006.

Walton, Jonathan L., *Watch This! The Ethics and Aesthetics of Black Televangelism*, New York and London: New York University Press, 2009.

Ware, Frederick L., *Methodologies of Black Theology*, Cleveland, OH: Pilgrim Press, 2002.

Warrior, Robert Allen, 'A Native American Perspective: Canaanites, Cowboys, and Indians', in R. S. Sugirtharajah (ed.), *Voices from the Margin: Interpreting the Bible in the Third World*, London and Maryknoll, NY: SPCK/Orbis, 1997, pp. 277–85.

Watkins Ali, Carroll A., *Survival and Liberation: Pastoral Theology in African American Context*, St Louis: Chalice Press, 1999.

Weems, Renita J., *Battered Love: Marriage, Sex, and Violence in the Hebrew Prophets*, Minneapolis: Fortress, 1995.

Weems, Renita J., *Just a Sister Away: A Womanist Vision of Women's Relationships in the Bible*, Philadelphia: Innisfree Press, 1988.

Wesley, John, *Thoughts Upon Slavery*, first published in 1774, republished by the Racial Justice Office of the Methodist Church for the Bicentenary of the Abolition of the Slave Trade Act (1807), London: Methodist Church, 2006.

West, Cornel, 'Black Theology and Marxist Thought', in Wilmore and Cone (eds), *Black Theology 1966–1979*, pp. 552–67.

West, Cornel, 'Black Theology of Liberation as Critique of Capitalist Civilisation', in James H. Cone and Gayraud S. Wilmore (eds), *Black Theology: A Documentary History, Volume Two, 1980–1990*, Maryknoll, NY: Orbis, 1993, pp. 410–25.

West, Cornel, *Prophecy Deliverance! An Afro-American Revolutionary Christianity*, Louisville, KY: Westminster John Knox, 2003.

West, Cornel, *Race Matters*, Boston: Beacon, 1993.

West, Gerald, *Biblical Hermeneutics of Liberation*, Maryknoll, NY: Orbis, 1991.

West, Traci C., *Disruptive Christian Ethics*, Louisville, KY: Westminster John Knox, 2006.

Westfield, Nancy Lynne, 'Called Out My Name, or Had I known You Were Somebody: The Pain of Fending Off Stereotypes', in Nancy Lynne Westfield (ed.), *Being Black, Teaching Black: Politics and Pedagogy in Religious Studies*, Nashville, TN: Abingdon, 2008, pp. 61–78.

Westfield, N. Lynne, *Dear Sisters: A Womanist Practice of Hospitality*, Cleveland, OH: Pilgrim Press, 2001.

Westfield, N. Lynne, 'Life-Giving Stories: The Bible in a Congregation', in Vincent L. Wimbush (ed.), *African Americans and the Bible: Sacred Texts and Social Textures*, London and New York: Continuum, 2000, pp. 577–87.

Wilkinson, John, *Church in Black and White: The Black Christian Tradition in 'Mainstream' Churches in England: A White Response and Testimony*, Edinburgh: St Andrew Press, 1994.

Williams, Delores, *Sisters in the Wilderness: The Challenge of Womanist God-Talk*, Maryknoll, NY: Orbis, 1993.

Williams, Demetrius K., *An End to This Strife: The Politics of Gender in African American Churches*, Minneapolis: Fortress, 2004.

Williams, Eric, *Capitalism and Slavery*, London: André Deutsch, 1983.

Williams, Lewin, *Caribbean Theology*, New York: Peter Lang, 1994.

Willis, Lerleen, 'All Things to All Men? Or What Has Language to Do with Gender and Resistance in the Black Majority Church in Britain', *Black Theology in Britain* 4:2 (2002), pp. 195–213.

Willis, Lerleen, 'The Pilgrim's Process: Coping with Racism through Faith', *Black Theology* 4:2 (2006), pp. 210–32.

Willows, David, *Divine Knowledge: A Kierkegaardian Perspective on Christian Education*, Aldershot: Ashgate, 2001.

Wilmore, Gayraud S., *Black Religion and Black Radicalism: An Interpretation of the Religious History of Afro-American People*, 2nd edn, Maryknoll, NY: Orbis, 1983.

Wilmore, Gayraud S., *Pragmatic Spirituality: The Christian Faith through an Africentric Lens*, New York: New York University Press, 2005.

Wimberly, Anne S., *Soul Stories: African American Christian Education*, Nashville, TN: Abingdon, 1996.

Wimberly, Edward P., *Moving from Shame to Self-Worth: Preaching and Pastoral Care*, Nashville, TN: Abingdon, 1999.

Wimbush, Vincent L. (ed.), *African Americans and the Bible: Sacred Texts and Social Textures*, New York and London: Continuum, 2000.

Wimbush, Vincent L., *The Bible and African Americans: A Brief History*, Minneapolis: Fortress, 2003.

Witvliet, Theo, *A Place in the Sun: An Introduction to Liberation Theology in the Third World*, London: SCM, 1985.

The Womanist Theology Group, 'A Womanist Bibliodrama', in Paul Grant and Raj Patel (eds), *A Time To Act: Kairos 1992*, Birmingham: A Joint Publication of Racial Justice and the Black and Third World Theological Working Group, 1992, pp. 25–32.

Woodson, Carter G., *The Mis-Education of the Negro*, Trenton, NJ: Africa World Press, 1990 [1933].

Wright Jr, Jeremiah A., 'Doing Black Theology in the Black Church', in Linda E. Thomas (ed.), *Living Stones in the Household of God: The Legacy and Future of Black Theology*, Minneapolis: Fortress, 2004, pp. 13–23.

Young, Josiah U., *A Pan African Theology*, Trenton, NJ: Africa World Press, 1992.

Young, Josiah U., *Dogged Strength within the Veil*, Harrisburg, PA. Trinity Press International, 2003.

Young, Josiah, 'Envisioning the Son of Man', *Black Theology* 2:1 (2004), pp. 11–17.

Name Index

Reddie, Anthony G. xiin2, xviin9, 4n11, 4n16, 6n24, 8n31, 11n42, 12n44, 13n45, 18n56, 20n59, 22n67, 23nn69, 71, 24n75, 29n5, 30n6, 32n8, 42n39, 47n45, 49n49, 53n56, 54nn 57, 59, 56n61, 60n3, 61n6, 63n7, 65n16, 72nn32, 33, 73nn34, 35, 74n37, 75n43, 77n48, 80n54, 81n57, 81n61, 95n26, 98n31, 105n46, 108 57, 110n64, 111nn65, 66, 67, 112nn70, 71, 129n41, 143n12, 147n21, 16272, 163n74, 167n88, 176n9, 178n20, 179n21, 186nn34, 35, 188n37, 189n39, 190n43, 196nn58, 59, 197n61
Reddie, Richard S. 90n8
Reid-Salmon, Delroy A. 32nn8, 9, 108, 132n49, 157n56
Rivera, Mayra 47n47
Roberts, J. Deotis xii, 122n20
Robertson, Pat 151
Rodney, Walter 19n58, 120n14
Rogers, Donald B. 194n55
Ross, Rosetta E. 97n30
Rowland, Christopher 156n50

Sant'Ana, Antonio 3n8
Segovia, Fernando F. 47n47, 167n89, 168n91, 169n92
Segundo, Juan Luis 21n66
Sharpe, Sam 11
Sheerattan-Bisnauth, Patricia 178n18
Sherwood, Marika 7n28
Shier-Jones, Angela 189n38
Shockley, Grant S. 152n37, 194
Singleton III, Harry H. 21n66
Sivanandan, A. 8n30
Smith, Theophus H. 81, 115n3
Smith, Yolanda Y. 115n3
Smith Jr, Archie 4n16, 20n62, 115n3
Smith Jr, Robert L. 128
Sobrino, Jon 11
Spencer, William David 9n33, 21n63, 64n10
Stewart, Dianne M. 93, 115n3, 179n23
Stewart III, Carlyle Fielding 115n3
Stinehelfer, Jeffrey N. 50n51
Sturge, Mark 71n29

Sugirtharajah, R. S. 17n51, 47n47, 143n8, 144n15, 154nn43, 44, 168n91, 169n92, 178n21, 183n29
Susin, Luiz Carlos 3n5, 6n26, 154n43, 166n87
Sutcliffe, John 192n45

Terrell, JoAnne Marie 33, 189
Thomas, Elaine E. 159n64
Thomas, Linda E. 25n78, 115n3
Thomas, Oral A. W. 45, 167, 178–179
Thomas, Stacey Floyd xivn5
Tillich, Paul 66, 68
Tlhagale, Buti 2, 3n9, 148n24
Tomlin, Carol 105
Townes, Emilie xivn5, 21n65, 147, 159, 160
Tracy, David 66, 68
Tribble Sr, Jeffrey L. 128
Trible, Phyllis 192n44
Troupe, Carol 30n6, 85n2, 119n13, 121–2, 176n9
Turner, Henry McNeal 38

Vincent, Theodore G. 6n27

Walker, Robin 5n22
Walton, Heather 68n22, 79n53
Walton, Jonathan L. 104n44, 163n76, 164, 166n85
Ward, Francis 68n22, 79n53
Ware, Frederick L. 1n1, 10n39, 39n32, 123, 123nn25, 27
Wareing, Helen 189n38
Warrior, Robert Allen 17n51
Weber, Max 38
Weems, Renita J. xivn5, 185n33
Wesley, John 126
West, Cornel 5n17, 158
Westfield, Nancy Lynne 50, 51n52, 100
Wilkinson, John L. 144n14
Williams, Delores S. xivn5, 64, 91, 92, 189–90
Williams, Eric 4n14
Williams, Lewin L. 1, 149
Willis, Lerleen 51n54, 105
Willows, David 15n47

Index

gospel 157
linked with Rastafarianism 70, 77
as the 'Logos' 182, 184, 185, 186
pentecostalist perceptions 70–1
personal experience of 54
power 96–9
presence 132
revelation of God 130
role 10–11
solidarity with humanity 139
suffering 33–5
transformative work 122
truth claims about 103–4
White Christ 138
White Jesus 111
Jesus Dub (Beckford) 65–71
Jesus Is Dread (Beckford) 70, 82, 129
Job 190
Job (book) 136
John's Gospel 183
Prelude 182
Jones, Jim (religious patriarch) 198
Judaea (Roman colony) 169

Kelly Miller Institute 82
King Jr, Martin Luther 8, 25n76, 77, 89,
90, 103, 122
Kingdom of God 8–9, 167, 170
Cone's views 155
Kingsway Christian Centre (UK) 166n86
knowledge, power's influence on 20
Koresh, David (religious patriarch) 198

lamentation 135–6
liberation 10
liberation theologies 3, 8, 159
liberative praxis 164
Black Theology as xiii, xvi
liberative spirituality 56–7
'limbo spaces' 110, 111
the 'Logos' 182, 184, 185, 186
Luke's Gospel 168, 169
lynchings, comparisons with Jesus'
sufferings 34–5

Malcom X 91
Mandela, Nelson 89

Mark's Gospel
crowd in 61n5, 96–7, 100–1, 105
Jesus' ministry 103
Marley, Bob 41
Marxism
Cone's use 155, 158
West's views 158
Mary (mother of Jesus) 134, 135, 136
media, manipulation of truth 147
mega-churches 163–4, 165–6
Methodist Church, sponsorship of re-
search into Black children's religious
awareness 72–4
Moses 51–4, 55, 56
music, and faith 66, 67–8

'name it and claim it' ethic 164
Nanny of the Maroons 53, 91
National Committe of Negro Churchmen, on Black Power 141–2
neighbour, love for 131
neo-Pentecostalism 163–7
challenges to 167–70
non-Christian religious traditions
118–19

Obama, Barack 24–5
Old Testament 43, 45
oppression, tri-partite oppression 98
oral traditions 197
organized religion, Black Theology's
criticisms 142–3
orthodoxy 28, 175, 182–3, 184
orthopraxis 28, 63–4
'outside looking in' approach 65, 67, 68,
69, 80, 83

'participative Black Theology in Britain'
76–7
passive radicalism 18–19, 130
patriarchy 198
Abraham 188–91, 193, 197, 198
Pentecostalism 124–5, 163
Beckford's views 64–6, 67–71, 129–30
influence on Beckford 64–6
neo-Pentecostalism 163–7
Pharoah, as authority figure 51–4, 55